Riding the Green Wave

Financial Conflicts of Interest
in Industry-Sponsored
Clinical Research

Riding the Green Wave

Financial Conflicts of Interest in Industry-Sponsored Clinical Research

Patricia M. Tereskerz

University Publishing Group
Hagerstown　　　Maryland

University Publishing Group, Inc.
Hagerstown, Maryland 21740
(240)420-0036 *www.UPGBooks.com*

© 2007 by University Publishing Group
All rights reserved. No part of this publication may be reproduced, stored in a retrieval system, or transmitted, in any form, or by any means, electronic, mechanical, photocopying, recording or otherwise, without the prior written permission of University Publishing Group.

This work was supported by a grant from the National Library of Medicine, project number: 1 G13 LM07512-01.

Disclaimer:
While every effort has been made to assure the accuracy of the material contained in this book as it relates to its subject matter, the author and publisher make no warranties, representations, guarantees, either express or implied, regarding the content of this book. The completeness, content, accuracy, or currency of the information contained in this book, or its fitness or suitability for any particular purpose, is not guaranteed. The material contained in this book is presented with the understanding that the publisher and author do not render any legal advice or service. Because of the rapidly changing nature of the information contained in this book, such information contained in this publication may become outdated. As a result, anyone using this material must always research original sources of authority and update information to ensure accuracy. In no event will the author or publisher be liable for any direct, indirect, or consequential damages resulting from the use of this material and expressly disclaim any liability for such use. If the user of this book, does not agree to the terms of this disclaimer then said user should not use the book.

Printed in the United States of America
ISBN 1-55572-084-6

For Terry, Taylor, Carly, and Polly

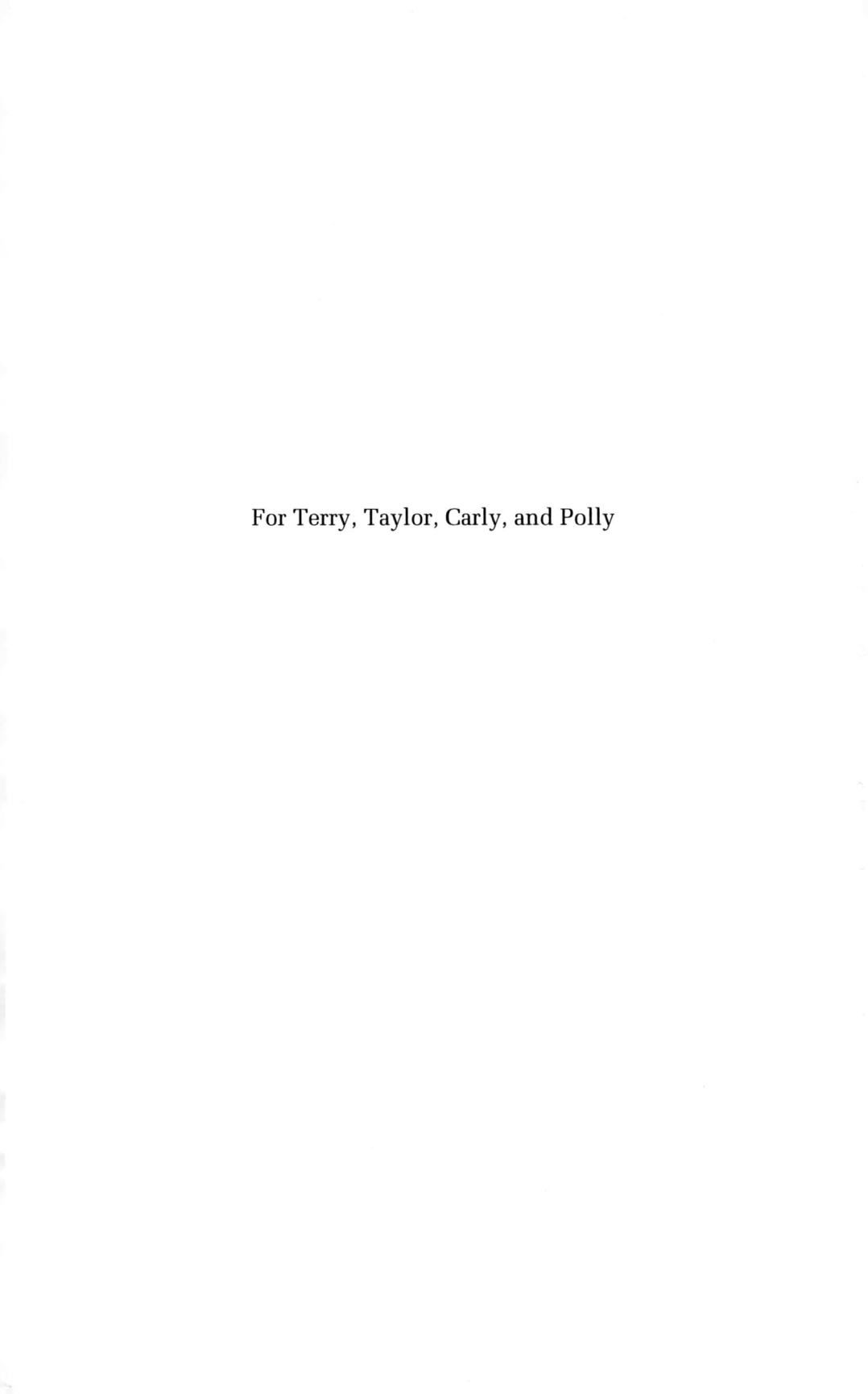

Contents

Acknowledgments *ix*

Abbreviations *xi*

Introduction *1*

1 An Overview of Clinical Research Funding and Conflicts of Interest: Defining a Financial Conflict of Interest *7*

2 How Financial Conflicts of Interest in Clinical Research Evolved: A Recent Passage through Time *29*

3 The Fallout: Realizing the Effects of Financial Conflicts of Interest in Clinical Research *43*

4 Policies and Regulations on Conflicts of Interest in Research *61*

5 Beyond Federal Regulations: Legal Ramifications of Financial Conflicts of Interest in Clinical Research *81*

6 A Recent Clinical Trial Involving Financial Conflicts of Interest: Applying Traditional Legal Theories *101*

7 Is There a Constitutional Right to be Treated with Dignity within the Context of Medical Experimentation? *109*

8 Financial Conflicts of Interest and Potential Statutory or Regulatory Violations *135*

9   The Other Side of the Coin: Potential Liability
    for Overly Restrictive Employment Policies   *149*

10 Developing a New Model: Preserving Scientific
    Objectivity, Trust, and the Informed Choices of
    Human Subjects   *153*

Appendices

A   The Nuremberg Code   *169*

B   World Medical Association Declaration of Helsinki   *171*

C   The Belmont Report   *179*

D   45 Code of Federal Regulations Part 46 Including
    Subpart A, the "Common Rule," and Supporting
    Subparts B, C, and D   *191*

Acknowledgments

I would like to acknowledge the financial support of the National Library of Medicine in underwriting this work.

I am also most grateful for the encouragement and mentoring provided by Jonathan Moreno during the course of this project and for the support of my colleague Ann Mills. I am greatly indebted to Leslie LeBlanc for her outstanding contribution in editing of this book.

Many thanks also to Dave Hudson who has afforded me the opportunity to put what I have learned through this research into practice.

And, as always, my heartfelt thanks and gratitude to my husband and children who have enthusiastically and lovingly encouraged and supported my academic endeavors.

Abbreviations

AAHRPP	Association for the Accreditation of Human Research Protection Programs
AAMC	Association of American Medical Colleges
AMA	American Medical Association
BMJ	*British Medical Journal*
AUTM	Association for University Technology Managers
CEJA	Council on Ethical and Judicial Affairs (of the American Medical Association)
CEO	chief executive officer
CFR	*Code of Federal Regulations*
CRADA	Cooperative Research and Development Agreement
CTI	Cell Therapeutics, Incorporated
DHHS	Department of Health and Human Services
FCA	Food, Drug and Cosmetic Act
FDA	Food and Drug Administration
FOIA	Freedom of Information Act
GAO	General Accounting Office
ICMJE	International Committee of Medical Journal Editors
HRPP	human research protection program
IHGI	Institute for Human Gene Research
IPA	institutional patent agreement
IRB	institutional review board
IV	intravenous
JAMA	*Journal of the American Medical Association*
MMR	measles, mumps, and rubella vaccine
NEJM	*New England Journal of Medicine*
NHRPAC	National Human Research Protections Advisory Committee
NIH	National Institutes of Health
NRBI	National Research Brokerage Institute

NSF	National Science Foundation
OHRP	Office for Human Research Protections
OIG	Office of the Inspector General
OMB	Office of Management and Budget
OTC	ornithene transcarbamylase
OPRR	Office for Protection from Research Risks
PhRMA	Pharmaceutical Research and Manufacturers of America
PHS	Public Health Service
PTX	pentoxifylline
RAC	Recombinant DNA Advisory Committee (NIH)
RFP	request for proposal
SEC	Securities and Exchange Commission
WMA	World Medical Association

Introduction

It is hard to find a week when the issue of financial conflicts of interest in clinical research do not make the headlines. Newspapers and journals are filled with articles discussing various types of financial conflicts and how they are detrimental to the research enterprise. Yet, at the same time, major institutions such as Harvard have once again considered whether to relax policies on financial ties to pharmaceutical companies.[1] In addition, the *New England Journal of Medicine* has changed its policy for those writing reviews and editorials, so that authors may not have any "significant" financial interest in a company (or its competitor) that makes a product discussed in the article.[2] Previously, such writers could not have "any" such financial interest. In making this decision, the editors lamented: "We would prefer that therapeutic research not be funded directly by commercial entities, but we are not the decision makers in this matter."[3] Contrast these developments with what is being written in the lay press: "Should research scientists who have financial stakes in the products they are writing about be forced to disclose those ties? To which the average person might reasonably respond, 'Of course they should.' But the more pertinent question is why scientists with financial stakes in the outcome of scientific studies are allowed anywhere near those studies, much less reviewing them in elite journals."[4]

The U.S. is floundering in its management of financial conflicts of interest. Rather than speaking with one voice, we have embarked on a course that has various organizations taking different paths.[5]

This book focuses on the conflicts that emerge from the relationship between private industry and primarily academic institutions and investigators conducting *clinical* research. Examples of conflict in other scientific areas are discussed to the extent they are applicable to clinical research.

In the past, most support for clinical research was provided through government grants. As a result, research institutions had no vested financial interest in the outcome of studies. The landscape has changed appreciably. Today, industry is a major underwriter of clinical research. As noted by highly regarded academicians, there is no place where the collapse of the wall between academia and industry is more notable than in the area of biomedical research.[6]

Today, private industry funding for biomedical research has outpaced that from public sources — most clinical studies, for example, that involve bringing new drugs from the bench to the bedside are financed by pharmaceutical companies, with 79 percent of money for clinical drug trials in the U.S. coming from industry.[7] Drug companies spend about $30 billion a year on drug research and development.[8]

Financial conflicts of interest occurring in clinical research encompass far more than those associated with industry-sponsored research. For example, the National Institutes of Health (NIH) has been under scrutiny for a policy instituted under former director Harold Varmus, MD, that encouraged NIH researchers to collaborate with pharmaceutical and biotech companies and exempted some NIH employees from federal regulations restricting financial ties to industry. Reports that government scientists violated ethics rules on collaborating with pharmaceutical companies, led to the enactment in 2005 of very stringent, yet controversial, ethics regulation for NIH investigators.[9] Because industry plays such a prominent role in funding research and has the potential to greatly impact the integrity of research, financial conflicts of interest associated with industry sponsorship is the sole focus of this book. It is intended primarily for an academic audience of clinical investigators, institutional review board members, and healthcare administrators. Attorneys practicing in this area may find it to be a useful resource.

Introduction 3

One of the goals of the book is to provide a concise survey, in one place, of the literature on financial conflicts of interest in clinical research as a resource for those in academia to consult. The topic is a complex one, with a vast literature that is not easy to summarize, since it has been addressed by different disciplines.

The book is organized around the theme that the regulatory and legal frameworks that exist to manage conflicts of interest in clinical research are inadequate. The argument advanced is that this situation exists primarily because the methods chosen to manage conflicts of interest are palliative, but do not afford a cure. It is further argued that until the underlying pathology is addressed, a satisfactory cure will not be in the offering.

Because it is often difficult, even for seasoned researchers, to imagine all of the various financial arrangements that can result in a conflict of interest, the book begins by lamenting the lack of a uniform definition of financial conflict of interest and by providing an overview explaining how clinical research is typically funded, so the readers will have a common understanding of how the various types of conflicts of interest described in the chapter have emerged. This is followed by a brief discussion of the conceptual framework that a definition of financial conflicts of interest should rely upon, as well as a definition of financial conflicts of interest as used in this book.

Chapter 2 is devoted to a description of the historical statutory and regulatory framework that provided incentives for financial conflicts of interest and allowed them to flourish in clinical research.

Having established common ground for gaining insight into what financial conflicts of interest are and how they emerged, the book will begin to lay the foundation for its argument that a new model to manage conflicts of interest is needed, by describing how financial conflicts of interest adversely impact research. Empirical data and discussion of anecdotal cases illustrate this.

With the magnitude of the problem of conflicts of interest now put into perspective, chapter 4 discusses existing policies, laws, and regulations that are in place to manage financial conflicts of interest and their limitations. Discussion of the appropriate approach to take when faced with financial conflicts of interest has been intense.[10] There is no current comprehensive document or policy guidance for those engaged in healthcare, medical research, or policy making to review concerning the appropriate means to handle conflicts of interest. While there has been excellent review of this subject earlier by several scholars,[11] there is no current publication that takes into account the numerous legislative, regulatory, and policy changes discussed herein that have recently been undertaken to deal with financial conflicts of interest occurring in the clinical research setting.

Chapters 5 through 8 go further to bolster the argument that new ways are needed to manage financial conflicts of interest by discussing the potential such conflicts pose for legal liability. The less obvious legal ramifications of financial conflicts of interest in clinical research are addressed, including potential liability under existing case law, as well as the potential for violating lesser known regulatory and statutory provisions. Having developed the argument that (a) conflicts of interest have been shown to be problematic and are associated with untoward research practices and results; (b) existing statutory and regulatory means to deal with financial conflicts of interest are inadequate to remedy the problem; and (c) financial conflicts of interest pose considerable legal risks for the unwary, the foundation is built upon which the book culminates in proposing a new model that is intended to address many of the limitations of the existing policy framework.

The model is premised upon a conceptual framework that avoids financial entanglements that present conflicts of interest, rather than providing remedies to ameliorate their "fallout" once they exist. The model develops a way for industry and academia to create liaisons that do not compromise traditional scientific principles and ethical values that promote the public well-being.

We are in the process of telling a story concerning our management of financial conflicts of interest in clinical research. No doubt, the power that money wields is not easily moved. However, ethical standards of research should not be forced to bend to accommodate the profit motive and must remain intractable in the face of political and economic pres-

Introduction

sure. As one commentator has concluded, researchers must encourage and nurture trust or "they may well find themselves bereft of their professional status."[12]

NOTES

1. Associated Press. (6/9/2003). Harvard may relax policies on financial ties to drug companies. Available at *http://www.boston.com*.

2. J Drazen, G Curfman. Financial associations of authors. N Engl J Med 2002; 346 (24):1901-02.

3. *Id.*

4. S Brownlee. Doctors Without Borders. Washington Monthly. April 2004.

5. H Moses, JB Martin. Academic relationships with industry: A new model for biomedical research. JAMA 2001; 285:933-35; Association of American Universities. Framework document on managing financial conflicts of interest. Available at *http:www.aau.edu/reports/frwkFFCOI.html*; G Blumenstyk. University group offers new guidelines to govern potential research conflicts. Chron of Higher Educ October 19, 2001 Guidelines for Dealing with Faculty Conflicts of Commitment and Conflicts of Interest in Research (Washington DC; AAMC, 1990); M Angell. Is academic medicine for sale? New Engl J Med 2000; 342:1516-18; MK Cho, R Shohar, A Schissel, et al. Policies on faculty conflicts of interest at US universities. JAMA 2000; 284:2237-38; SV McCrary, CB Anderson, J Jakovljevic, et al. A national survey of policies on disclosure of conflicts of interest in biomedical research. New Engl J Med 2000; 343:1621-26; B Lo, LE Wolf, A Berkeley. Conflict-of-interest policies for investigators in clinical trials. New Engl J Med 2000; 343:1616-20; PhRMA adopts principles for conduct of clinical trials and communication of clinical trial results. Available at *http://www.phrma.org;* F Davidoff and others. Sponsorship, authorship, and accountability. New Engl J Med 2001; 345:825-6; L Guterman. 12 Medical journals issue joint policy on research supported by business. Chron Higher Educ October 5, 2001; International Committee of Medical Journal Editors. Uniform requirements for manuscripts submitted to biomedical journals. Available at *http://www.*

icmje.org; 21 CFR 54 et seq.; Public Health Service. Responsibility of applicants for promoting objectivity in research. Available at *http://grants.nih.gov/grants/guide/notice-files/not95-179.html* 1995.

6. JB Martin, DL Kasper. In whose best interest? Breaching the academic-industrial wall. N Engl J Med 2000; 343: 1646-49.

7. S Kaplan and S Brownlee. Dying for a cure: Why cancer patients often turn to risky experimental treatments — and wind up paying with their lives. U.S. News & World Report. Oct. 11, 1999 at 34.

8. DM Birch, G Cohn. Standing up to Industry as Corporations Increasingly Hold their Purse Strings, Many Researchers Feel Pressed to Deliver Favorable Results. Baltimore Sun. June 26, 2001. WL 6163085.

9. D Willman. Stealth merger: Drug companies and government medical research; Some of National Institutes of Health's top scientists are also collecting paychecks and stock options from biomedical firms. Increasingly such deals are kept secret. Los Angeles Times. December 7, 2003. Available at Westlaw 68902911. Alliance for Human Research Protection. Ex-NIH director lifted conflict of interest rule, now favors limits on drug-company ties. Available at *http://www.ahrp.org.* March 14, 2004; DG McNeil. Review finds scientists with ties to companies. *New York Times.* July 15, 2005. For final NIH ethics regulation and related information go to *http://www.nih.gov/about/ethics/COI.htm.*

10. S Krimsky. Conflict of interest and cost-effectiveness analysis. JAMA 1999; 282:1474-75; CD DeAngelis. Conflict of interest and the public trust. JAMA 2000; 284:2237-38, and articles cited therein.

11. M Rodwin. Medicine, Money, and Morals : Physicians' Conflicts of Interest. Oxford University Press. New York. 1993; RJ Porter, TE Malone. Biomedical Research: Collaboration and Conflict of Interest. The Johns Hopkins University Press. Baltimore and London. 1992; RG Spece, DS Shim, AE Buchanan. Conflicts of Interest in Clinical Practice and Research. Oxford University Press. New York, 1996.

12. N Moore. What doctors can learn from lawyers about conflicts of interest. BU L Rev 2001; 81:445-56.

1

An Overview of Clinical Research Funding and Conflicts of Interest: Defining a Financial Conflict of Interest

> He entreats us to regard the human vessel — the single most venerated and protected subject in any civilized society — as equal with the basest commercial commodity. He urges us to comingle the sacred with the profane. He asks much.
> — *Justice Armand Arabian, Moore v. Regents*

Modern science and medicine provide researchers with opportunities to enhance their financial wealth significantly through entrepreneurial activities. In some cases, the temptation proves too great, and research subjects suffer as a consequence. Newspaper headlines and journals are filled with articles discussing various types of financial conflicts, such as "Teenager's Death is Shaking up the Field of Human Gene-Therapy Experiments,"[1] and "Safeguards Get Trampled in Rush for Research Cash."[2] It has been said that "research ethics was born in scandal and reared in protectionism."[3] Today, we are devising the scientific, legal, and ethical parameters to deal with financial conflicts of interest in the research setting.

To understand the theoretical framework and arguments developed in this book, it is important to understand what constitutes a financial conflict of interest and why financial conflicts of interest matter.

This chapter explains why financial conflicts of interest jeopardize the future of clinical research. It laments the lack of an accepted and uniform definition of *financial conflict of interest* and provides a conceptual basis and a definition of financial conflict of interest. Because it may be difficult for even the most experienced clinical researchers to imagine all of the various arrangements that can result in a financial conflict, this chapter also provides illustrations of different types of financial arrangements that are often seen in clinical research that may constitute a conflict of interest.

WHY DO FINANCIAL CONFLICTS OF INTEREST MATTER?

Physicians and other medical researchers are sentries at the portals of life and death. We trust them with that which is most precious to us. In the past, the Norman Rockwell image of compassionate physicians and medical researchers whose sole allegiance was to patients and research subjects was commonplace. The respect and trust granted to these professionals were commensurate with the role they played. Today, this image has been tainted, in some instances, by financial conflicts of interest.

Financial conflicts of interest represent only one of several areas encompassing research integrity and the protection of human subjects. Yet, these conflicts present a serious and complicated challenge to the future of clinical research and to the preservation of the public's trust in research objectivity.[4]

It has been estimated that about 18,000,000 people are human research subjects in the U.S. alone each year.[5] Financial conflicts of interest in research are serious because they have the potential to harm individual research participants. On a more global scale, financial conflicts undermine trust in the research infrastructure upon which clinical medicine rests.[6]

The effect that financial conflicts of interest may have in undermining trust in clinical research has been previously discussed. Trust is the foundation upon which our research infrastructure, and particularly clinical research, have been built. As Thomas Bodenheimer, MD, noted, "If we are going to rely on the trust of patient subjects, of human volunteers, of taxpayers, to participate in research, we have to not only rely and build on their trust but to build a system that is trustworthy."[7]

Recent research reports that a declaration of competing interests may have a significant adverse effect on how readers view the credibility of published research.[8]

Public perception that financial conflicts compromise trust in researchers and research institutions may cause individuals to be less willing in the future to continue to participate in clinical research. Consequently, financial conflicts of interest may have serious, long-reaching effects on the future of clinical research.

DEFINING FINANCIAL CONFLICT OF INTEREST IN CLINICAL RESEARCH

What, then, is a financial conflict of interest in clinical research? This is a good question, as there is no uniform definition used throughout the literature. U.S. Public Health Service (PHS) regulations do not define financial conflicts of interest, leaving it to the discretion of institutions receiving PHS funding to determine which significant financial interests constitute conflicts of interests that must be reported to the NIH and "managed, reduced, or eliminated."[9]

A report by the U.S. General Accounting Office (GAO) on financial conflicts of interest in research states that a conflict between academia and industry exists when the relationship between them compromises, or appears to compromise, an investigator's professional judgment and independence in the design, conduct, or publication of research.[10]

According to Marc Rodwin, JD, PhD, "Conflicts of interests have the capacity to cause harm; the injury may not have yet occurred."[11] This is true to a degree. Just because a conflict of interest exists, this does not mean that the researcher or research institution engaged in conduct that actually harmed or injured a human subject.

As this author has previously stated, "The mere presence of a conflict of interest, whether acted upon or not, in all likelihood always injures the integrity of clinical research and researchers. In the public's psyche, the imagined influence a conflict may have on judgment may be just as damaging to the integrity of clinical research as any real influence."[12] Therefore, any financial incentives that have either the appearance of compromising or actually compromise a researcher or a research institution's objectivity should be avoided, so that independent judgment and objectivity are preserved.

In general, a financial conflict of interest may be defined as "any financial arrangement that compromises, has the capacity to compromise, or has the appearance of compromising, trust in clinical research."[13] It is again emphasized that, embraced within this definition, are two integral components: financial arrangements (a) that actually compromise a researcher's judgment or those (b) that only have the appearance of compromising or the ability to compromise judgment.

Because it is difficult to foresee all of the various financial entanglements between sponsors and researchers that may occur in clinical research and lead to conflict, the following section provides actual illustrations of some of the various arrangements that often lead to financial conflicts of interest.

DESCRIPTION OF TYPES OF FINANCIAL CONFLICTS OF INTEREST ASSOCIATED WITH INDUSTRY-SPONSORED RESEARCH

Financial conflicts of interest in the research setting have been described as an inevitable collision "between profit and objectivity,"[14] as the primary fiduciary duty of business is to produce profits for its stockholders, while the primary fiduciary duty of physician researchers and other clinical researchers is to research participants and the public good. Various authors have described the different types of conflicts of interest that may exist.[15]

Recently, this author reviewed the various types of financial conflicts of interest in clinical research,[16] and the following summarizes this description. Financial relationships between medical researchers and industry come in a variety of packages. For example, researchers at universities or other research institutions are often provided grant support to study or collaborate in developing a company's drugs, devices, or other products. Because universities, particularly public institutions, are always in need of funding, researchers' jobs often depend on their ability to garner outside grants to support themselves.

The funds for industry grants are channeled through an institution, which provides the credibility that researchers need. From a practical standpoint, institutions serve as a researcher's banker, in that it usually takes a "cut off the top" of the grant in the form of indirect costs for administrative and fixed costs, and then doles the money back out to cover the costs of the research. This often includes significant and long-term salary support for investigators and their research staffs. Although it is a circuitous mechanism by which a researcher receives support, it can nevertheless be, and often is, a major source of clinical investigators' livelihoods. This arrangement is not publicly transparent, and conceals that while technically researchers are employees of the university or research institution, they are often fully or substantially paid by a third party, such as industry. In some instances a university researcher's entire career and livelihood may have been almost wholly subsidized by industry. Clearly, it is easy to understand the dilemma such a relationship poses in the reluctance of researchers to take a position that is adverse to the interests of the sponsor underwriting the researcher's work.

Researchers who are studying a sponsor's product also are often simultaneously compensated by the sponsor to serve as consultants or join the company's advisory boards and speakers' bureaus. Both institutions and researchers may also enter into patent and royalty agreements with industrial sponsors.

In addition, researchers who are supported by an industrial sponsor may be listed as authors for articles that are ghostwritten by the sponsor.[17] As one expert on financial conflicts of interest in research has been quoted as saying, "Here we are entering the world of guests and ghosts. . . . Known instances are becoming common, as is the practice of paying big names to appear on the byline in place of the ghosts, though they contributed nothing except their prestige."[18] Survey results indicate that 19 percent of articles named authors who did not meet the criteria for authorship of the International Committee of Medical Journal Editors, and 11 percent were ghost-written by unnamed authors.[19]

Clinical researchers may also promote drugs and devices at company-sponsored symposia or accept expensive gifts and trips from companies that are, at the same time, providing researchers grants to study their products. Finally, there is the arrangement that has raised the most eyebrows, and received the most media attention: many researchers are given stock or equity interests in the companies whose products they are studying. In some instances, the researcher and/or the research institution establish their own start-up company to manufacture products that they have discovered through their research endeavors. Published research involving an analysis of articles from major medical journals indicates that 34 percent of lead authors held personal financial interests in their research,[20] and about 68 percent of academic institutions held equity in start-up businesses that sponsored faculty research.[21]

Sponsors of pharmaceutical medical devices have offered investigators financial incentives for enrollment of participants into a study.[22] While these enrollment fees are intended to cover the cost of subjects' participation, they typically are in excess of the costs. In academia, the excess funds are often used to support personnel, travel to meetings, or laboratory supplies and equipment. In contrast, within the private practice environment, the dollars often remain with the researcher.

Other kinds of incentive payments present similar concerns, such as finder's fees to physicians for referring patients to participate in clinical trials.[23] In an article intended to raise awareness of how serious the issues surrounding finder's fees are, the authors reported that physicians involved solely in commercial research have divulged annual incomes of more than $1,000,000 with profits of more than $300,000.[24] Finder's fees to parents to increase the enrollment of children in research have increased from $16,000 in 1997 to $45,000 in 2001.[25]

Such incentives are important tools for the sponsors of clinical trials, because they allow tight enrollment deadlines that keep costs down, and increase the potential profitability of the drug or device being studied, by permitting sponsors to meet the ever-increasing demand for research subjects to fill clinical trials.[26] However, these incentives may encourage enrollment of subjects who do not meet inclusion criteria for participation in the research. There have been reports that research participants involved in studies in which such financial incentives were used received drugs to treat conditions that they did not have, or participants were not told that the drug was experimental.[27]

Time is money when getting a new drug to market. Each day's delay in getting approval from the U.S. Food and Drug Administration (FDA) costs, on average, a reported $1.3 million.[28] Adverse research reports can impose tremendous costs on a company hoping to market a new drug or device. There are major incentives for industry research sponsors to try to influence the research process.

Such financial entanglements compromise or have the appearance of compromising an investigator's judgment in conducting related research. These arrangements give rise to conflicts of interest.

The ethical dilemma this poses is that, to receive industry funding, researchers must satisfy their sponsors, who in turn must make their stockholders happy. This transforms what once were academic and scientific endeavors, renowned for their objectivity, into corporate research. At times, such arrangements may require a researcher to agree that research findings that are important to science and to the public well-being, but deleterious to corporate supporters, will remain secret.[29] Results of one survey found that 27 percent of those with industry funding experienced delays of more than six months when publishing study results.[30] It has been estimated that 30 to 50 percent of contracts submitted by companies to investigators have clauses that control the publication of results in an unacceptable way.[31]

In addition, drug and product companies, driven by the profit motive, may decline to fund clinically important research because the results may reduce sales of other products. Companies that devise studies to be undertaken by investigators may purposefully design studies that favor their product. Often industry will sponsor a study that compares a product with a placebo, rather than with another treatment modality, because it is likely that the company's product will be better than none at all, but may not compare well with existing regimens. As previously noted, it is the latter comparison that is needed for informed decision making as to which drug is best.[32] The response by industry to this criticism is often that FDA regulations sanction the use of placebo controls.[33] However, it must be noted that the FDA does not require the use of placebo as the only control and it supports trials that include active controls.[34]

Other tactics that have been identified as ways to favor the outcome of a drug or product being studied include the following.[35] Studies may be undertaken in a healthier population than the one for which the drug or device is intended or involve insufficient doses of competing drugs, use administration routes that favor the study drugs, or surrogate end points that may not correlate with important clinical end points.[36] In some cases, individual investigators have been denied access to all of the study data in a multi-institutional clinical trial.[37]

Most recently, editors of the *Journal of the American Medical Association* (*JAMA*) condemned the pharmaceutical industry when it halted a large study of high blood pressure drugs to save money.[38] *JAMA* published the incomplete study to underscore how unethical the practice was. Rennie, deputy editor of *JAMA*, stated, "How can a sponsor do this when everybody . . . particularly the patients, have given their energy, their blood, their bodies . . . and suddenly they're just blown off."[39]

These practices may be an added incentive fostering a current trend of reduced innovation by the pharmaceutical industry. Only about 15 percent of new drugs approved by the FDA in the last decade were novel chemicals or innovations that were a significant improvement over older drugs; most were modified versions of existing medicines.[40] However, during the same time period, consumer spending on prescription drugs more than doubled, with most of the increased spending being attributed to "copycat" drugs.[41] This unsettling trend is even more troubling, given that *Fortune* magazine's 2002 annual ranking of the Top 500 companies found that the 14 companies that comprise the "pharmaceuticals" category had a median profit, as a percent of revenue, of 18 percent — higher than the profit of any other industry sector.[42]

As this author has previously written:

> Another type of financial entanglement that has not yet been adequately addressed in the literature but which poses the potential for very serious fallout is major gifts of endowed professorships. When a company for whom an investigator is studying their product or an industry related product provides the investigator's university or institution with a substantial endowment to establish a chaired professorship for the investigator, the income from the invested endowment is then used to support in large part the investigator's salary for the duration of the faculty member's tenure.
>
> Gifts of such magnitude are particularly problematic because, although they are in theory to be given without restrictions, there is no question that there are unspoken expectations that the investigator will not take a position that is adverse to that of the benefactor. As Spece et al. (1996) note, "[A]ccepting a gift carries tacit obligations, including gratitude and reciprocation." These authors go on to cite several surveys whereby there is evidence that industry gift-giving may adversely affect judgment.
>
> Because such gifts are generally reserved for more senior faculty, the investigator who is the beneficiary of such a gift may, in turn, exert undue influence on junior faculty to prevent undertaking or reporting results of research which may be adverse to the interests of the donor. This type of endowment may be one of the most prudent, but least discussed, investments industry makes."[43]

When billions of dollars in potential corporate profits or losses are at stake, supporting an investigator who could otherwise wreak serious havoc with profits can be a sound investment for an industry involved in introducing an innovative product or attempting to suppress the introduction of such new products by competitors.[44]

The relationships that develop between researchers and private industry are not surprising, considering the pressures that affect researchers. With the increasing demand for biotechnology and the skyrocketing costs associated with bench and clinical research, the need for research funding has increased. It is easy to understand why many researchers have turned to private industry for funding, and why industry has willingly participated.

INSTITUTIONAL CONFLICTS OF INTEREST

Not only have individual investigators become entrepreneurs, but many academic institutions have entered the world of medical entrepreneuralism.[45] In his recent book, Sheldon Krimsky, PhD, argues strongly against the commercial environment in which academic research is now conducted.[46] Noting how research has long been ripe for "industrial colonization" to harvest much needed revenues, Krimsky argues that universities have been reinvented as corporations.[47] The commercialization of intellectual property that originated in universities that resulted in licensing agreements has generated more than $20 billion for the U.S. academic community.[48] Today, most universities have offices that are devoted solely to the transfer of technology to industry and are dedicated to facilitating business arrangements such as patenting and/or licensing agreements.

It is acknowledged that academic institutions routinely sign research contracts that do not meet adequate ethical standards; this has led to a call for an independent entity that will review research contracts for compliance with standards of ethical integrity.[49] Rarely have such agreements ensured the independence of investigators, the design of studies, the collection of data, the analysis or interpretation of data, or the right to publish results.[50]

As will be discussed in more detail in chapter 2, passage of the Bayh-Dole Act[51] encouraged collaboration between industry and academia by giving grantees and contract organizations the titles to inventions that resulted from federally funded research. However, at the same time, this legislation introduced new conflicts of interest by vesting patent rights in inventions that resulted from federally funded research with the institution and investigator, and encouraging commercialization of such inventions.[52] As the working group for the National Human Research Protections Advisory Committee

(NHRPAC) points out, this new category of financial relationships is problematic.[53] Members of institutional review boards, (IRBs) groups that are responsible for protecting research subjects and approving clinical study protocols, often include department chairs or other high-ranking officials who no doubt understand the value of such investments to the institution, and their judgment, approval, and oversight may be impaired, or may have the appearance of being impaired, when they consider a relevant protocol and have countervailing concerns for patents, stock prices, or other related financial interests, such as end-of-year bonuses. A recent article on a survey of Association of American Medical College faculty found that 47 percent of those serving on IRBs also served as consultants to industry.[54]

In 2001, *Draft Interim Guidance* (hereinafter, *Federal Draft Guidance*) from the U.S. Department of Health and Human Services (DHHS) concerning financial conflicts of interest in research expressed concern about these risks, noting that members of IRBs "may be subject to institutional pressures, whether implicit or explicit, to approve research activities in which the institution has either a financial stake or other interest in the outcome of the research."[55] However, as noted in a 2001 GAO report on financial conflicts of interest,[56] federal guidance is limited on managing institutional conflicts of interest, particularly those conflicts of interest that relate to university start-up companies. Most recently, the federal government's new 2004 *Final Guidance* recommends that institutions engaged in federally supported human research consider separating responsibilities for financial and research decisions and establishing conflict of interest committees, or their equivalents, to be responsible for addressing institutional financial interests in research.[57]

Others have articulated strategies to deal with institutional conflicts of interest. For example, Adil Shamoo, PhD, and David B. Resnick. PhD, wrote an essay that compares institutional and individual conflicts of interest and proposes strategies to manage institutional conflict of interests.[58] The Association of American Medical Colleges (AAMC) has issued the most comprehensive recommendations concerning institutional management of financial conflict of interests.[59] A primary tenet of the recommendations is that institutions should assure that the administrative responsibilities that are related to human subjects research are separated from those related to investment management and technology licensing. The report's final section addresses the responsibility of IRB members to disclose any financial interests that could appear to be affected in the course of their duties and recommends that institutions publicly disclose all conflicts of interest that have not been eliminated.

Others have previously suggested that institutions create a separate entity to manage institutional equity interest in research sponsors.[60] For example, the Association of American Universities Task Force on Research Accountability has recommended that decision making about financial and research activities be segregated and independently managed.[61]

In meeting the challenge of managing financial conflicts of interest in clinical research, it is instructive to look at other professions. Michel Davis, PhD and Andrew Stark, PhD completed serious philosophical analysis of a conceptual framework to explore conflicts of interest and provide excellent guides through comparison of a wide range of professions, including law, anthropology, literary and art criticism, investment banking, and medicine.[62] Only a brief explanation is provided here; the reader seeking a detailed and sophisticated discussion of the philosophical and conceptual bases of conflicts of interest is referred to Stark's work on conflicts of interest in American public life.[63]

Conflicts of interest in general have a "legal pedigree" that grew out of fiduciary law.[64] A *fiduciary* is "one who owes to another the duties of good faith, trust, confidence, and candor."[65]

In the legal profession, for example, there are extensive codes, legal ethics opinions, and disciplinary proceedings by courts and state bar associations that govern the ethical conduct of lawyers regarding conflicts of interest.[66]

> (a) A lawyer shall not enter into a business transaction with a client or knowingly acquire an ownership, possessory, security or other pecuniary interest adverse to a client unless: (1) the transaction and terms on which the law-

yer acquires the interest are fair and reasonable to the client and are fully disclosed and transmitted in writing in a manner that can be reasonably understood by the client; (2) the client is advised in writing of the desirability of seeking and is given a reasonable opportunity to seek the advice of independent legal counsel on the transaction; and (3) the client gives informed consent, in a writing signed by the client to the essential terms of the transaction and the lawyer's role in the transaction, including whether the lawyer is representing the client in the transaction. . . .[67]

There is no parallel structure of standards and enforcement mechanisms to regulate clinical research. The medical profession has not had a strong tradition of self-regulation regarding financial conflicts of interest.[68] For example, the American Medical Association (AMA) *Principles of Medical Ethics* does not address the topic.[69] However, there are advisory opinions of the AMA Council on Ethical and Judicial Affairs (CEJA) that discuss a physician's ethical responsibilities in clinical research.[70]

In comparing how the legal and medical professions manage conflicts of interest, Nancy J. Moore, JD, notes, "Unlike rule-oriented lawyers, physicians traditionally view professional ethics as a matter of 'individual conscience',"[71] which is, as Mark Rodwin, JD, notes, "a subject over which well-intentioned individuals can, and often do, disagree."[72]

In contrast to the rules-oriented approach embraced by the legal profession, Moore characterizes the medical method as follows: "Beginning with the Hippocratic oath, medical codes have emphasized the 'discretion' of the individual physician to decide what conduct is ethically required in particular cases. In addition, the codes articulate standards, guidance, or bases for moral reasoning, rather than setting forth compulsory rules. As a result, physicians have failed to formulate relatively specific standards to guide their conduct."[73] Not surprisingly, standard casebooks on medical ethics often do not address financial conflicts of interest occurring in the medical profession. Likewise, "many doctors bridle at the notion [that] clinical researchers are easily tempted to be 'unethical' when their self-interest is directly involved" and "resist precautionary measures that they believe unfairly taint the whole profession for the misdeeds of a few."[74]

As others have pointed out, "to lawyers . . . such thinking on the part of physicians reflects a fundamental misunderstanding of the underlying purpose of both fiduciary law and conflicts of interest rules. These legal regulations are designed to hold fiduciaries to a higher standard of conduct than nonfiduciaries as a means of preserving the trust that is the hallmark of the fiduciary relationship."[75]

Unfortunately, it has taken the haunting visages of Jesse Gelsinger[76] and other clinical research tragedies[77] to breathe life into the public movement to hold clinical researchers and research institutions accountable for the protection of human subjects in the face of financial conflicts of interest (see chapters 6 and 7).

One of the major impediments faced by those who have been charged with the development of policies and regulations to manage conflicts of interest is the lack of empirical data. It is unfortunate that policy makers have been asked to devise solutions that remedy concerns associated with financial conflicts of interest in research, when they have very limited information on the incidence, prevalence, and causes of such conflicts. Nor are there sufficient data regarding the efficacy of existing policies and regulations that have been designed to ameliorate such concerns. Policy makers travel uncharted territory without a compass.

It is not surprising there is no uniform policy guidance for those engaged in research or policy making concerning the appropriate means to handle conflicts of interest.

The challenge is to develop mechanisms to reconcile the pressures, motivations, and incentives introduced into research by private funding with traditional scientific principles and ethical values that promote public well-being. Financial incentives propel scientific and medical advance.[78] As William Raub, MD, of the DHHS stated; "Our challenge . . . is not to arrest or reverse these trends that attend the commercialization of research results. Rather, our challenge is to understand and modulate these trends, such that our traditional commitment, the protection of human research subjects, is continually reaffirmed in word and continually exercised in practice."[79]

NOTES

The epigraph at the beginning of this chapter is from *Moore v. Regents of Univ. of Calif.* 51 Cal.3d 120, 148, 793 P.2d 479,497, 1990 (Arabian J. concurring).

1. SG Stolberg. Teenager's Death is Shaking Up Field of Human Gene-Therapy Experiments. NY Times. January 27, 2000. 2000 WL 12394777.
2. MJ Berens, J Manier. Safeguards Get Trampled in Rush for Research Cash. Chicago Tribune. September 5, 1999. 1999 WL 2908989.
3. National Institutes of Health. Conference on Human Subject Protection and Financial Conflicts of Interest Transcript. J Sugarman. Raising Ethical Questions Concerning Conflict of Interest Throughout the Process of Clinical Research. August 16, 2000. Available at *http://ohrp.osophs.dhhs.gov/ conflictofinterest8-15.htm.*
4. PM Tereskerz. Research accountability and financial conflicts of interest in industry-sponsored clinical research: A review. Accountability in Research 2003; 10:137-58.
5. AE Shamoo. Adverse events reporting—The tip of an iceberg. Accountability in Research 2001; 8:197-218.
6. Tereskerz, see note 4 above.
7. National Institutes of Health. Transcript. Conference on Human Subject Protection and Financial Conflicts of Interest. A Non-Federal Perspective: Thomas S. Bodenheimer. Available at *http://www.ohrp.osophs.dhhs.gov/conflict of interest/ 8-15.htm.* August 15, 2000.
8. S Chaudhry, S Schroter, R Smith et al. Does declaration of competing interests affect readers' perceptions? A randomized trial. BMJ 2002; 325: 1391-92; S Schroter, J Morris, S Chaudhry et al. Does the type of competing interest statement affect readers' perceptions of the credibility of research? A randomized trial. BMJ 2004; 328:742-43; SYH Kim, RW Millard, P Nisbet, C Cox, and ED Caine. Potential research participants' views regarding researcher and institutional fi-

nancial conflicts of interest. J Med Ethics 2004; 30:73-9.

9. Tereskerz, see note 4 above; 42 CFR Pt. 50 Subpart F.

10. General Accounting Office (GAO) Report to the Ranking Minority Member, Subcommittee on Public Health, Committee on Health, Education, Labor, and Pensions, U.S. Senate. GAO-02-89. November 2001.

11. M Rodwin. Medicine, Money, and Morals. Oxford Univ Press 1993. Pg. 225.

12. Tereskerz, see note 4 above.

13. *Id.*

14. S Wolfe. Transcript. Conference on Human Subject Protection and Financial Conflicts of Interest. August 16, 2000 Plenary Presentation. Available at *http://ohrp.osophs.dhhs.gov/conflict of interest8-16.htm.*

15. CD DeAngelis. Conflict of interest and the public trust. JAMA 2000; 284:2237-38, and articles cited therein; RG Spece, DS Shim, AE Buchanan. Conflicts of Interest in Clinical Practice and Research. Oxford University Press. New York. 1996.

16. Tereskerz, see note 4 above.

17. International Committee on Medical Journal Editors. Uniform requirements for manuscripts submitted to biomedical journals. JAMA 1997; 277:927-34; TA Brennan. Buying editorials. New Engl J Med 1994; 331(10):673-75.

18. NIH, see note 3 above.

19. A Flanagin, LA Carey, PB Fontanarosa et al. Prevalence of articles with honorary authors and ghost authors in peer-reviewed medical journals. JAMA 998; 280:222-24.

20. S Krimsky, LS Rothenberg. Conflict of interest policies in science and medical journals: editorial practices and author disclosures. Science and Engineering Ethics 2001; 7:205-18.

21. AUTM Licensing Survey FY 1999: Survey Summary. Northbrook, Ill.: Association of University Technology Managers 2000.

22. Tereskerz, see note 4 above.

23. Office of Inspector General. Recruiting Human Subjects: Pressures in Industry Sponsored Clinical Research. 2000; Pgs. 1-79; Office of Inspector General. Recruiting Human Subjects: Sample Guidelines for Practice. Pgs. 1-23.

24. T Lemmens, P Miller. The human subjects trade: Ethi-

cal and legal issues surrounding recruitment incentives. J Med & Ethics 2003; 31:398-414.

25. *Id.*

26. Tereskerz, see note 4 above; Office of Inspector General. Recruiting Human Subjects, Sample Guidelines, see note 22 above.

27. LB Andrews. Money is Putting People at Risk in Biomedical Research. Chronicle of Higher Education. Mar. 10, 2000 at B4.

28. Office of Inspector General. Recruiting Human Subjects: Pressures, see note 23 above.

29. Chalmers. Underreporting research is scientific misconduct. JAMA 1990; 263:105-08.

30. D Blumenthal. Withholding research results in academic life science: Withholding evidence from a national survey of faculty. JAMA 1997; 277:1224-28.

31. CT Maatz. University physician-research conflicts of interest: The inadequacy of current controls and proposed reform. High Tech. LJ 1993 7:137-88.

32. Tereskerz, see note 4 above.

33. Food and Drug Administration. (2001). Guidance for Industry: Choice of Control Group and Related Issues in Clinical Trials.

34. Tereskerz, see note 4 above.

35. *Id.*

36. PA Rochon, PB Berger, M Gordon. The evolution of clinical trials: Inclusion and representation. 1998; CMAJ 159:1373-74; T Bodenheimer. Uneasy alliance — clinical investigators and the pharmaceutical industry. New Engl J Med 2000; 342:1539-44; LA Bero, D Rennie. Influences on the quality of published drug studies. Int J Technol Assess Health Care 1996; 12(2)209-37.

37. KA Schulman, DM Seils, JW Timbie et al. A national survey of provisions in clinical-trial agreements between medical schools and industry sponsors. N Engl J Med 2002; 347(17): 1335-41.

38. MP Bruce, D Rennie. Stopping Medical Research to Save Money. A Broken Pact with Researchers and Patients. JAMA 2003; 289:2128-31.

39. Associated Press. JAMA Decries Early End to Study.

WSJ April 23, 2003 at D4.

40. Associated Press. FDA Approved Fewer New Drugs Over Decade. Augusta Chron. A07. May 29, 2002.

41. *Id.*

42. Available at *http://www.fortune.com/lists*.

43. Tereskerz, see note 4 above; cite to Spece et al., in the quote, is: RG Spece, DS Shim, and AE Buchanan (1996). Conflicts of interest in clinical practice and research. New York: Oxford University Press.

44. R Holding. Safety Designs Proposed — But Not Produced. San Francisco Chronicle. April 14, 1998; W Carlsen. Virginia Scientist Leads Fight to Protect Health Care Workers. San Francisco Chronicle. April 14, 1998; CBS News: 60 Minutes. Contaminated Needles Pose Grave Danger to Health Care Workers. Transcript available at 2001 WL 8032808.

45. E Emanuel, D Steiner. Institutional conflict of interest. New Engl J Med 1995; 332:262-67.

46. S Krimsky. Science in the Private Interest: Has the Lure of Profits Corrupted Biomedical Research? Rowman and Littlefield 2003.

47. R Horton. The Dawn of McScience. New York Review of Books. Volume 51(4A) March 11, 2004.

48. Dueker's in PA Rochon, PB Berger, and M Gordon. The evolution of clinical trials: Inclusion and representation. 1998; CM AJ 159: 1373-74, citing Senator Birch Bayh. Keynote Address: Sixteen Years of Bayh-Dole. MIT Conference on Intellectual Property Rights: Corporate Survival and Strategic Advantage (Dec. 9-10, 1996).

49. G DuVal. Institutional ethics review of clinical study agreements. J Med Ethics 2004; 30:30-34.

50. *Id.*

51. Bayh-Dole Act, Pub L No. 96-517 (1980).

52. LB Andrews. Money is Putting People at Risk in Biomedical Research. Chron Higher Educ. Mar. 10, 2000 at B4.

53. Correspondence to Arthur J. Lawrence, Assistant Surgeon General from Mary Faith Marshall, Chairperson for NHRPAC dated 8/23/2001. Available at *http://ohrp.osophs.dhhs.gov/nhrpac/doc~report.htm*.

54. EG Campbell, JS Weitsman, B Clarridge et al. Characteristics of medical school faculty members serving on insti-

tutional review boards: Results of a national survey. Accountability in Research 2003; 78:831-35.

55. Public Health Service. Draft Interim Guidance. Financial Relationships in Clinical Research: Issues for Institutions, Clinical Investigators, and IRBs to Consider When Dealing with Issues of Financial Interests and Human Subject Protection. Available at *http://ohrp.osophs.dhhs.gov/nhrpac/mtg12-00/finguid.htm*. January 10, 2001.

56. GAO Report, see note 10 above.

57. Department of Health and Human Services. (5/03/04). Final Guidance: Financial relationships and interest in research involving human subjects: guidance for human subject protection. Replacing Department of Health and Human Services. (3/31/2003). Draft: Financial relationships and interest in research involving human subjects: guidance for human subject protection.

58. AE Shamoo, DB Resnik. (2003). Responsible Conduct of Research. Oxford University Press; AE Shamoo, DB Resnik. Conflict of interest and the university. Accountability in Research 2002; 9:45-64.

59. American Association of Medical Colleges. (October 2002). Protecting subjects, preserving trust, promoting progress II: Principles and recommendations for oversight of an institution's financial interests in human subjects research. Available at *http://www.aamc.org/members/coitf/*.

60. H Moses, JB Martin. Academic Relationships with Industry: A New Model for Biomedical Research. JAMA 2001; 285:933-35.

61. Association of American Universities, Task Force on Research Accountability. (October 2001). Report on individual and institutional financial conflicts of interest; Association of American Universities. Framework document on Managing Financial Coi's. Available at *http://www.aau.edu/reports/frwkCOI'S.html*.

62. M Davis, A Stark (Eds). Conflict of Interest in the Professions. 2002; A Stark. Conflict of Interest in American Public Life. Harvard University Press 2000.

63. A Stark. Conflict of Interest in American Public Life. Harvard Univ Press 2000.

64. RG Spece, Jr. et al. (Eds). Entrepreneurial Doctors and

Lawyers: Regulating Business Activities in the Medical and Legal Professions. In Conflicts of Interest in Clinical Practice and Research at 1996.

65. Black's Law Dictionary. 7th Ed. 1999.

66. See, e.g., American Bar Association, Model Rules of Professional Conduct.

67. Black's Law Dictionary, see note 65 above.

68. NJ Moore. What doctors can learn from lawyers about conflicts of interest. BU L Rev 2000; 81:445.

69. American Medical Association. Code of Medical Ethics and Current Opinions, in Rena A. Gorlin, Codes of Professional Responsibility: Ethics Standards in Business, Health, and Law 339, 341 (4th Ed. 1999). See also American Medical Association. Principles of medical ethics. 2001. Available at *http://www.ama-assn.org.*

70. Council on Ethical and Judicial Affairs. Gifts to physicians from the industry (opinion 8.061 of Dec. 3, 1990). JAMA 1991; 265-501.

71. N Moore. Entrepreneurial Doctors and Lawyers: Regulating Business activities in the Medical and Legal Professions, in Conflicts of Interest in Clinical Practice and Research at 183 (Roy G. Spece, Jr. et al. (Editors), 1996).

72. M Rodwin. The organized American medical profession's response to financial conflicts of interest: 1890-1992, 70 Milbank Q 705 (1992).

73. FH Miller. Trusting Doctors: Tricky business when it comes to clinical research. BU L Rev. 2001; 81:423-43.

74. *Id.*

75. Rodwin, see note 72 above.

76. Jesse Gelsinger was an 18-year-old participant in a Phase One safety trial of a gene transfer procedure. In a wrongful death claim that was subsequently settled for reportedly a substantial amount, Jesse's family claimed that the investigators failed to disclose, among other things, that the investigators had financial ties to the company whose product was being tested for safety in the clinical trial. Dr. Wilson, the director of the University of Pennsylvania's Institute for Gene Therapy, held ownership interest in the company whose product was evaluated in the trial. J Washburn. Informed Consent. One Lawyer's Assault on the Medical Research Establishment.

Washington Post. December 30, 2001.

77. Stolberg, see note 1 above; Hippocrates Meets Mammon. The Economist Newspaper Ltd. Sept. 22, 1990, Pg. 95.

78. Office of Research Integrity. Reported Misconduct Activity Increases for 2nd Consecutive Year. Available at *http://ori.dhhs.gov/html*.

79. National Institutes of Health. Conference on Human Subject Protection and Financial Conflicts of Interest. Transcript. WF Raub. Perspective from the DHHS. Available at *http://www.ohrp.osophs.dhhs.gov/conflict of interest/8-15.htm*. August 15, 2000.

2

How Financial Conflicts of Interest in Clinical Research Evolved: A Recent Passage through Time

> Academic science has been a public resource, a repository for ideas, and a source of relatively unbiased information. Industrial connections blur the distinctions between corporations and the university, establishing private control over a public resource. Problems of . . . proprietary rights are inherent in these new relationships and hold serious implications for both academic science and the public interest.
> — *Dorothy Nelkin*

In this chapter we explore the question of why conflicts of interest in clinical research have become more prevalent. The chapter examines the political and historical factors behind current financial conflicts of interest in clinical research.

HISTORIC BACKGROUND

In the past, relatively little academic research was funded by private industry, and the majority of funds were from government grants.[1] Historically, as beneficiaries of public funds, universities were viewed as sanctuaries for research conducted in a quest for knowledge to benefit society. As such, researchers and universities were not burdened by concerns about the economic ramifications of a clinical trial's outcome.[2] In other words, the engine driving the academic train was the pursuit of scientific knowledge, not financial gain. Today there are various pockets of funding that sustain research and help propel the academic train.

FUNDING SOURCES

Federal research grants constitute a major source of funding for clinical research. This funding is usually channeled through an institutional employer such as a university or medical center. The federal grants cover the cost of research, including salary support for the investigators that is proportionate to the amount of time devoted to the research. Academic institutions such as universities benefit from this type of funding in several ways. Economically, institutions are compensated for housing the research, via payments for indirect costs by the government to the institution; these payments often amount to approximately 50 percent or more of the total direct costs of conducting the research.

This stream of funding is one of the most sought after by academic institutions, because it is associated with a high degree of prestige. Because grant funding from federal agencies such as the National Institutes of Health (NIH) or the National Science Foundation (NSF) is highly competitive and peer reviewed, the amount of such federal funding an institution has in its coffers is considered an important component in acquiring and sustaining a high ranking. This, in turn, affects the institution's ability to attract the best students and faculty who procure the funding in the first place, creating a circle of synergy.

As previously noted, industry is also now a major player in subsidizing various types of research in the United States. Pharmaceutical, food, and automotive companies, as well as the electronics industry, to mention only a few, conduct a substantial amount of research *outside of academic settings*. Of the $170 billion spent on research and development in 1995, private industry paid for 59.4 percent, the federal government for 35.5 percent, and 5.1 percent came from other organizations, such as foundations or universities.[3]

While the federal government has been the foremost source of funding for clinical research in the past, today it is surpassed by private industry, and there is a definite trend for a greater percentage of this research to be supported by the private sector.[4] Recent research reports that 28 percent of faculty members in the life sciences receive funding from private sponsors.[5] As stated in the foreword to this book, the proportion of private sector funding for healthcare research rose from 42 percent in 1986 to 52 percent in 1995, representing a threefold increase, from $6 to $19 billion dollars.[6]

However, most funding for all types of *academic* research still comes from the federal government, and NIH is the leading source. In the year 2000, the Association for University Technology Managers (AUTM) reported $29.5 billion dollars in sponsored research expenditures from 190 reporting institutions. Of this, 61 percent of research expenditures were funded by the federal government and 9 percent by industry.[7] Over the past 10 years, 67 to 71 percent of research expenditures were made by the federal government, while the amount from industry remained about the same, 8 to 9 percent.[8]

Yet financial entanglements with industry have become pervasive.[9] Several reasons have been offered.[10] Expenditures on medical treatment greatly exceed research and development spending, and the number of NIH grant applications has steadily increased, leading to increased competition for the decreasing amount of funds available. This has created greater pressure for institutions to seek funds from other sources. Various financial liaisons with industry such as licensing agreements, for example, have helped to fill this gap;[11] 70 percent of active licenses of universities that responded to an AUTM survey were in the life sciences.[12]

THE UNION BETWEEN ACADEMIA AND INDUSTRY

Marcia Angell, MD, outlines the reasons for the coalescing of the once distinct borders between academia and industry.[13]
1. There has been a need to facilitate technology transfer of new drugs and devices from the laboratory to the marketplace.
2. Academic medical centers need the money, as many are "bleeding red ink as a result of reduction in Medicare and

the hard bargaining of other third-party payers to keep hospital costs down."[14]
3. In the past, academic institutions had a monopoly when it came to performing clinical trials for industry for several reasons: (a) lack of in-house expertise in industry; (b) available populations of patient research subjects at academic hospitals; and (c) the credibility and prestige of academic publications necessary to market industry's products.

However, the model has changed, and academia's position has been substantially weakened by competition from for-profit contract-research organizations and site-management organizations. Because there is evidence that the commercial sector completes trials more efficiently, in terms of both time and money, the percentage of industry money for clinical trials that is dedicated to academic centers has dropped from 80 percent in 1991 to 40 percent in 1998.[15]

These are the reasons that a marriage between academia and industry, within the realm of clinical research, was necessary. But, as described in the next section, it was a major shift in national policy, accomplished through the enactment of a series of laws, that facilitated this union and allowed the relationship to flourish.

BACKGROUND

The Patent and Trademark Law Amendments Act, commonly referred to as the Bayh-Dole Act of 1980 (P.L. 96-517), and the subsequent amendments included in P.L. 98-620 that were passed in 1984, were the primary catalysts for the change in the way we subsidize a large portion of clinical research.

Joseph B. Martin, MD, PhD, notes that the seeds of the current debate in "breaching the wall between academia and industry" emerged as early as the late 1700s. He recounts the following story.[16]

> Benjamin Waterhouse, one of the three full-time professors at Harvard Medical School, received a copy of Edward Jenner's Inquiry into the Causes and Effects of the Variolae Vaccinae. Armed with new knowledge of the efficacy of cowpox vaccination for the prevention of small-

pox, Waterhouse proposed to test the vaccine in Boston, and if successful, to develop a monopoly under which he would inoculate New England children for a fee. After receiving three cowpox preparations from England, Waterhouse inoculated first his son Daniel, then six other members of his household. He next carried out a clinical study in which 19 children were inoculated twice, then exposed to smallpox for 20 days in a Boston hospital. Not one child came down with smallpox — surely one of the most successful clinical trials of all time, "whatever modern day ethicists might say about the impropriety" but the medical school's two other professors, John Warren and Aaron Dexter, were outraged at Waterhouse's behavior, which they saw as self-serving. Dissent engendered by this and other events led in 1812 to the expulsion of Waterhouse from the faculty, despite former U.S. president Thomas Jefferson's active support of Waterhouse as the founding father of vaccination in the United States. [Citations omitted.][17]

In the 1920s, there were not many U.S. universities involved in the commercialization of research discoveries to private industry. But, for the most part, the wall between academia and industry had not begun to crumble. By and large, as a concept, the transfer of technology from academia to industry is associated with a report entitled *Science — The Endless Frontier*, written by Vannevar Bush for President Franklin D. Roosevelt in 1945.[18] Bush recognized that increasing the transfer of knowledge from basic science to industry held significant promise in terms of economic value. This report emerged around the time that the U.S. military had placed special training and development projects at various universities to assist with the World War II effort, such as the Manhattan Project, established by the U.S. in 1941 as a secret program to develop an atomic bomb. The report was influential in stimulating increased funding of research by the federal government and the formation of the NIH, NSF, and the Office of Naval Research.[19]

The massive infusion of federal dollars to universities was accompanied by a significant amount of federal regulation and an "ever-more-Byzantine" regulatory structure of government, creating an uncoordinated maze of regulations, eventually resulting in 26 different sets of agency regulations on government funding of academic research.[20]

In the 1960s and 1970s there was considerable concern about the lack of success by the federal government in promoting the commercialization of research emerging from federally funded university research. By 1980, the government had title to approximately 28,000 patents, but fewer than 5 percent were licensed to industry for development of commercial products, a situation with serious economic ramifications, as well as ethical concerns that potential cures were not reaching patients.[21] As Kenneth S. Dueker, JD, succinctly states:

> It seemed intuitive that if tax dollars paid for the research behind an invention that the government should own it. The problem was that government ownership of patents did not result in these inventions truly being in the public domain. Few companies were willing to take licenses on government-held patents. Thus, the government had "possession without enjoyment" of this property. To the chagrin of the federal government, the primary impediment to the public use of government-sponsored innovations was the government itself. . . . Thus, while the government held title to inventions in the putative name of public interest, valuable tax dollars actually were squandered on ideas that were inaccessible to those who could put them to viable use, a true "tragedy of the common." [Citations omitted.][22]

As this author has previously written,

> Because the hurdles were so great for research institutions to surmount the presumption of federal title, and, in addition, few had the institutional infrastructure to associate with commercial partners, it was feared by the 1970's that the United States was losing its competitive edge by failing to capitalize on its own innovations. Consequently and ironically, U.S. tax dollars subsidizing research ultimately provided an advantage to foreign economic competitors (Duecker, 1997). In an effort to remove the barriers to tech-

nology transfer, Congress enacted a succession of laws that would allow the federal investment in research, then emerging as an important national asset, to reap greater financial returns. In order to facilitate the commercialization of this research into technology, these laws provided opportunities for both research institutions and researchers to share in the ownership and the potential profitability of the products resulting from the transfer of technology from the scientific bench to the marketplace.[23]

THE BAYH-DOLE ACT

Enter the 1980 Bayh-Dole Act, which unlocked the federal maze of bureaucracy that stymied the transfer of technology from the research lab to industry.[24] In 1978 Senators Birch Bayh (D-Indiana) and Robert Dole (R-Kansas) introduced a bipartisan bill that ultimately became the Bayh-Dole Act. This act removed the barriers to the transfer of research technology from the ivy-covered walls of academe to private industry. In 1980, the Bayh-Dole Act was passed. Regulations clarifying provisions of the Act appeared in 1987.[25] As Senator Bayh noted:

> The foundations for the technology transfer and patent policies embodied in Bayh-Dole can be traced back almost 200 years to the Lewis and Clark expedition. . . . [Thomas] Jefferson realized that allowing Lewis and Clark to publish their own journals would accelerate the settlement and commercialization of the region. Jefferson thought that knowledge generated through the use of federal funds would more quickly become of practical use to the general public if those who discovered this information were given the financial incentives to commercialize that knowledge.[26]

Passage of this act was not without intense debate: "The record shows that the debate included such issues as whether exclusive licenses would lead to monopolies and higher prices; whether taxpayers would get their fair share; whether foreign industry would benefit unduly; and whether ownership of inventions by a contractor is anti-competitive. From the beginning, it was obvious that economic interests rather than academic science interests were the driving forces for the change in governmental policy."[27]

The Bayh-Dole Act allowed universities and small businesses to participate in the financial ownership of inventions that were the result of federal funding, and to be direct participant in the commercialization of the inventions, by patenting products and permitting exclusive licensing by the university to industry. The statute required that the royalties accrued by a university must be shared with the inventor, and all of the remaining balance, less expenditures for patenting, licensing, and other incidental expenses, must be used to support scientific research and education. The intent was that the licensing of new inventions from universities to industry would enhance the manufacture of products in the U.S. and stimulate domestic economic growth.

THE FEDERAL TECHNOLOGY TRANSFER ACT

The Federal Technology Transfer Act, passed in 1986, offered private industry the opportunity to gain rights to intellectual properties that were the result of its collaboration with scientists in federal laboratories.[28] Beginning in 1988 and 1989, NIH laboratories entered into the what are known as Cooperative Research and Development Agreements (CRADAs), which were provided for in this statutory scheme. CRADAs are contracts in which a company contributes funds and expertise to a federal laboratory in exchange for rights to any resulting patentable inventions. Under this Act, the government is required to share at a rate of no less than 15 percent of total royalties resulting from CRADAs with the scientist who discovered the technology.[29] This Act followed the Stevenson-Wydler Technology Act of 1980, which required federal laboratories to develop the capacity to transfer technology to industry.[30] As a result of this Act, all federal agencies established Offices of Research and Technology Transfer.

REALIZING THE EFFECTS OF FEDERAL LEGISLATION

There seems to be little disagreement that there has been a sharp increase in U.S. university patenting and licensing following passage of the legislation discussed. In fiscal year 2000, the number of new U.S. patent applications filed rose 15 percent, continuing an upward trend in the number of applications filed each year for the last 10 years.[31]

Most commentators tend to immediately conclude that the Bayh-Dole Act was responsible for this trend. There has been little empirical study of this assertion. At least one set of investigators, however, has undertaken a statistical analysis of the increased patenting activity by examining three academic institutions that were the leading recipients of licensing and royalty income during the 1990s, and concluded that the growth in patenting activities since 1981 in these universities represents "an acceleration of a trend that predated the passage of Bayh-Dole. . . . Nevertheless, Bayh-Dole did serve an important role in legitimizing these practices and accelerating these trends. . . ."[32] The authors also acknowledge, "The passage of this law almost certainly hastened the entry by many universities . . . into patenting and licensing activities that they formerly avoided as a matter of policies."[33]

However, these authors make the argument that the Act should be viewed within the context that it was only one component of a broad U.S. policy shift toward improved protection of intellectual property rights.

Other contemporaneous factors confound the picture and make it difficult to determine exactly to what degree the Bayh-Dole Act caused the increase in university patenting and licensing. These factors include:

1. The growth of federal financial support for biomedical research, beginning in the late 1960s.
2. The related rise in biotechnology research, beginning in the early 1970s.
3. A series of at least 14 other laws passed by Congress that strengthened intellectual property protection;[34]
4. The 1980 U.S. Supreme Court's Decision in *Diamond v. Chakrabarty*,[35] upholding the validity of a broad patent in the then-new biotech industry, which opened the door to patenting organisms, molecules, and other biotechnological techniques.
5. Establishment of the Court of Appeals for the Federal Circuit in 1982 to serve as the court of final appeals in patent

cases, which is recognized as a champion of patent-holder rights.

The Court of Appeals for the Federal Circuit has upheld patent rights in about 80 percent of cases argued before it, representing a substantial increase from the 30 percent rate before its creation.[36]

These developments, and particularly the Bayh-Dole Act, have been viewed as the great catalysts that spurred universities to become "engines of economic growth," by supplying industry with research, new products, and processes.[37] The concern, however, is that when newspaper headlines read, "Scientists' 'Publish or Perish' Credo Now 'Patent and Profit' — 'Recombinant U.' Phenomenon Alters Academic Culture" that the pendulum may have swung too far.[38]

It seems clear that an infusion of industry dollars is needed to sustain academic research, and that this has improved clinical practice in some areas. The Council on Governmental Relations cites a few examples originating from federally funded universities, including:
- Artificial lung surfactant for use with newborn infants,
- Cisplatin and carboplatin cancer therapeutics,
- Citracal® calcium supplement,
- Haemophilus B conjugate vaccine,
- Metal alkoxide process for taxol production,
- Neupogen® used in conjunction with chemotherapy,
- The process for inserting DNA into eukaryotic cells and for producing proteinaceous materials,
- Tecombinant DNA technology, and
- Trusopt® ophthalmic drops used for glaucoma.[39]

Others have also cited magnetic resonance imaging, positron-emission tomography, and microscopic surgical approaches.[40]

Many advances in medical research would not have been realized without industry support. Such collaboration allows for the rapid transfer of technology that fosters development of new products and benefits society greatly. In addition, in many instances industry-sponsored research is conducted in an ethical manner. This having been said, it must be recognized that research discoveries are not always translated into clinical practice. In fact, the need to better translate research discoveries into measurable improvements in healthcare has been clearly described by the Institute of Medicine and other healthcare leaders. Accordingly, the Agency for Healthcare Research and Quality and the Veterans Administration have programs that are solely devoted to encouraging research that addresses the translation of research into improved quality care, safety, and healthcare outcomes.[41]

The issue becomes, how does our society insure that research will be conducted in a manner that preserves the public's trust in research objectivity and assures the safety of research subjects? A new model will be proposed in chapter 10 to help resolve this dilemma within the realm of clinical research.

NOTES

The epigraph cited at the beginning of this chapter is from Dorothy Nelkin, *Science as Intellectual Property: Who Controls Research?* available at *http://www.aaup.org/publications/Academe.*

1. PM Tereskerz. Research accountability and financial conflicts of interest in industry-sponsored clinical research: A review. Accountability in Research 2003; 10:137-58.

2. JP Liebeskind. Risky Business. Universities and Intellectual Property. Academe (quoting Dorothy Nelkin, *Science as Intellectual Property: Who Controls Research?*). Available at *http://www.aaup.org/publications/Academe.*

3. A Shamoo, D Resnik. "Collaboration between Academia and Private Industry." Responsible Conduct of Research. Oxford University Press 2002.

4. PC Kuszler. Curing conflicts of interest in clinical research: Impossible dreams and harsh realities. Widener L Symp J 2001; 8:115.

5. CT Maatz. University physician-research conflicts of interest: The inadequacy of current controls and proposed reform. High Tech. LJ 1993 7:137-88.

6. *Id.*

7. AUTM. Licensing Survey FY 2000. Available at *http://*

www.autm.net.

8. Kuszler, see note 4 above.

9. JB Martin, DL Kasper. In whose best interest? Breaching the academic-industrial wall. N Engl J Med 2000; 343: 1646-49.

10. Council on Governmental Relations. The Bayh-Dole Act: A Guide to the Law and Implementing Regulations. September 1999; Tereskerz, see note 1 above.

11. KS Dueker. Biobusiness on campus: Commercialization of university-developed biomedical technologies. Food and Drug L J 1997; 52:453.

12. Tereskerz, see note 1 above.

13. M Angell. Is academic medicine for sale? New Engl J Med 2000; 342: 1516-18.

14. *Id.*

15. T Bodenheimer. Uneasy alliance—clinical investigators and the pharmaceutical industry. New Engl J Med 2000; 342:1539-44.

16. Martin and Kasper, see note 9 above.

17. Bodenheimer, see note 15 above.

18. V. Bush. Science — The Endless Frontier, *http://www.nsf.gov/od/lpa/nsf50/vbush1945.htm.*

19. Dueker, in PA Rochon, PB Berger, M Gordon. The evolution of clinical trials: Inclusion and representations. 1998; CMAJ 159: 1373-74, citing Senator Birch Bayh. Keynote Address: Sixteen Years of Bayh-Dole. MIT Conference on Intellectual Property Rights: Corporate Survival and Strategic Advantage (Dec. 9-10, 1996).

20. *Id.*

21. *Id.*

22. *Id.*

23. Tereskerz, see note 1 above; the citation to Dueker is to KS Dueker. Biobusiness on campus: Commercialization of university-developed biomedical technologies. Food and Drug L J 1997; 52:453.

24. Bayh-Dole Act, Pub L No. 96-517 (1980).

25. 37 CFR Section 401 (2002).

26. Dueker, see note 19 above.

27. *Id.*

28. P.L. 96-580.

29. *Id.*

30. 15 USCA Sections 3701-1715 (2002).

31. Kuszler, see note 4 above.

32. DC Mowery, RR Nelson, BN Sampat, AA Ziedonis. The growth of patenting and licensing by U.S. universities: An assessment of the effects of the Bayh-Dole Act of 1980. Available at *http://www.sipa.columbia.edu.*

33. *Id.*

34. ML Katz, JA Ordover. R & D competition and cooperation. *Brookings papers on economic activity: Microeconomics* 1990; 1990: 137-92.

35. 447 U.S. 303, 100 S.Ct. 2204, 1980.

36. Mowery, see note 32 above.

37. *Id.*

38. T Abate. "Scientists' 'Publish or Perish' Credo Now 'Patent and Profit' — 'Recombinant U.' Phenomenon Alters Academic Culture." San Francisco Chronicle. Aug. 18, 2001 at D1.

39. Dueker, see note 11 above.

40. AUTM, see note 7 above.

41. AHQR and VA Announce Research Priority: Translating Research Into Practice. Press Release, February 19, 2002. Agency for Healthcare Research and Quality. Rockville, Md. *http://www.ahrq.gov/news/press/p2002/tripaper.htm.*

3

The Fallout: Realizing the Effects of Financial Conflicts of Interest in Clinical Research

> The biotechnology revolution has moved us literally or figuratively, from the classroom to the boardroom and from the *New England Journal* to the *Wall Street Journal*.
> — Leon Rosenberg, Princeton University

WHY CONFLICTS OF INTEREST NEED TO BE STUDIED: MAGNITUDE OF THE PROBLEM

In this chapter, a factual foundation is provided to support the central theme of this book — a new model to manage conflicts of interest is needed. This is done through a review of empirical data and a discussion of anecdotal cases. Here the approach is the same as that used by lawyers when first presenting a case to a jury; first the facts are presented, and, in subsequent chapters, the application of the facts to existing laws will take place. While the empirical data reviewed are of no doubt more significant import from an academic perspective in developing the argument, the anecdotal cases are presented because they breathe life into the problem. They humanize the dilemma that financial conflicts present by painting a picture of real-life research tragedies that accompany financial conflict. Such depictions are more memorable and elicit a greater response than statistical recitations.

BACKGROUND

The debate over researchers engaging in enterprises that could compromise the integrity of research findings began in the mid 1980s. This controversy accompanied the tremendous growth that occurred in the past several decades in biomedical science. Biotechnology began to be viewed as big business around 1980 and now embraces more than 500 companies that have annual sales in the billions of dollars.[1] In the process, the integrity of clinical research has, in some instances, been compromised.

Financial conflicts of interest in clinical research have been described by the Association of American Medical Colleges (AAMC) as the single issue that poses the "greatest threat to maintaining public trust in biomedical research."[2]

Researchers now often serve several masters — the institution where they work, those who provide them with research funding, and research subjects. It has long been acknowledged that "No servant can serve two masters: for either he will hate the one, and love the other; or else he will hold to the one and despise the other."[3] As one nursing researcher said, "In 20 short years, science 'morphed' from its noble traditions of public good to its present, somewhat tarnished, reputation."[4]

In part, this flawed image is due to changes in how we go about the business of funding research. As two science journalists stated in their book on scientific fraud, *Betrayers of the Truth*, "the roots of fraud lie in the barrels, not the bad apples that occasionally roll into public view."[5] The same may be said of divided loyalties that affect clinical research.

As noted in chapter 1, the entrepreneurial temptation has been compelling, and there is a noticeable trend in which academic liaisons with industry appear to be gaining greater momentum.[6] Over the past decade, the financial ties between biomedical researchers and industry have grown, with private firms increasing their spending on biomedical research at a greater rate than the federal government.[7] In a recent investigation, the Inspector General's Office noted that there has been "Transformation of clinical research into a traditional business model" and documented the often highly unethical and possibly illegal recruitment practices of subjects for clinical trials.[8]

Marcia Angell, MD, former editor of the *New England Journal of Medicine,* concluded that while most medical schools have guidelines concerning financial relationships between faculty and industry, the rules are "quite relaxed and are likely to become even more so."[9] In support of this statement, Angell pointed out that Harvard Medical School, noted for having strict guidelines governing potential financial conflicts of interests, was in the process of softening its guidelines. Following publication of Angell's editorial and other intense scrutiny by the press, Harvard decided to keep its ethics guidelines in place.[10] Most recently, as previously noted, Harvard is once again considering whether to relax policies on financial ties to pharmaceutical companies.[11]

Angell goes on to describe an article on antidepressant drugs in the *New England Journal of Medicine (NEJM),* in which the authors' ties with the industry that manufactured the drugs were so extensive, it would have taken too much space to disclose them in *NEJM.* Therefore, the ties were summarized on the *NEJM* website. She described the difficulty that *NEJM* had in this instance, and others, in finding individuals to write editorials on articles evaluating drugs because there were so few investigators who did not have financial ties to companies that make the drugs at issue. In an unusual letter to readers, *NEJM* announced that it had violated its own disclosure guidelines by publishing drug evaluations written by doctors who had conflicts of interest 19 times since 1997.[12]

It must be remembered that journals have their own financial conflicts of interest. For example, a recent *Washington Post* story reported on an article that was critical of the increased use of an expensive medicine used for transplant patients that was rejected for publication by *Dialysis and Transplantation,* the most widely circulated journal in the field, because the journal's marketing department objected to publishing it, and overruled the editor's decision to publish it.[13] Even more troubling is a recent study that found that less than 1 percent of scientists who publish drug research findings report their financial ties to the company whose product they researched.[14]

One may certainly posit that just because there are incentives to allow conflicts of interest to mar scientific or clinical judgment, it does not necessarily follow that these concerns are realized. However, recent reports indicate that several of the nation's foremost researches have yielded to the allure of biomedical profits at the expense of patient care, as described below. While it is unknown whether scientific misconduct occurs more frequently among physicians, compared with other scientific researchers, it is noteworthy that the most publicized cases of such misconduct have involved physicians conducting biomedical research.

THE EMPIRICAL EVIDENCE

The evidence goes far beyond the anecdotal case reports described and includes empirical data, albeit limited, that demonstrate that financial conflicts of interest exist to the detriment of clinical research and society. As biomedical research and the profession of medicine have embraced a business or market model, public perception of biomedical research and healthcare has changed.

Historically, universities have been seen as important in a system of checks and balances, in which academic scientists have been the objective players. Public scrutiny has come to the fore as the business of biomedical research has resulted in several recent tragic outcomes, including several highly publicized deaths, in which investigators had financial entanglements or a personal stake with the financial sponsor of the research. The stories of the victims of these tragedies have been well publicized, and will be discussed throughout this book; they have been important factors in undermining the public's trust in biomedical research.

The effects of conflicts of interest emerging from the research setting are particularly troubling because damaging and injurious results from inappropriately managed conflicts can adversely affect the treatment of thousands of patients. Clinical investigators' results often establish a gold standard of treatment that is followed worldwide.[15] Consequently, any results tainted by a researcher's own financial interests may have serious and long-reaching effects, and, for this reason, are particularly egregious.

While anecdotal reports of the tragic results of clinical trials that have been plagued by financial conflicts of interest are emotionally gripping and may have broad public or political appeal, empirical data provide a more rational basis for justifying the need for research to address the issue of financial conflicts of interest in research. A meta-analysis of 37 studies concerning financial conflicts of interest concludes that industry-sponsored studies are significantly more likely to reach favorable conclusions to the sponsor than studies that are not supported by industry, that relationships involving industry-sponsored research are "pervasive and problematic," and that management of such conflicts is in a "state of flux."[16] This meta-analysis points to the concern about the influence that industry sponsorship has on the integrity of research involving the efficacy of drugs.

While the authors of this meta-analysis also cite several studies that found industry-sponsored research to be similar in quality with other research, they point out that these studies were limited, in that they used assessment instruments based on methodological criteria such as blinding and randomization, which, while important, "fall short" of assessing a study's overall quality, which would also require consideration of, for example, the questions studied and the use of appropriate control therapies.

Lexchin and colleagues undertook a meta-analysis of 30 studies to assess whether the funding of studies by the pharmaceutical industry was associated with outcomes that were favorable to the sponsor, and whether the methods used were different, relative to sponsorship. The authors conclude, "Systematic bias favours products which are made by the company funding the research. Explanations include the selection of inappropriate products to compare with the products being investigated and publication bias."[17] None of the 13 studies that analyzed reported methods found that the studies funded by industry were of poorer quality. However, the authors make the point that this does not guarantee the absence of bias in industry studies, since outcomes could be influenced by factors left out of the quality scores that were studied.

In addition, as previously described by this author,[18] the medical literature is replete with individual articles expressing concern about the undue influence that industry dollars have on the integrity of medical research. Bodenheimer summarized several such findings.[19]

Stelfox and colleagues: Researchers whose work supported the safety of calcium-channel antagonists had a higher frequency of financial relationships with manufacturers of the drugs than those who did not support their safety.[20]

Davidson and colleagues: Research findings favoring a new therapy versus a traditional one were more likely if the study was funded by the new therapy's manufacturer.[21]

Bero and colleagues: Articles from symposia sponsored by a single drug company were more likely to have outcomes that were favorable to the sponsor's drugs than articles without industry support.[22]

Friedberg and colleagues: 38 percent of studies with non-profit funding reached unfavorable conclusions about cancer drugs, compared to only 5 percent of industry-sponsored pharmoeconomic studies of the cancer drugs.[23]

Rochon and colleagues: Trials of non-steroidal anti-inflammatory drugs always reported the sponsor's product equal or superior to the product to which it was compared.[24]

Kjaergard and colleagues: Randomized clinical trials published in the *British Medical Journal (BMJ)* involving pharmacological and non-pharmacological products from 12 specialties reported that there was a significant association between the authors' conclusions and financial competing interests; whereas, personal, academic, and political competing interests were not significantly associated with the authors' conclusions.[25] As the authors of this study point out, it is likely that this finding is true for studies published in journals other than the *BMJ* because, in fact, other major journals publish a much higher portion of trials funded by the pharmaceutical industry than *BMJ*.[26]

While the empirical data presented do not prove a causal relationship between industry sponsorship and results, but instead look only to associations, there are now enough data from many different sources to raise serious questions and

The Effects of Financial Conflicts of Interest

concerns about the propriety and ethical ramifications of industry-sponsored research.

In addition, there may be some less obvious negative ramifications. Research by Blumenthal and colleagues indicates that, in the academic setting, when faculty members receive more than two-thirds of their research support from industry, that:

1. They are less academically productive than those receiving a lower level of support.
2. Their published articles are less influential than those by researchers with no industrial support.
3. They are significantly more likely than those without industrial support to report that trade secrets resulted from their work and that they took commercial considerations into account when choosing research topics.[27]

These results are consistent with other literature summarized by Cho and colleagues, who report that faculty who have industry ties are more likely to report research that is favorable to the sponsor, are more likely to conduct lower quality research, and are less likely to disseminate their results to the scientific community.[28]

As this author has previously stated,

> Because research protocols funded by industry often do not undergo the same rigorous peer review as those submitted to governmental entities such as NIH, for example, it provides a much less formidable means by which to obtain funding for those researchers whose work may not otherwise withstand the scrutiny of highly competitive peer review required by other funding sources. Comparatively, industry funding is easy money that may inure to those who may be better at networking than engaging in scientific research. In this regard, the public good is harmed in that the limited resources available for research are not being channeled to the most qualified researchers. It also allows industry the opportunity to design studies that are likely to produce favorable results for their products that would have otherwise never withstood the scrutiny of a purely objective evaluation.[29]

When the bar is lowered in terms of the requirements that a drug or device must meet to pass muster, the quality of such products is likely lower than it otherwise would have been if such products were subjected to rigorously objective scientific protocols.

ANECDOTAL CASES

Deplorable episodes have arisen that unfortunately have involved some of the most prestigious medical journals and research institutions in the country. The following provides a review of selected cases of financial conflicts of interest when the ramifications from such conflicts were just beginning to receive public attention.[30] These cases are reviewed because they breathe life into empirical evidence. They are important because it is likely that the public reacts to cases such as these, and they are a major component in undermining public trust in the research enterprise.

RETIN-A

In 1988 the *Journal of the American Medical Association* *(JAMA)* published a report concerning Retin-A, a drug that, according to the article, held great promise as it reduced wrinkles in aging skin and may have prevented skin cancer.[31] The report led to tremendous coverage of the drug in the lay press, which, in turn, resulted in record sales. Subsequently, the report became the subject of a congressional committee report that cited the drug trial as one of 10 egregious instances of alleged or proven misconduct in biomedical research.[32] The editors of *JAMA* did not know that the authors of the article had failed to mention their considerable economic ties to the firm manufacturing Retin-A. As it turns out, the researchers conducted the study employing methodology that may have biased results in favor of Retin-A. A panel of NIH experts appointed to assess the drug concluded that the efficacy of Retin-A as applied to aging skin had not been proven.

EXPERIMENTAL TEST FOR CANCER

Duke University has also been tarnished by a conflict of interest episode. In 1986 a woman with a history of breast cancer underwent surgery for abdominal cancer that was nonexistent.[33] The patient also needlessly underwent radiation therapy for cancer diagnosed in her ribs, meaning that she would be unable to receive any additional radiation therapy in the future if she were to develop cancer again, because she had already received the maximum exposure allowed. The cancer was diagnosed by an experimental test developed by Duke pathologist William Johnston, MD, who was chief of the Cytopathology and Cytogenetics Division at Duke University. Johnston reportedly used hundreds of the tests a month and received $15,000 a month in extra fees, despite admonitions from his department chairman to use the method frugally. A lawsuit involving this episode was settled.

VITAMIN A LOTION

Harvard Medical School did not remain unscathed.[34] A research fellow, Scheffer Tseng, MD, conducted clinical trials of a vitamin A lotion used in the treatment of a condition known as dry eye, the underlying etiology of which may be the result of several diseases that can ultimately destroy the cornea and result in blindness. The results of Tseng's works were never published. His findings indicated that the ointment was not an effective treatment. As it turns out, Tseng and his supervisor, Kenneth Kenyon, owned large blocks of stock in Spectra Pharmaceutical Services, a company formed to purchase the patent rights of the vitamin A treatment, and, when the company went public in 1985, there were strong incentives to cover up the inconclusive results of their research that involved Tseng's treatment of his patients with additional drugs, and to change dosages without his patients' consent. It is reported that Tseng and his relatives made more than $1 million selling Spectra stock.[35] Tseng and Kenyon were charged by the state medical board with the following:
1. Violating Harvard's conflict of interest policy in owning stock in a product they were using in their research,
2. Failing to follow guidelines to protect study patients,
3. Failing to inform the public that vitamin A was not working as expected to relieve the dry eye problem,
4. In Tseng's case, treating patients with a substance not approved for human use without their consent.

The magistrate concluded that Tseng did not engage in fraudulent or unethical behavior. However, despite finding by the magistrate that Tseng violated hospital policy and study protocol in conducting the research, the charges were dropped against both physicians, with the chairman of the medical board stating, "We don't really have to exactly follow what [the magistrate] decides. . . . There was no patient harm and so . . . we felt that this was really the best thing to do."[36]

OTITIS MEDIA TREATMENT

A saga that unfolded at the University of Pittsburgh involved a pediatric researcher, Charles Bluestone, MD, who received $3.5 million in research funds and more than $250,000 in honoraria and travel fees from pharmaceutical companies with interests in a study he was conducting to evaluate the efficacy of amoxicillin in the treatment of children's ear infections.[37] The original study was funded by NIH for $17.5 million.

In 1984, the Otitis Media Research Center, directed by Bluestone, had an accumulated deficit of approximately $300,000. Bluestone wrote letters to three drug companies asking if they would be willing to have their products evaluated against amoxicillin. Several companies agreed and contributed about $3.4 million to support clinical trials. Once the new sponsors were added, Bluestone, who had concluded that amoxicillin was effective when compared with a placebo in the treatment of ear infections in children, made changes to the original study design to include two new costly antibiotics in the trial. These changes disturbed Erdem Cantekin, MD, a co-investigator, who challenged Bluestone's conclusions. Cantekin claimed, "It was a fraudulent study. . . . This isn't a question of scientific interpretation. They made certain changes to make the drugs look better." Cantekin argued that the end point for measuring whether or not treatment was successful should be at eight weeks, while Bluestone contended that it should be at four weeks. Apparently, the data indicated that, after four weeks, a small percentage of children receiving the antibiotics had healthier ears than those taking a placebo, while at eight weeks there was no difference. Then, in 1985, with their data complete, Cantekin and Bluestone arrived at opposite conclusions based on the study data. Bluestone judged antibiotics useful for ear infections while Cantekin did not.

Bluestone, the senior investigator, wrote the official paper reporting the study results and submitted it to the *New England Journal of Medicine*. Cantekin drafted a separate report of the study with his own conclusions and submitted it to the journal. *NEJM* asked officials at Pittsburgh to choose one paper for publication, and university officials responded that only Bluestone was authorized to publish the data.

According to a story about this debacle that appeared in the *Wall Street Journal*, over the next five years Cantekin's accusations were considered and rejected by several panels, including three university committees that exonerated Bluestone. One NIH inquiry found Bluestone should have been more forthright about his acceptance of private funding when applying for NIH grants, but that his conduct was excused, while another recommended that Bluestone be placed on five years administrative oversight for "having analyzed the data from NIH-funded research in a manner biased toward the effectiveness of the antibiotics he had evaluated with public monies."[38]

In 1990, the congressional Subcommittee on Human Resources and Intergovernmental Relations, which held hearings on scientific misconduct in research, was highly critical of both the University of Pittsburgh and Bluestone for handling Cantekin's claims, and found that most troubling was that Cantekin's dissenting report had been, in essence, censored. The subcommittee concluded, "Evidence of the ineffectiveness of antibiotics would have been available to physicians and the public several years ago, if the medical school had not prevented Dr. Cantekin from publishing them."[39]

In the ensuing years, as the dispute continued, several independently financed studies found that, for most ear infections, antibiotics are little more effective than no treatment at all, and that serious consequences result from too many children taking too many antibiotics, in the form of drug-resistant strains of bacteria.[40] This has caused many physicians to prescribe shorter courses of treatment, or to wait to see if an infection doesn't resolve in a few days, and if it does not, only then prescribing antibiotics.[41]

In the years following Cantekin's original allegations, millions of dollars and thousands of hours were spent on this controversy, and the story still hasn't ended; 15 years later, Cantekin is broke and has been, for all practical purposes, exiled by the university for his whistleblowing activity. Cantekin filed a whistleblower lawsuit.

Cantekin had avoided the legal system until the 1991 case discussed above was brought, and he would not consider a financial settlement with the university. His lawyer stated, "The first thing Pittsburgh did when they found out [Dr. Cantekin] had retained me was to dispatch a lawyer to my office with a checkbook. . . . The lawyer closed the door and asked, 'What does he want?' But for [Dr. Cantekin], it wasn't a question of money. You couldn't settle with him because you couldn't settle the scientific issue."[42]

THE TISSUE PLASMINOGEN ACTIVATOR EPISODE

Tissue plasminogen activator (tPA) is a genetically engineered drug approved by the Food and Drug Administration in 1987 and produced by Genentech.[43] It is used to destroy blood clots following myocardial infarction. A known side-effect of the drug is that both low and high doses may result in brain hemorrhage. The tPA episode outlined below chronicles just how high the stakes can become when economic forces are factored into the medical decision-making equation.

During the years 1983 to 1989, scientists from 13 universities and five laboratories were involved in conducting clinical trials of tPA that were sponsored by the NIH. Published results from the tPA trials led many physicians to believe that tPA was superior to streptokinase, an alternative treatment that received FDA approval prior to tPA. The study results received favorable press, leading many in the medical community to believe tPA was the drug of choice.

Treatment with tPA at that time cost approximately $2,000 more per patient than streptokinase, and, looking only at the U.S., the two drugs competed for a share in a potential market of 500,000 patients. Consequently, to justify the more than $1

billion a year difference in deeming tPA the treatment of choice, the scientific data supporting tPA as the drug of choice would have to be compelling.

TPA's future appeared rosy. The jury was in, with a published report in the prestigious *New England Journal of Medicine,* finding tPA to be superior to streptokinase in the treatment of heart attack victims through its ability to open occluded arteries.[44] The value of Genentech stock rose from $18 to $28 a share during the month in which the article appeared.

Then, the unthinkable happened. A congressional report citing egregious episodes in medical conduct appeared and implicated the tPA trials. It was revealed that at least 13 of the researchers, three of whom were instrumental in designing the tPA trials, owned stock in Genentech or had options to buy the stock at a discount, which, the congressional committee concluded "could have created a conflict of interest."

Examining the presentation of results in the *NEJM* article did not allay concerns of conflicts of interest. The article, its critics argued, accentuated data that were favorable to tPA and failed to mention findings that were not as promising. For example, the investigators failed to indicate that no significant differences existed between patients receiving tPA and those receiving streptokinase in terms of the functioning of the heart's left ventricle, an important predictor of mortality related to the dissolution of blood clots.[45] Even more importantly, the study failed to report that both tPA and streptokinase produced a systemic effect on blood that could lead to hemorrhaging. This serious side-effect remained unpublished by the NIH grantee researchers until 1987/1988, at which time several articles published by other researchers had already brought attention to this serious untoward effect.

Evidence brought forth at the congressional hearing disclosed that twice during the trials researchers increased the doses of tPA without informing patients. The increased dosages caused intracranial hemorrhages in five of 311 patients, and three of these patients died as a result. Major bleeding was also observed in 41 of the remaining patients, ultimately leading to a decision to reduce the recommended dosage.

It was further revealed that the consent forms used in most of the hospitals participating in the tPA trials failed to mention that tPA was an experimental drug, not yet approved by the FDA, that could produce lethal side-effects resulting from bleeding in some cases. Consent forms used in most all of the study institutions were remarkably similar, because the original model form was designed by Elliot Grossbard, MD, a Genentech employee.

Obviously, researchers always have a vested interest in enrolling a sufficient number of individuals to participate in their studies to yield meaningful results. However, when scientific enthusiasm is compounded by financial interests, the incentive to enroll a sufficient number of study subjects becomes even more compelling. The failure of the consent forms in the tPA trials to represent the potential risks was admittedly wrong, according to the director of NIH's Office for the Protection from Research Risks.[46]

The final blow in the tPA saga came when a 1989 study by the original NIH-funded researchers and a 1990 study conducted by scientists with no financial ties reported tPA and streptokinase to be equally efficacious in the treatment of heart attack victims.[47] The congressional hearing found that the research literature on tPA contained repeated examples of evaluations presenting a more favorable outcome for tPA by scientists with relationships with Genentech, compared to those without such associations.

After such reports, it might be reasonable to assume that there would be little likelihood of similar incidents down the road. However, we continue to learn about investigators' financial conflicts of interest that are associated with untoward results, compromising trust in the research enterprise. For example, in 2004, *The Lancet* revealed a financial conflict of interest in research that linked an increasing rate of autism in children to vaccine for measles, mumps, and rubella (MMR).[48] The editors at *The Lancet* were unaware that, at the time of publication, the researcher received funds from lawyers investigating whether parents of children with autism could sue for compensation, based on an alleged link between autism and the MMR vaccine. The editor stated that the journal may not have published the research if this conflict had been known.

NOTES

The epigraph at the beginning of chapter 3 is from L. Daniels. *Commercialization of Human Tissues: Has Biotechnology Created the Need for an Expanded Scope of Informed Consent?* 27 Calif. W. L. Rev. 209, 210 (quoting) Leon Rosenberg. *Using Patient Materials for Product Development: A Dean's Prospective.* Clinical Research 1985; 33:452-53.

    1. D Hamilton. White Coats, Black Deeds; The New Scientific Method: Lie, Cheat, and Get Good PR, 22 (3) Washington Monthly 23 (April 1990) (on Lexis).
    2. RP Kelch. Maintaining the public trust in clinical research. N Engl J Med. 2002; 346:285-87.
    3. MA Rodwin. Strains in the fiduciary metaphor: Divided physician loyalties and obligations in a changing health care system. Am. J L & Med 1995; 21:243-57 (FN11 *quoting* Luke 16:13 (King James).
    4. VP Tilden. Preventing scientific misconduct — times have changed. Nursing Res 2000; 49:243.
    5. W Broad, N Wade. *Betrayers of the Truth*. New York, Simon and Schuster 1982.
    6. E Boyd, L Bero. Assessing faculty financial relationships with industry. JAMA 2000; 284:2209-14.
    7. PN Ossorio. Pills, bills and skills: Physician-researcher's conflicts of interest. Widener L Symp J 2001; 8:75-103.
    8. Office of the Inspector General. Recruiting Human Subjects: Sample Guidelines for Practice, pgs. 1-23.
    9. M Angell. Is academic medicine for sale? New Engl J Med 2000; 342:1516-18.
    10. S Nadi. Harvard keeps its ethics guidelines (news). Nature 2000; 405 (6786):497.
    11. Associated Press. (6/9/2003). Harvard may relax policies on financial ties to drug companies. Available at *http://www.boston.com*.
    12. WM Bulkeley. Publication Broke Rules on Disclosure. The Wall Street Journal. February 24, 2000. 2000 WLWSJ 3019181.
    13. S Vedantam. Business, Science Clash at Medical Journal. Washington Post. February 7, 2004.

14. SG Stolberg. Scientists Often Mum About Ties to Industry. NY Times. April 25, 2001.

15. PM Tereskerz. Research accountability and financial conflicts of interest in industry-sponsored clinical research: A review. Accountability in Research 2003; 10:137-58.

16. JL Bekelman, L Yan, CP Gross. Scope and impact of financial coi's in biomedical research. JAMA 2003; 289:454-65.

17. J Lexchin, LA Bero, B Djulbegovic, O Clark. Pharmaceutical industry sponsorship and research outcome and quality: systematic review. Br Med J 2003; 326:1167-70.

18. Tereskerz, see note 15 above.

19. T Bodenheimer. Uneasy Alliance — clinical investigators and the pharmaceutical industry. New Engl J Med 2000; 342:1539-44.

20. HT Stelfox, G Chua, K O'Rourke, AS Detsky. Conflict of interest in the debate over calcium-channel antagonists. N Engl J Med 1998; 338:101-6.

21. RA Davidson. Source of funding and outcome of clinical trials. J Gen Intern Med 1986; 1:155-158.

22. LA Bero, D Rennie. Influences on the quality of published drug studies. Int J Technol Assess Health Care 1996; 12:2009-37.

23. M Friedberg, B Saffran, TJ Stinson, W Nelson, CL Bennett. Evaluation of conflict of interest in economic analyses of new drugs used in oncology. JAMA 1999; 282:1453-57.

24. PA Rochon, PB Berger, M Gordon. The evolution of clinical trials: Inclusion and Representation. 1998; CMAJ 159: 1373-74.

25. LL Kjaergard, B Als-Nielsen. Association between competing interests and authors' conclusions: Epidemiological study of randomized clinical trials published in the BMJ 2002; 325:249.

26. Editor's Choice. Western medicine: A confidence trick driven by the drug industry? BMJ 2002; 325:7358.

27. D Blumenthal, DG Campbell, N Causion, LK Seashore. Participation of life-science faculty in research relationships with industry. New Engl J Med 1996; 335:1734-39.

28. M Cho, R Shohara, A Schissel, R Drummond. Policies on faculty conflicts of interest at US universities. JAMA 2000;

284:2203-8.

29. Tereskerz, see note 15 above.

30. The sources for the facts presented in the cases discussed in this section are cited in the first sentence of each section.

31. Hippocrates Meets Mammon. The Economist Newspaper Ltd. Sept. 22, 1990 at 95; H.R. 1-101-688, 101st Congress, 2d Sess. At 24 (1990).

32. H.R. at 5. The study quoted in this article followed one by the original TIMI Study group also ultimately finding no difference in the two drugs. *See* TIMI Study Group. Comparison of Invasive and Conservative Strategies After Treatment with Intravenous Tissue Plasminogen Activator in Acute Myocardial Infraction, New Engl J Med 1989; 320:218. The 1990 international study confirmed the 1989 TIMI Study groups' results and reported that streptokinase was as effective as t-PA in terms of reducing mortality even though tPA costs 10 times more. *See* HR 101-688, 101st Congress, 2d Session at 24 (1990). Negative medical reports were accompanied by unfavorable press of the drug and dramatic drops in the value of Genentech stock. *See id.;* L. Altman, *Study Finds No Difference in 2 Heart Attack Drugs*, N.Y. Times (March 30, 1989); M. Waldholz, *Genentech Heart Drug Dealt Critical Blow*, Wall St. J (March 30, 1989).

33. P. Gosselin. Doubts Grow Over Doctor's Favored Cancer Test. Boston Globe a1, June 9, 1989.

34. P Gosselin. Flawed study helps doctors profit on drug. Boston Globe at 1, October 19, 1988. Editorial: A medical-research sullying. Boston Globe at A3, October 23, 1988; D Kong. Charges against 2 dropped. Eye researchers had been accused of ethical violations. Boston Globe at 50, April 13, 1992.

35. Hippocrates, see note 31 above.

36. *Id.*

37. Cho et al., see note 28 above; Hippocrates, see note 31 above; C Crossen. The Treatment: A Medical Researcher Pays for Challenging Drug-Industry Funding. He Said Antibiotics Weren't Good for Kids' Earaches; His Peers Found Otherwise. Wall Street Journal January 3, 2001.
at A1.

38. Crossen, see note 37 above.

39. *Id.*
40. *Id.*
41. *Id.*
42. *Id.*
43. Cho, see note 28 above; Hippocrates, see note 31 above.
44. *TIMI Study Group: The Thrombolysis in Myocardial (TIMI) Trial.* New England J of Med 1985; 312:932.
45. H.R. 1-101-688, see note 31 above. *at* 20. The congressional committee noted that this finding was not reported until 1987. *See* F Sheehan. The Effect of Intravenous Thrombolytic Therapy on Left Ventricular Function. Circulation 75:817 (1987).
46. *Id.*
47. H.R. 1-101-688, see note 31 above.
48. R Horton. A statement by the editors of The Lancet 2004; 363 (9411):820-21.

4

Policies and Regulations on Conflicts of Interest in Research

> Financial advisers who sell you insurance or mortgages are required by the rules to tell you how much commission they will earn as a result of your custom. But doctors who ask patients under their care to take part in a clinical trial are under no obligation to reveal how much they might earn as a result of their patients agreeing to take part in the trial. Can this be right?
> — *Jammi N. Rao and L.J. Sant Cassia*

The preceding chapter put the magnitude of the problem of financial conflicts of interest into perspective. This chapter will explain the need for a new model to manage financial conflicts, and describe how existing policies, laws, and regulations to manage financial conflicts are insufficient. This chapter will move from the presentation of factual information to the application of law to the facts.

There has been much discussion on financial conflicts of interest in the recent medical literature, and many professional societies are in the process of developing, or have developed, policies. Several professional organizations have published position papers or opinions in related areas concerning the relationship between the pharmaceutical industry and physicians.[1]

THE POSITIONS TAKEN BY
PROFESSIONAL ORGANIZATIONS AND JOURNALS

The appropriate approach to take when faced with financial conflicts of interest has received widespread attention, with various perspectives presented in the medical literature.[2] Experts have proposed models for managing academic relationships with industry.[3]

As early as 1990, the Association of American Medical Colleges (AAMC) defined institutional and individual responsibilities concerning conflicts of interest in research.[4] More recently, the AAMC Task Force on Financial Conflicts of Interest in Clinical Research met to develop guidelines for addressing financial conflicts of interest. AAMC has issued reports dealing with individual and institutional conflicts of interest.[5] The guidelines identify circumstances in which researchers with financial conflicts of interest may be allowed to participate in research; institutional responsibilities for oversight and management of conflicts of interests; and the individual responsibilities of faculty, staff, and students with regard to such conflicts. A core principle underlying the guidelines is that *the welfare of the patient is paramount*.[6]

The Association of American Universities developed a mechanism to manage investigators' conflicts of interests,[7] and, in 2000, formed the Task Force on Research Accountability, which issued a report on improving the protection of human research subjects.[8] This association has recommended that no investigator who has a financial interest in the research should participate in studies involving human subjects, "except in compelling circumstances." Under such circumstances, research subjects should be told of the investigator's financial interests, and the institution should monitor the researcher's involvement and insure that a review board monitors the study.[9]

The American Society of Gene Therapy has implemented one of the most stringent conflict of interest policies for all principal investigators conducting gene therapy research. The policy states, "all investigators and team members directly responsible for patient selection, the informed consent process and/or clinical management in a trial must not have equity, stock options, or comparable arrangements in companies sponsoring the trial. The American Society of Gene Therapy requests its members to abstain from or to discontinue any arrangement that is not consonant with this policy."[10] Adding to the burgeoning field of organizations assessing human research protection activities and conflicts of interest is the Association for the Accreditation of Human Research Protection Programs (AAHRPP), a nonprofit organization that offers accreditation to institutions engaged in research involving human participants, which has a separate set of standards, including those involving financial conflicts of interest.[11]

In addition, PhRMA (Pharmaceutical Research and Manufacturers of America), which represents leading research-based pharmaceutical and biotechnology companies, adopted a set of principles governing the conduct and reporting of clinical trials.[12] These principles add little substantively to the field and are, in essence, a reiteration of existing regulatory requirements and guidelines adopted by other groups.

Most recently, several of the world's most prominent medical journals announced a uniform policy intended to assure the independence of researchers' work, supported by businesses.[13] The journals agreed that they would reject manuscripts by authors who did not have control of either the data or the decision to publish.[14] Most journals have not had such policies in place. In July 2001, a report that looked at policies of research journals regarding conflicts of interests found that, of 1,396 journals sampled, representing 61,134 articles, only 181 had a conflict of interest policy.[15] In addition, as discussed earlier, less than 1 percent of scientists publishing drug research findings report their financial ties with the company whose product they researched.[16]

In 2001, the International Committee of Medical Journal Editors issued revised *Uniform Requirements for Manuscripts Submitted to Biomedical Journals,* which require full disclosure of the sponsor's role in research and assurance that investigators are independent of the sponsor, that investigators are responsible for the design and conduct of the trial with independent access to all trial data, and that investigators control editorial and publication decisions. In an effort to preserve public trust, the guidelines were issued to promote integrity.[17] Unfortunately, a study[18] that assessed compliance with the guidelines found that academic institutions regularly participated in industry-sponsored research that did not adhere to the guidelines and that institutions "rarely ensure that their investigators have full participation in the design of trials, unimpeded access to trial data, and the right to publish their findings."[19] In addition, leading NIH-funded medical schools agreed on guidelines to strengthen conflict of interest policies for schools, hospitals, and research institutes.[20]

GOVERNMENT REGULATIONS AND INITIATIVES

The U.S. Department of Health and Human Services (DHHS) has regulations pertaining to financial interests in biomedical research. The rules are divided into those covering federally funded research and those governing privately funded research.[21] The U.S. Public Health Service (PHS) and the Food and Drug Administration (FDA) have had regulations requiring financial disclosure for clinical investigators in place since 1995 and 1998, respectively.[22] In addition, regulations for protection of human research subjects have been adopted by 17 different departments and independent agencies of the federal government. Oversight within DHHS for federally funded or regulated biomedical research is the responsibility of three entities: the National Institutes of Health (NIH), the FDA, and the Office for Human Research Protections (OHRP).

THE NATIONAL INSTITUTES OF HEALTH

NIH is responsible for assuring that the research it funds complies with the applicable DHHS regulations[23] on individual investigators' financial interests. Accordingly, organizations funded by PHS must do the following:
1. Maintain and enforce written policies on financial conflicts of interest,
2. Inform investigators of these policies, and
3. Require investigators, their spouses, or dependent children to disclose any significant financial interests in entities that may be affected by the research.

Policies and Regulations

These interests are defined as those that would be affected by research or in entities whose financial interests reasonably appear to be affected by research, including salaries (not from the applicant institution) over 12 months or equity interests greater than $10,000 or 5 percent ownership in one entity, royalties or other payments greater than $10,000 in the next year, and patents. It is left to the discretion of institutional officials to determine whether a significant financial interest constitutes a conflict of interest. If it is determined that such an arrangement presents a conflict of interest, the institution must then report the conflict of interest to the PHS and explain whether the conflict has been "managed, reduced or eliminated." These latter terms are not defined by PHS regulations, but examples of strategies to manage the conflicts are provided.

THE U.S. FOOD AND DRUG ADMINISTRATION

The FDA is charged with insuring that clinical investigators' financial interests and arrangements do not interfere with the reliability of data that is submitted in support of applications for marketing drugs, biological products, or medical devices.

The FDA published a final rule in 1999 that acknowledged that investigators' financial interests in the outcome of a study may be a source of bias depending on the following:
1. The way payment is arranged,
2. Whether the investigator has a proprietary interest in the product, or
3. Whether the investigator has an equity interest in the study sponsor.[24]

Consequently, federal regulations now require that submission of a marketing application to the FDA must be accompanied by certification that the investigator did not have certain types of financial interests, or, alternatively, the investigator must disclose them. This information is used by the FDA, together with information submitted on the purpose of the study, its design, and information obtained from on-site inspections, to assess the reliability of the data that are submitted. Unlike the PHS regulations, FDA regulations require disclosure of payments made by the study sponsor to the investigator or the investigator's institution of any amount greater than $25,000 over and above costs to conduct the study, or an equity interest an investigator has in a publicly traded company sponsoring the research greater than $50,000.[25] The FDA may consider clinical studies and data resulting from them inadequate, if, among other factors, steps have not been taken in the design, reporting, and analysis of data to minimize bias that could include financial conflicts of interest.[26]

OFFICE FOR HUMAN RESEARCH PROTECTIONS

OHRP, located in the Office of the Assistant Secretary for Health, was established in 2000 and assumed the human research protection functions of the former Office for Protection from Research Risks (OPRR) that was part of NIH. OHRP is responsible for overseeing research conducted or funded by DHHS that involves human research subjects.[27] Research that is not federally funded or does not involve research or products requiring federal approval is not necessarily subject to OHRP oversight and regulations regarding financial interests and human subject protection. DHHS regulations do not discuss directly investigators' financial conflicts of interests. A recent report issued by the General Accounting Office (GAO) concludes,[28]

> However, the regulations do require a university's IRB [institutional review board] which reviews research proposals involving human research subjects, to weigh a study's risks and benefits to participants, and review the study's participant consent form, as part of its review of the research. Because financial conflicts of interest may affect the risk-benefit analysis, the purpose of the IRB review implies consideration of them. While the actual IRB review of a research proposal may not explicitly consider financial conflicts of interest, IRB's have the right to request and review information about investigators' financial interests that might pose risks to subjects, and they may require an investigator to disclose significant financial interest to the research subjects in the consent form.[29]

Policies and Regulations

The U.S. Secretary of Health and Human Services has announced several further initiatives that are intended to protect human research subjects. One involves identifying new and improved ways to manage financial conflicts of interest that could compromise the objectivity of research or the safety of research subjects.[30] In January 2001, DHHS offered a draft guidance to assist clinical investigators and institutions with potential and actual conflicts of interest and to facilitate disclosure in consent forms.[31] In 2004, new final guidance was issued addressing the management of financial conflicts of interest.[32]

LIMITATIONS OF EXISTING GOVERNMENTAL REGULATIONS

While the existing measures described above are appropriate, there are still troubling issues that have not been adequately addressed. This author has previously summarized these weaknesses, many of which are outlined below.[33]

1. LACK OF CONSISTENCY

There is lack of consistency among the various governmental regulations, that is, there is no uniform national standard by which to manage financial conflicts of interest in clinical research. For example, disclosure levels for defining a significant financial interest are different for the FDA and PHS.

2. DISCLOSURE AFTER RESEARCH

Financial interests must be disclosed before conducting research for the PHS, but, for the FDA, disclosure is required after the research has occurred and product approval is sought.

3. REGULATIONS ARE NOT EXPLICIT

Existing regulations do not explicitly state which information investigators or institutions should share regarding financial conflicts of interest with human research subjects.

4. LACK OF PRESCRIPTIVE REQUIREMENTS

Neither FDA nor PHS regulations contain proscriptive requirements regarding the types of financial interests that may be held. Indeed, as noted, the PHS regulations do not even define conflict of interest. Therefore, it is left to the discretion of the funded institution to determine which significant financial interests constitute conflicts of interests that must be reported to the NIH and managed, reduced, or eliminated.

5. DISCLOSURE NOT ALWAYS REQUIRED

Disclosure is required only for those financial interests related to research proposed for funding by the PHS or National Science Foundation (NSF). This leaves a tremendous gap in coverage for financial interests related to privately funded research, where the greatest conflicts of interest likely exist.[34] Even when disclosure is required by PHS regulations, it must be made only to institutional officials, not to the public. A GAO report found that, of five universities studied, all limited review of investigator disclosure forms to university officials or a designated committee, and one university removed the names of investigators from the disclosure forms before giving them to the conflict of interest committee for review.[35]

6. REQUIREMENTS NOT LINKED

PHS and FDA regulations on financial conflicts of interest are not directly linked to the regulations on human subjects protection; therefore, information on financial entanglements is not necessarily conveyed to IRBs for consideration when they review research proposals.

7. DEFINITION OF CONFLICT NOT SPECIFIED

Under federal regulations, an IRB member may not participate in the review of any project if the member has a conflicting interest, except to provide information requested by the IRB. Again, however, these regulations do not specify what constitutes a financial conflict of interest and leaves it to the IRBs to have clear procedures in place for recusal of IRB members for deliberating or voting on protocols for which there is a potential or actual conflict of interest.

8. LACK OF DETAILED GUIDANCE

Neither the PHS or NSF guidelines nor the DHHS interim guidance on financial conflicts of interest provide detailed

Policies and Regulations

guidance on appropriate ways of addressing institutional conflicts of interest, particularly with regard to university associated start-up companies.

9. CHANGES OFTEN NOT TRACKED

Compensation terms or financial arrangements may change during the course of a study; however, such new arrangements are not usually considered by an IRB or conflict of interest committee.[36]

The federal draft guidance discussed earlier was issued to provide guidance to institutions, IRB, and investigators to address financial relationships and interests in research involving human subjects. This document is valuable, in that it identifies the issues and questions that should be addressed by these factions, but it is limited regarding to how to determine which relationships cause conflict and how to manage those that do.

One of the challenges faced by those who are charged with developing of policies to manage conflicts of interest is the lack of representative national data. Data are limited to study samples that may not be representative of the national experience, making it difficult to efficiently channel resources for educational efforts and regulatory initiatives. Data exist but are not easily accessible. For example, the FDA collects information concerning financial arrangements between sponsors and investigators for covered studies (OMB No. 0910-0396), yet these data are not in a database. Reported conflicts are managed on a case-by-case basis; therefore, there is no analysis of how various financial entanglements have been managed in the past. The only potential mechanism for accessing all of this information is a Freedom of Information Act (FOIA) request, which is a tedious process that can take more than a year to receive the information requested.

REALITY CHECK: CURRENT UNIVERSITY CONFLICT OF INTEREST POLICIES

A study at Stanford University examined conflict of interest policies at 89 major research institutions and found that while most had written policies that were more extensive than the federal regulations, there was great variation among the policies' requirements.[37] Most were not specific about which types of relationships with industry were permitted or prohibited. These findings are consistent with recent studies conducted by McCrary and colleagues[38] and Lo and colleagues,[39] as well as a GAO report generated in 2001.[40] The GAO visited five universities — the University of California, Los Angeles; the University of North Carolina, Chapel Hill; the University of Washington, Seattle; Washington University, St. Louis; and Yale University, New Haven — and performed an in-depth study of these institutions' financial conflict of interest policies and processes. the 20 universities were selected from 483 institutions of higher education that received NIH research funding in fiscal year 1999 that were involved in a high degree of technology transfer, such as patenting and licensing of new technologies. The GAO found the following.

1. EXISTING COMMITTEES

The universities studied had conflict of interest committees that oversaw the development and implementation of financial conflict of interest policies and procedures. But the institutions had broad policies and procedures in place to comply with the PHS regulations regarding investigators' financial conflicts of interest.

2. PUBLIC AND PRIVATE

In general, the policies applied to both publicly and privately funded research.

3. VARIATION

There was considerable variation in the policies developed by universities regarding the types of financial relationships considered to be manageable ones; there were differences in threshold amounts, timetables, and processes for disclosure.

4. STRATEGIES EMPLOYED DIFFERENTLY

Management strategies for conflicts were similar among the universities and included required disclosure, monitored

Policies and Regulations   71

research, and/or required divestiture of financial interest, but they employed these strategies differently.

5. MULTIPLE LOCATIONS, FORMATS

Oversight data regarding investigators' research activities and financial interests were kept in multiple offices, files, and formats within each of the universities, making it difficult to assure that conflicts were identified and appropriately managed.

6. SELF-CERTIFICATION

The universities generally allowed investigators to self-certify that they complied with the institution's own financial conflict of interest policies.

7. WEAK DATA

All of the universities studied had difficulty providing basic data on investigators' financial conflicts of interest with regard to clinical research involving human subjects.

8. INVOLVEMENT OF IRBs

IRB involvement in reviewing financial conflicts of interest varied greatly, ranging from a reviewing investigators' disclosure statements to obtaining verbal information through informal exchanges between IRB members and a conflict of interest committee.

9. LACK OF SAFEGUARDS

Each university's conflict of interest policy stated that failure to comply with the institution's conflict of interest policy was cause for disciplinary action, but none of the universities had any safeguards to verify that there had been full disclosure by investigators.

10. NEED FOR IMPROVEMENT

In general, the universities acknowledged a need for better coordination of information.

The five universities did have policies and procedures that addressed certain aspects of institutional conflicts of interest.

One must ponder why institutions have been reluctant to adopt stringent policies to protect research subjects against conflicts of interest. The answer is likely to be complex, and to reflect many different parameters, including political pressure from physicians, researchers, and industry not to interfere, and the difficulty inherently involved in unraveling complex issues within the realm of conflicts of interest. However, perhaps the leading impediment is the lack of empirical data. There are no nationally representative data describing how prevalent such conflicts are, and there is no research data on whether current policies and regulations are effective in managing the conflicts.

Another likely reason is that, until recently, there have been few legal incentives to assure that conflicts of interests do not compromise the integrity and objectivity of research. One reason for the paucity of litigation in this area is the inability of research subjects to discover the conflicts. The clandestine nature of financial entanglements has made this discovery almost impossible.

IRBS AND FINANCIAL CONFLICTS OF INTEREST

Since their inception in the 1970s, IRBs, widely recognized as being overworked, have diligently attempted to fulfill their role of protecting human research subjects.[41] However, in the past few years, there has been an extraordinary amount of government and media scrutiny regarding IRB oversight of biomedical research due to the following.[42]

1. INADEQUATE OVERSIGHT

The release of a series of reports from the Office of the Inspector General (OIG) concluding that IRBs were providing inadequate oversight.[43]

2. LACK OF ENFORCEMENT

A series of suspensions or significant restrictions by federal regulators of research programs involving human subjects by the FDA or the federal office then known as the Office for Protection from Research Risks (OPRR), after the involved in-

Policies and Regulations

stitutions were found not to be following regulations designed to protect research subjects.

3. PUBLIC AWARENESS
Increased public awareness concerning failures to protect human subjects.

4. RELOCATION OF AUTHORITY
The decision to relocate OPRR from NIH to the Office of the Secretary of the DHHS, renaming the office the Office for Human Research Protections (OHRP), and upgrading the position of its director.[44]

Human research protections programs (HRPPs) are vital to protecting human research subjects.[45] Encompassed within the realm of HRPPs are IRBs, which are required to do the following:

1. MINIMIZE RISK
Determine that the risks of research are minimized and reasonable when compared to anticipated benefits.

2. ASSURE EQUITY
Assure equitable selection of subjects.

3. ENSURE INFORMED CONSENT
Ensure that informed consent is obtained from prospective research subjects.[46]

The means by which HRPPs and their IRBs or conflict of interest committees should deal with financial conflicts of interest in institutions and investigators is an extremely complicated subject that has received considerable national attention. One of the major problems confronting HRPPs in general and IRBs, in particular is *the lack of definitive guidance regarding how to consider and manage these conflicts.*

A great deal of attention is now being focused on the consideration that IRBs should extend to the financial conflicts of interest that a research institution or investigator may have. There is no regulatory requirement for IRBs to consider such financial conflicts of interests.[47] In addition, there are no regulatory requirements as to what, if anything, should be disclosed to human subjects concerning financial conflicts of interest.[48] However, it is unlikely that IRBs will be able to avoid consideration of financial conflicts of interest in the future for the following reasons.

1. LEGAL ARGUMENTS

While there is no specific regulatory requirement for IRBs to consider financial conflicts of interest, legal arguments have been set forth claiming that various elements of federal regulations impose a duty upon IRBs to consider financial conflicts of interest. For example, federal regulations state that there must be a "description of any benefits to the subject or to others which may reasonably be expected from the research."[49] In addition, a portion of the informed consent regulations states that an investigator should seek "consent only under circumstances that provide the prospective subject or the representative sufficient opportunity to consider whether or not to participate and that minimize the possibility of coercion or undue influence."[50] Arguably, these provisions may implicitly require that IRBs consider financial conflicts of interest. It has been estimated that, in actual practice, only 25 percent of IRBs routinely deal with financial conflicts of interest during their deliberations.[51]

2. LEGISLATION

A bipartisan bill, the Human Research Subject Protections Act, introduced in the U.S. House of Representatives (HR 4697), is likely indicative of future requirements and would clearly make the role of IRBs more prevalent in considering and managing financial conflicts of interest.[52]

3. FEDERAL GUIDANCE

Finally, perhaps the most compelling indication that IRBs will have increasing responsibilities in gauging conflicts of interest is the most recent guidance from OHRP,[53] which delineates specific recommendations concerning how IRBs should screen members for financial conflicts of interest, as well as recommendations that IRBs should perform the following tasks.

- Determine if the methods used to manage financial conflicts of interest are adequate to protect human subjects;
- Determine when an IRB requires additional information on financial interests that could affect human subjects, and mechanisms to obtain this information; and
- Take necessary action to minimize risks and the kind, amount, and level of detail of information regarding financial arrangements/funding to be disclosed to subjects.

Clearly, this guidance recommends that substantial responsibility concerning the identification and management of financial conflicts of interest rests with IRBs.

One of the impediments to the provision of definitive federal guidance concerning IRBs and financial conflicts of interest is, again, the lack of empirical data. It is ironic that policy makers have been asked to devise solutions to remedy the concerns associated with financial conflicts of interest in research with limited data about the incidence, prevalence, and causes of such conflicts and how they are currently being managed by IRBs. Nor is there sufficient data regarding the efficacy and feasibility of proposed federal guidance that has been designed to ameliorate such concerns. And, certainly, there are no data on what IRB chairs, members, and institutional officials view as the appropriate role for IRBs to play in the identification and management of financial conflicts of interest.

NOTES

The epigraph at the beginning of this chapter is from JN Rao, LJ San Cassia. Ethics of undisclosed payments to doctors recruiting patients in clinical trials. BMJ 2002; 325:36-37.

1. American College of Physicians. Physicians and the pharmaceutical industry [Position Paper] Ann Intern Med 1990; 112:624-26; M Angell. Is academic medicine for sale? N Engl J Med 2000; 342:1516-18; MK Cho, R Shohar, A Schissel et al. Policies on faculty conflicts of interest at US universities. JAMA 2000; 284:2237-38; SV McCrary, CB Anderson, J Jakovljevic et al. A national survey of policies on disclosure

of conflicts of interest in biomedical research. N Engl J Med 2000; 343:1621-26; B Lo, LE Wolf, A Berkeley. Conflict-of-interest Policies for Investigators in clinical trials. New Engl J Med 2000; 343:1616-20.

2. S Krimsky. Conflict of interest and Cost-effectiveness analysis. JAMA 1999; 282:1474-75; CD DeAngelis. Conflict of interest and the public trust. JAMA 2000 284:2237-38 and articles cited therein.

3. H Moses, JB Martin. Academic relationships with industry: A new model for biomedical research. JAMA 2001; 285:933-35; DG Nathan, DJ Weatherall. Academic freedom in clinical research. N Engl J Med 2002; 347:1368-71.

4. AAMC. Guidelines for Dealing with Faulty Conflicts of Commitment and Conflicts of Interest in Research (Washington DC., 1990).

5. AAMC. Protecting subjects, preserving trust, promoting progress I: Policy and guidelines for the oversight of individual financial interests in human subject research. December 2001. Available at *http://www.aamc.org*; AAMC. Protecting subjects, preserving trust, promoting progress II: Principles and Recommendations for Oversight of an institution's financial interests in human subjects. October 2002. Available at *http://www.aamc.org*.

6. RP Kelch. Maintaining the public trust in clinical research. New Engl J Med 2002; 346:285-87.

7. Association of American Universities. Framework Document on Managing Financial Conflicts of Interest (*http:www.aau.edu/reports/frwkCONFLICTOFINTEREST.html*).

8. Association of American Universities. Report on University Protections of Human Beings Who Are the Subjects of Research (Washington, D.C., 2000).

9. G Blumenstyk. University Group Offers New Guidelines to Govern Potential Research Conflicts. Chron of Higher Educ. October 19, 2001.

10. American Society of Gene Therapy. Policy of the American Society of Gene Therapy on Financial Conflict of Interest in Clinical Research. Adopted April 5, 2000. Available at *http://www.asgt.org/policy/index.html*.

11. AAHRPP. Sponsor Standard IV-3. Available at *http://*

Policies and Regulations

www.aahrpp.org/sponsor.

12. PhRMA adopts principles for conduct of clinical trials and communication of clinical trial results. Available at *http://www.phrma.org.*

13. F Davidoff and others. Sponsorship, authorship, and accountability. New Engl J Med 2001; 345:825-6.

14. L Guterman. 12 Medical Journals Issue Joint Policy on Research Supported by Business. Chron Higher Educ. October 5, 2001.

15. S Krimsky, LS Rothenberg. Conflict of interest policies in science and medical journals: editorial practices and author disclosures. Science and Engineering Ethics 2001; 7:205-18.

16. SG Stolberg. Scientists often mum about ties to industry. NY Times. April 25, 2001.

17. International Committee of Medical Journal Editors. Uniform requirements for manuscripts submitted to biomedical journals. Available at *http://www.icmje.org.*

18. Guterman, see note 14 above.

19. Stolberg, see note 16 above.

20. Harvard Medical School Office of Public Affairs. News Release. Leading NIH-Funded Medical Schools Agree on Guidelines that Would Strengthen Conflict of Interest Policies of Virtually all Schools, Hospitals, and Research Institutes. Available at *http://www.hms.harvard.edu/news/releases/020801conflict.html.* February 8, 2001. Consensus Statement on Conflict of Interest Policies for Academic Institutions. Available at *http://www.hms.harvard.edu/news/releases/conflict_guidelines.html.*

21. PM Tereskerz. Research accountability and financial conflicts of interest in industry-sponsored clinical research: A review. Accountability in Research 2003; 10:137-58.

22. 21 CFR 54 et seq.; Public Health Service. Responsibility of Applicants for Promoting Objectivity in Research. Available at *http://grants.nih.gov/grants/guide/notice-files/not95-179.html* 1995.

23. 42 CFR pt. 50 Subpart F.

24. FDA. Guidance, Financial Disclosure by Clinical Investigators. Available at *http://www.fda.gov/oc/guidance/financialdis.html.*

25. 21 CFR pt. 54, and applicable portions of parts 312, 314, 320, 330, 601, 807, 812, 814, and 860.

26. 21 CFR Section 54.1(b) (2002).

27. 45 CFR pt. 46.

28. General Accounting Office (GAO) Report to the Ranking Minority Member, Subcommittee on Public Health, Committee on Health, Education, Labor, and Pensions, U.S. Senate. GAO-02-89. November 2001.

29. *Id.*

30. D Shalala. Protecting research subjects: What must be done. N Engl J Med 343 (11) 2000.

31. Public Health Service. Draft Interim Guidance. Financial Relationships in Clinical Research: Issues for Institutions, Clinical Investigators, and IRBs to Consider When Dealing with Issues of Financial Interests and Human Subject Protection. Available at *http://ohrp.osophs.dhhs.gov/nhrpac/mtg12-00/finguid.htm.* January 10, 2001.

32. Department of Health and Human Services. (5/03/04). Final Guidance: Financial relationships and interest in research involving human subjects: guidance for human subject protection. Replacing Department of Health and Human Services. (3/31/2003). Draft: Financial relationships and interest in research involving human subjects: guidance for human subject protection.

33. Tereskerz, see note 21 above.

34. General Accounting Office Report, see note 28 above.

35. *Id.*

36. Correspondence to Arthur J. Lawrence, Assistant Surgeon General from Mary Faith Marshall, Chairperson for NHRRPAC dated 8/23/2001.

37. Cho et al., see note 1 above.

38. McCrary et al., see note 1 above.

39. Lo et al., see note 1 above.

40. General Accounting Office Report, see note 28 above.

41. The Nat'l Comm'n for the Protection of Human Subjects of BioMedical and Behavioral Research. DHEW Pub. No. (OS) 78-0012. The Belmont Report: Ethical Principles for the Protection of Human Subjects of Research (1978). Available at *http://ohrp.osophs.dhhs.gov/humansubjects/guidance/blemont.htm.*

42. JA Goldner. Dealing with conflicts of interest in biomedical research: IRB oversight as the next best solution to the abolitionist approach. Symp J L Med & Ethics 2000; 28:379.

43. Office of Inspector General. Institutional Review Boards: Their Role in Reviewing Approved Research. (June 1998).

44. J Brainard. Physician May Lead New Human-Research Office. Chron Higher Educ. May 26, 200 at A41.

45. JA Goldner. An overview of legal controls on human experimentation and the regulatory implications of taking Professor Katz seriously. St. Louis U Law J 1993; 38:63-134.

46. National Institutes of Health. Financial conflicts of interest and research objectivity: issues for investigators and institutional review boards. June 5, 2000. Available at *http://grants.nih.gov/grants/guide/notice-files/NOT-OD-00-040.html.*

47. 45 CFR 46.111 (1991); 21 CFR Section 56.111 (1991).

48. 21 CFR Section 50.25 (1981); 45 CFR Section 46.116C (1991); 45 CFR Section 690.116C (1991).

49. *Id.*

50. 21 CFR Section 50.20 (1981); 45 CFR Section 46.116 (1991); 45 CFR Sections 690.116 (1991).

51. SG Stolberg, see note 16 above.

52. Status as of 1/2004. H.R. 4697. Introduced 5/9/2002. Referred to the House Committee on Energy and Commerce. Referred to the Subcommittee on Health.

53. DHHS. Draft Guidance Document. Financial Relationship and Interests in Research Involving Human Subjects: Guidance for Human Subject Protection. Federal Register 60(61) 15457-460. March 31, 2003.

5

Beyond Federal Regulations: Legal Ramifications of Financial Conflicts of Interest in Clinical Research

> For years, medical researchers were largely immune from lawsuits. But the death of Jesse Gelsinger in 1999 changed all that. Lawsuits were unheard of eight to 10 years ago.... Now, it's the hot topic.
>
> — *Janet Richardson, attorney for drug and medical device manufacturers*

As outlined in chapter 4, there is limited federal regulation of financial conflicts of interest regarding investigators, research institutions, and institutional review boards (IRBs). Consequently, in daily practice, we often hear from researchers or even IRB members that there is no specific law or regulation that precludes this or that type of financial arrangement, or that requires disclosure, and, therefore, there is no exposure to liability for me or my institution. This is wrong. In short: *the legal obligations associated with clinical research go far beyond the plain language of the limited statutory and regulatory requirements.*

The preceding chapter outlined the plain language of existing statutes, regulations, and policies and their limitations; this and the following three chapters further the argument that new ways are needed to manage financial conflicts by show-

ing that they pose considerable potential for legal liability. One of the most problematic aspects of the current scenario is that the potential for liability is most often not apparent to those who are most likely in harm's way. This chapter will describe the potential pitfalls:
1. Beyond the regulatory and statutory environments, there is the common (case) law, which may impose duties on researchers and research institutions that go beyond the regulatory and statutory schemes.
2. Statutory and regulatory requirements from other areas of the law that, on their surface, would not seem likely to be applicable can be imposed to manage financial conflicts of interest.
3. Provisions of regulations and statutes that pertain to the protection of human subjects that do not explicitly address financial conflicts of interest can, and have been, interpreted to include such conflicts.

In the next several chapters, we will explore various common law remedies that have been used to address financial conflicts of interest. First, *fiduciary duty* and *informed consent* will be considered under tort law. Applicable statutory schemes, other than those directly regulating financial conflicts of interest in research will be examined; insider trading and consumer protection laws are two examples that may apply to various circumstances involving financial conflicts of interest in clinical research.

Because consideration of financial conflicts of interest under the common law is a relatively new topic, there is little legal authority from court decisions. Therefore, recent pleadings filed by attorneys in leading clinical trial cases involving financial conflicts of interest will be used to explore the theories on which they rely to pursue their claims.

THE PHYSICIAN RESEARCHER AND FIDUCIARY DUTY TO PATIENTS: CONTRACT THEORY

When a patient engages the services of a physician, and the physician accepts the patient for treatment, a contractual relationship, which may be either expressed or implied, is

Legal Ramifications

created, and the rights and obligations of both parties are subject to contract law.[1]

Embedded in the relationship between a physician and a patient is the underlying predicate that the physician possesses special knowledge and highly technical skills that are used in diagnosis and treatment. Comparatively speaking, the patient usually lacks the necessary knowledge and skills the physician maintains, and the patient has, therefore, sought the services of the physician, that are vitally important to the health and life of the patient.[2]

Considering the vulnerability of a person in ill health and the virtual monopoly a physician has on knowledge that may be used to treat a patient, it is recognized that a patient could easily be subjected to the dominion, control, and undue influence of a physician. Consequently, contractual transactions between physicians and patients are carefully examined by the courts when an incident arises questioning the propriety of such arrangements, to assure that fairness is preserved. Traditionally, any arrangements between physician and patient are scrutinized far beyond those transactions in which parties are considered to be dealing at arm's length,[3] and any arrangement that compromises the fiduciary relationship between a physician and a patient is usually viewed as being in opposition to public policy, unenforceable, and void.[4]

A PHYSICIAN'S FIDUCIARY DUTY TO PATIENTS: NEGLIGENCE AND THE INFORMED CONSENT DOCTRINE

Tort law[5] also recognizes that a patient usually becomes highly dependent upon a physician's judgment, and the relationship that emerges is a fiduciary one in which mutual trust and confidence between physician and patient are essential to maintain the relationship.[6] Given the patient's dependence on the physician's knowledge and skill, certain obligations arise under tort law on the part of the physician to protect the patient's vulnerability. Among those obligations is the rendering of due care to the patient.[7] Intertwined with this duty is the physician's responsibility to inform the patient of his or her condition and to obtain the patient's consent to medical treatment. This is commonly recognized as the *doctrine of informed consent*.[8]

The perception of what constitutes "informed" consent is central to the conflicts of interest issue. Understanding the principles behind the informed consent doctrine is helpful because so much of the current debate surrounding financial conflicts of interest in clinical research revolves around which financial entanglements with sponsors should be disclosed.

The hallmark of the theory of informed consent rests upon the concept that patients have a right to exercise dominion and control over their bodies and to be reasonably informed of material elements of treatment that may affect their decisions on whether to submit to treatment.[9] Several courts have premised the duty to disclose on the fiducial characteristics of the physician-patient relationship.[10]

The requirement of patients' consent to medical treatment was recognized as early as the late eighteenth century.[11] The doctrine of informed consent requires that, in the absence of emergent conditions, a physician must obtain consent before treating a patient.[12] Critical to the concept of informed consent is that, for the consent to be valid, it must be "informed." It is generally agreed that physicians must reveal the following information before treating a patient:

- A description and purpose of the treatment or procedure,
- Potential risks and benefits,
- Reasonable alternative treatments and their attendant risks and benefits, and
- Potential risks involved in foregoing treatment.[13]

Informed consent, as both a legal and an ethical doctrine, reflects the principle of *patients' autonomy*.[14] As of the late twentieth century, the right to self-determination concerning healthcare has been tantamount to a fundamental right.[15] However, this has not always been the case. Until the mid-1900s, medical decision making was guided by the principle of *beneficence*, which eventually coalesced into *paternalism*, whereby a physician's opinion regarding what is in a patient's best interest took precedence over that of the patient.[16] The conception of patients' autonomy emerged with the social

Legal Ramifications

movement of bioethics in the 1960s and 1970s.[17] It was during this time that informed consent emerged as the legal vehicle by which patients could override the pervasive paternalism that had become entrenched in the medical community.

In 1957, the phrase "informed consent" first appeared in a legal opinion, in which the court held, "a physician violates his duty to his patient and subjects himself to liability if he withholds any facts which are necessary to form the basis of an intelligent consent by the patient to the proposed treatment."[18] However, cases dealt with consent primarily within the context of whether a physician had a patient's consent to perform a procedure or whether the physician had committed a *battery*, which refers to intentional or offensive touching of another without consent, long before 1957. For example, it was within this context that Justice Cardozo's opinion in *Schloendorff v. Society of New York Hospital* contains one of the most memorable quotes concerning a patient's right to self-determination:

> Every human being of adult years and sound mind has a right to determine what shall be done with his own body, and a surgeon who performs an operation without his patient's consent commits an assault, for which he is liable in damages.[19]

The basis for most modern-day legal claims for failure to obtain informed consent has been rooted in *negligence*. To prove negligence, within this context, a plaintiff must demonstrate the following:
- The existence of a duty, recognized by law to adhere to a standard to protect others against unreasonable risks;
- That a breach of the duty occurred;
- A causal connection between the breach and the resulting injury or damages.[20]

Prior to the 1970s, the *professional standard* was the basis for judging whether informed consent was required. Professional standard refers to what a reasonable practitioner would do under similar circumstances. However, with *Canterbury v.*

Spence[21] and *Cobbs v. Grant*,[22] a new standard was adopted requiring the physician to disclose information that a *reasonable person*, not a reasonable physician, in the patient's circumstances would consider material to a treatment decision. The line of cases following this latter approach to informed consent is premised on the notion that while a decision to treat may seem clear to a physician, it is a patient's, not a physician's, prerogative to determine a patient's interests and to decide whether or not to accept treatment. Given that a patient's relationship with the physician is a fiduciary one, a physician has obligations that extend beyond those of arm's length transactions to inform a patient of all of the information that a patient would have a right to expect under the circumstances.[23]

In the United States, the legal requirements for disclosure produced a checkerboard of jurisprudence, with about one-half of the states adopting the "reasonable person" standard set out in *Cobbs*, and the remaining states continuing to adhere to the "professional" or medical community standard.[24]

Clearly, the question that emerges within the conflict of interest scenario is what yardstick should be used to measure whether or not a researcher has a duty to disclose any conflicts of interest to a patient.

As applied to financial conflicts of interest in clinical research, the issue becomes whether a researcher is legally required or has a duty to divulge relevant conflicts that may affect clinical decision making before treating a patient. The following discussion considers how the judiciary has addressed this issue.

THE RESEARCHER'S DUTY TO SUBJECTS

While there has been a long-standing and rather clear delineation of the duty that physicians owe to the patients they treat, the duty of a researcher, who also may or may not be a research subject's treating physician, has not been clearly defined. From the legal perspective, it has not been clear what type of duty a researcher has to a research subject. In other words, what, if any, legal duty emerges from the special relationship that exists between researcher and human subject? Is

Legal Ramifications

this relationship tantamount to the physician-patient relationship within the clinical treatment setting?

Why is this issue of *duty* so important? Because, within the legal context, "there can be no negligence where there is no duty that is due; for negligence is the breach of some duty that one person owes to another."[25] It has been only relatively recently that this issue has been considered by the judiciary. In the first case involving this issue, a Maryland appellate court considered a case involving nontherapeutic research.[26] The case involved a study intended to determine how effective varying degrees of lead paint abatement were, by measuring dust levels and the extent to which healthy children's blood became contaminated with lead over a two-year study period.[27] In essence, as the court stated, the "researchers intended that the children be the canaries in the mines but never clearly told the parents."[28]

Among the issues before the court were whether informed consent agreements in nontherapeutic research projects constitute special relationships, giving rise to duties a researcher has to a research subject, and whether governmental regulations create duties on the part of researchers to human subjects out of which special relationships can arise. The court found the following.

1. A special relationship is created between researchers and human subjects, which is used by the researchers by the very nature of the research, and that out of this special relationship, an attendant duty emerges.
2. Governmental regulations that protect human research subjects can also create duties on the part of researchers toward human subjects, out of which a special relationship arises.
3. Informed consent agreements in nontherapeutic research can constitute contracts as well as special relationships and, if they are breached, may give rise to negligence claims.
4. Importantly, the court also ruled that a parent or surrogate cannot consent for a child, or other persons under a legal disability, to participate in nontherapeutic research when there is any risk of injury or damage to the subject.

FIDUCIARY DUTY AND INFORMED CONSENT AS APPLIED TO THE CONFLICT OF INTEREST ISSUE IN THE RESEARCH SETTING

As noted earlier, the effects of financial conflicts of interest emerging from the research setting may go far beyond those that arise within the context of direct patient care. Conflicts of interest that biomedical researchers face pose serious threats to the integrity of medical practice, because damaging and injurious results from inappropriately managed conflicts can adversely affect the treatment of thousands of patients whose physicians base their clinical decisions on tainted research results. But the damage goes even beyond this: one of the most serious consequences is that such conflicts can compromise the integrity of or trust placed in the entire research infrastructure. At any point in time, there are at least 14,000 clinical trials underway.[29] Cases involving financial conflicts of interest that are associated with tragic outcomes often become highly visible, and, when viewed through the lens of the public's eye, may result in what many fear will be a chilling effect on scientific advancement, as the pool of willing volunteers dissipates.[30] One study found that a majority of individuals suffering from various diseases thought the following.
1. Knowing about financial conflict of interest information was "extremely" or "very" important.
2. Disclosing financial conflicts of interests should be part of informed consent.
3. A sizable minority were wary of participating in studies in which financial conflicts of interest existed.[31] Contrast this with the incongruent findings of a study assessing the policies of academic medical centers on disclosure of financial conflicts to research participants; only 48 percent of the academic medical centers had policies mentioning disclosure of financial conflicts to research participants, resulting in circumstances ripe for legal liability.[32]

The California Supreme Court addressed the conflict of interest issue within the context of a case involving a physician who had a financial interest in the research he was undertaking. In *Moore v. The Regents of the University of Cali-*

fornia,[33] a patient who underwent treatment for leukemia filed action against his physician, among others, alleging that the cells extracted from the patient's body were used in lucrative medical research without his consent. The patient alleged two claims — first, that the physician failed to disclose pre-existing research and economic interests that the physician had in the cells before he obtained consent from the patient for the medical procedure used to extract the cells. This failure, the plaintiff claimed, resulted in a breach of the physician's fiduciary duty to his patient. The second allegation made by the plaintiff was that the use of the cells constituted conversion (wrongful possession).[34]

BREACH OF FIDUCIARY DUTY CLAIM

At the trial level, the court granted leave to amend.[35] In a subsequent proceeding, the court again sustained the defendant's objection to the legal sufficiency of the plaintiff's claim without leave to amend.[36] The court of appeals reversed.[37] The issue before the California Supreme Court was whether the plaintiff's complaint stated facts that were sufficient to sustain a lawsuit.[38]

The plaintiff, John Moore, was diagnosed with hairy-cell leukemia and later went to the Medical Center of the University of California at Los Angeles for treatment.[39] Upon hospitalization, large amounts of the plaintiff's blood, bone marrow aspirate, and other bodily substances were withdrawn by his physician, David W. Golde, MD, who confirmed the diagnosis.[40] At that time, Golde was cognizant that various blood products were of great value and that blood containing such substances could result in considerable commercial and scientific benefits.[41]

Golde told Moore that he recommended that Moore's spleen be removed, suggesting that the surgery would be necessary to save his life.[42] However, before the procedure, Golde made arrangements to retain portions of the plaintiff's spleen to be used in research that was unrelated to the plaintiff's case.[43] Neither Golde nor his research associate informed Moore of their research plans or obtained his permission to use his spleen for this purpose.[44]

Moore's spleen was removed, and he subsequently traveled to the medical center on numerous occasions from his home in Seattle for seven years at the direction of Golde, who represented that the visits were necessary for his care.[45] Upon each of these visits, Golde withdrew samples of blood, serum, skin, bone marrow aspirate, and sperm. During this time period, Golde and his colleagues were engaged in the conduct of research on Moore's cells, and they planned to benefit financially and competitively by maintaining exclusive access to the cells through their relationship with the plaintiff.[46] Moore was never cognizant that this activity was underway.[47]

By 1979, Golde had established a cell line using the plaintiff's cells, and the university applied for a patent on the cell line. As an inventor, Golde and his colleague would share in the royalties.[48] Subsequently, Golde mediated agreements so commercial development of the cell line and derivative products could be undertaken. With one agreement, Golde became a paid consultant who acquired the rights to 75,000 shares of stock plus $330,000, to be paid over a three-year period, which was to include a portion of his salary. In exchange, Golde agreed that the company would have exclusive access to the materials and his research performed on Moore's cell line.[49] Following this initial agreement, Golde added another company, Sandoz, to the contract, whereby the amount paid to Golde was increased by $110,000.[50]

In considering the issue of whether Golde's activities constituted a cause of action for breach of fiduciary duty and lack of informed consent toward the plaintiff, the court held that the plaintiff's allegations were sufficient to state a cause of action against Golde on grounds of either a breach of a fiduciary duty to disclose facts material to the patient's consent or in terms of performing medical procedures without obtaining the patient's informed consent.[51]

California follows the reasonable patient standard of when informed consent is required, discussed earlier.[52] The court applied this standard in the *Moore* case and held:

> Indeed, the law already recognizes that a reasonable patient would want to know whether a physician has an economic interest that might affect the physician's professional

judgment. As the Court of Appeals has said '[c]ertainly a sick patient deserves to be free of any reasonable suspicion that his doctor's judgment is influenced by a profit motive. . . .

[A] physician who treats a patient in whom he also has a research interest has potentially conflicting loyalties. This is because medical treatment decisions are made on the basis of proportionality — weighing the benefits *to the patient* against the risks *to the patient*. . . . A physician who adds his own research interests to this balance may be tempted to order a scientifically useful procedure or test that offers marginal, or no benefits to the patient. The possibility that an interest extraneous to the patient's health has affected the physician's judgment is something that a reasonable patient would want to know in deciding whether to consent to a proposed course of treatment. It is material to the patient's decision and, thus, a prerequisite to informed consent. . . . Accordingly, we hold that a physician who is seeking a patient's consent for a medical procedure must, in order to satisfy his fiduciary duty and to obtain the patient's informed consent, disclose personal interests unrelated to the patient's health, whether research or economic, that may affect his medical judgment.[53]

The court went on to determine that the plaintiff stated a cause of action both as to the surgical removal of Moore's spleen and for the withdrawal of blood and other bodily fluids on subsequent office visits absent consent.[54] Interestingly, regarding other defendants who were named in the case who were not physicians, the court held that none of these individuals was involved in a fiduciary relationship with Moore, and, therefore, had no duty to obtain his consent.[55]

CONVERSION CLAIM

Moore's conversion claim[56] was based on the theory that he continued to possess property rights in the cells removed from his body and that he never agreed to allow his cells to be used in medical research. Moore alleged that the unauthorized use of his cells would constitute conversion in that, as a result of the property interest he had in the cells, he also had a proprietary interest in each of the products that the defendants created from his cells.[57]

In this instance, the court refused to expand the theory of conversion to allow Moore to establish a cause of action under this doctrine.[58] The court cited three basic reasons why a claim should not be allowed under the traditional doctrine of conversion.

1. There was no judicial precedent to support Moore's claim.
2. Existing California statutes limit continuing interest of a patient in cells removed from the body.
3. The cell line and products derived from it were factually and legally distinct from Moore's cells.[59]

Consequently, the court determined that if the conversion action were to lie, the court would have to enlarge the theory of conversion to embrace Moore's claims.[60] The court, however, refused to expand the theory, on policy grounds. The court found that, on balance, a finding of conversion would only result in an undesirable incentive to decrease medical research initiatives, while not offering the plaintiff substantially more protection than currently afforded through the doctrine of informed consent.[61]

ANALYSIS OF THE *MOORE* DECISION

The boom in the biotechnology industry has altered traditional incentives and relationships between physicians, researchers, and patients. As outlined in chapter 2, statutory provisions have assisted in stimulating this change.[62] The Patent and Trademark Amendment Act provided universities and nonprofit institutions with patent rights to inventions that resulted from federally funded research.[63] In addition, the Supreme Court's decision in *Diamond v. Chakrabarty* held for the first time that a live, human-made micro-organism was patentable.[64] As would be expected, after these developments, there was a large increase in the amount of capital invested in biotechnology involving human tissues, and 50 percent of the institutions that responded to a survey on tissue use indicating that they used patients' tissue and fluids in their research.[65]

Legal Ramifications

As Daniels, a physician, notes in her article on the commercialization of human tissues, these statutory provisions were not accompanied by any companion legislation to protect the patient/physician fiduciary relationship.[66] Current federal regulations and statutes[67] do not require a physician to disclose the possible commercial value and use of excised body tissue or fluids.[68] It was, therefore, inevitable that a case such as *Moore* would occur.

The *Moore* decision is praiseworthy on several grounds. It recognizes the essence of the fiduciary relationship between the physician and patient and honors the foundations of the informed consent doctrine. While decisions such as *Moore*, which upheld the right of action when a physician fails to inform a patient of the conflicting financial interests that he or she may have, will instill incentives for physicians to disclose conflicts of interest, informed consent alone is not sufficient to protect patients for the following reasons.

The pragmatic parameters of *Moore* are of limited effectiveness. The judiciary cannot go beyond the limits of its power. The realities of medical practice require more than the judiciary alone can provide. Informed consent will protect, for the most part, only those patients who are undergoing nonemergent treatment. Yet, it is often under emergent conditions, when physicians are treating the most critically ill patients, that protection from conflicts of interest is most essential.

Take, for instance, the tPA episode described in chapter 3. tPA is a drug that is used under emergent and life-threatening circumstances. Picture, if you will, a member of your family collapsing as a result of myocardial infarction. The ambulance comes; you and your family member are rushed to the hospital. The gurney is rolled into a treatment room, and a heart monitor is hooked up while other diagnostic tests are underway, in a sea of confusion. The physician comes up to you and tells you that there is a blockage of a primary vessel, and he would like to use tPA to remove it. Is it reasonable to believe that during this extremely intense moment, when every second is of the essence, that a physician will stop and explain to you that he or she has a financial interest in the drug, as many tPA researchers did? Of course not. Given the emergent circumstances, the physician may not even be required to obtain consent under the doctrine of informed consent if, on balance, the physician thinks (and probably would be justified in doing so) that the risk of conflict of interest may not be of material interest under the circumstances, or, alternatively, that the medical standard of disclosure does not require this disclosure under the circumstances.[69]

Furthermore, if the patient is unconscious, and no family member is present, the informed consent requirement would be waived under current legal doctrine.[70] Clearly, then, the *Moore* holding leaves a major gap in the area in which informed consent is, perhaps, most necessary — making life and death decisions under emergent circumstances.

Even in the treatment of patients with chronic conditions, however, disclosure of conflicts of interest may not adequately protect patients. As one author suggested, given the limited medical knowledge patients have and the trust and dependence they place in their treating physicians, disclosure does not insure the patient will truly appreciate the ramifications of a conflict of interest.[71] Some may conclude that a physician's financial interest in diagnostic devices or research is merely a continuation of the physician's practice, and "Just like Victor Kiam and the Remington Razor — he thought it was so great, he bought the company."[72]

A further difficulty is the inequitable distribution of power between the physician and patient. Patients may be reluctant to challenge a physician's recommendation. This concern becomes even more compelling when it is considered in tandem with the fact that patients are usually in extremely vulnerable and compromised positions, with their health and welfare at stake, when they consult a physician and enroll in a clinical trial. Therefore, even if patients are informed of the risks, they may be unwilling to challenge the physician's or researcher's authority by refusing a treatment, whether the physician or researcher has a financial interest in the therapy or not.

While there are several statutory provisions that provide some protection for patients against conflicts of interest in their relationships with physicians, this legislation addresses primarily the clinical, rather than the research, setting.

A Common Law Approach Does Not Provide Adequate Protection

As discussed above, common law has always tenaciously guarded the fiduciary relationship between physician and patient when any questionable financial arrangement has been challenged. Courts have repeatedly struck down arrangements that compromise the integrity of the relationship between doctor and patient. However, common law alone is unable to adequately protect patients. Relatively few cases have been brought that contend that a breach of fiduciary duty has occurred. This lies in stark contrast to the number of lay and congressional reports of serious transgressions in fiduciary duties, suggesting that current legal treatment has obviously failed to cure the existing ills faced by the medical profession.

The *Moore* case illustrates at least one reason why few cases have emerged in this area — the inability of patients to discover the conflict. The clandestine nature of financial entanglements makes it virtually impossible for a patient to ascertain if the fiduciary relationship with a physician has been compromised. In *Moore*, the plaintiff underwent treatment for more than seven years before he discovered that his physician was requiring follow-up visits in part to satisfy the physician's avarice.[73]

In cases such as *Moore,* the trust of patients is being abused, and patients are harmed, often for long periods, without their knowledge — it is an unchecked silence. By its very nature, the problem requires a prophylactic rather than a curative approach.

As such, the argument that some have posed — that physicians' investment in areas that pose conflicts is a mere continuation of the fee for service system inherent to the medical profession — falters.[74] In this regard, Arnold Relman, former editor of the *New England Journal of Medicine*, stated,

> Whatever conflicts of interest may exist in the fee for service relation between doctor and patient are clearly visible to all concerned and have long been accepted by society. When patients have any doubts they are free to seek other advice. The situation is different when physicians seek income beyond fee for service and make business ar-

rangements with other providers. . . . Such arrangements introduce a new and unnecessary conflict.[75]

Even if detection were not problematic, and the common law supplied a sufficient remedy, it must be asked whether increasing litigation through the common law approach is the best answer. As Representative Pete Stark (D-California) points out: "Doctors are often complaining about lawyers and litigation — with good cause. However, the amount of litigation in every jurisdiction that would be needed to achieve . . . desired results is absolutely mind-boggling."[76]

The ethics of the medical profession cannot and should not bend to accommodate the profit motive. Medical ethics cannot be held to a high standard only so long as it is politically and fiscally advantageous to follow the standard. Ethics are not a matter of convenience, but must remain intractable in the face of political and economic pressures. The propriety of the fiduciary relationship between physicians and other researchers and patients can only be adequately safeguarded by public policy and legislative enactments that protect patients against those in the medical profession who are blinded by the allure of profits, and those physician researchers who turn a deaf ear to the oath they once took to do no harm.[77]

When the profit motive is allowed to become a driving force in clinical research, to the point that human dignity is compromised and human lives are threatened, and the medical profession is slow to offer a remedy, it is time for legislative and regulatory bodies to step in and impose a resolution. It appears that this is exactly what is happening. A bipartisan bill before Congress would provide human subjects the right to know of researchers' conflicts of interest.[78] The proposed legislation requires disclosure by researchers conducting studies with federal dollars to disclose conflicts of interest to research subjects and institutional review boards, and similarly, members of IRBs would be obligated to report their financial ties with industry to academic institutions. The proposed legislation also applies the "Common Rule," a set of federal research regulations, to federally funded research conducted at hospitals, academic institutions, and contract research organizations (see appendix D for the text of the "Common Rule").[79]

Legal Ramifications

The bill also would require federal officials to harmonize the diverse federal regulations concerning conflicts of agencies set forth by various federal agencies as described in chapter 4.

NOTES

The epigraph cited at the beginning of chapter 5 is from A Dembner. Lawsuits Target Medical Research. The Boston Globe. 8/12/02, quoting Janet Richardson, a Los Angeles lawyer who defends drug and medical device manufacturers.

1. *See e.g., Spencer v. West*, 126 So. 2d 423 (La. App. 1960); 97 ALR2d 1224.
2. *Hummel v. State*, 210 Ark 471, 196 S.W.2d 594 (1946) *Adams v. Ison*, 249 S.W.2d 791 (Ky. 1952); 132 ALR 379; 61 Am Jur 2d § 166.
3. *Campbell v. Oliva*, 424 F.2d 1244 (6th Cir. 1970); *Kopprasch v. Stone*, 340 Mich 384, 65 N.W.2d 852 (1959); *Houghton v. West*, 305 S.W.2d 407 (Mo. 1957); *Re: Estate of Hendricks*, 110 N.W.2d 417 (N.D. 1961).
4. 61 Am Jur 2d § 166.
5. A tort is defined as a civil wrong for which there is usually a remedy.
6. *Stacey v. Pantano*, 177 Neb 694, 131 N.W.2d 163 (1964); 61 Am Jur 2d §187.
7. *See generally*, 61 Am Jur 2d §188.
8. *See generally*, 61 Am Jur 2d §187.
9. *Schloendorff v. Society of New York Hospital*, 211 NY 125, 105 N.E. 92 (1914); *Bing v. Thunig*, 2NY2d 656, 163 NYS2d 3, 143 N.E.2d (1957); 61 Am Jur 2d §188.
10. *Berkey v. Anderson*, 1 Cal. App. 3d 790, 82 Cal. Rptr. 67 (1969); *Woods v. Brumlop*, 71 NM 221, 377 P.2d 520 (1962); *Miller v. Kennedy*, 11 Wash. App. 272, 522 P.2d 852 (1974). *See also* 61 Am Jur 2d §187.
11. Daniels (citing *Slater v. Baker and Stapleton* 95 Eng. Rep. 860 (K.B. 1767).
12. *See* generally, 61 Am Jur 2d §187 and citations therein.
13. 61 Am Jur 2d at 219.
14. 51 Cal. 3d at 120, 271 Cal. Rptr. at 147, 793 P.2d at 480.
15. *Id.*

16. *Id.*

17. *Id.*

18. *Salgo v. Leland Stanford Jr. Univ. Board of Trustees*, 317 P.2d 170 (Cal. App. 1957).

19. *Schloendorff v. Society of New York Hospital*, 105 N.E.92 (N.Y. 1914).

20. GI Strausberg, RD Getz. Health Care Workers with AIDS: Duties Rights, and Potential Tort Liability. Baltimore L Rev 21:285.

21. *Canterbury v. Spence*, 464 F.2d 772 (D.C. Ci 1972), *cert. denied*, 409 U.S. 1064 (1972).

22. *Cobbs v. Grant*, 8 Cal. 3d 299, 502 P.2d 1, 104 Cal. Rptr. 505 (1972).

23. *Canterbury*, 464 F.2d at 786 (Footnote 20).

24. JF Daar. Informed consent: defining limits through therapeutic parameters. Whittier L Rev 1995; 16:187.

25. *West Virginia Central RR Co. v. Fuller*, 96 Md. 652, 666, 54 A. 669 671 (1903).

26. *Grimes v. Kennedy Krieger Institute, Inc.*, 366 Md. 29, 782 A.2d 807 (2001).

27. See note 25 above.

28. *Id.*

29. M Milford. Lawsuits Attack Medical Trial. As Claims Arise, Some Fear Tests Will Lose Public Support. Natl L J Aug 20, 2001.

30. PM Tereskerz. Research accountability and financial conflicts of interest in industry-sponsored clinical research: A review. Accountability in Research 2003; 10:137-58.

31. SYH Kim, RW Millard, P Nisbet, C Cox, and ED Caine. Potential research participants' views regarding researcher and institutional financial conflicts of interest. J Med Ethics 2004; 30:73-9.

32. KP Winfurt, MA Dinan, JS Allsbrook et al. Policies of academic medical centers for disclosing financial conflicts of interest to potential research participants. Academic Medicine 2006; 81:113-18.

33. *Moore v. Regents of the University of California*, 51 Cal. 3d 120, 271 Cal. Rptr. 146, 793 P.2d 479 (1990).

34. *Moore v. Regents of the University of California*, 51 Cal. 3d at 120, 271 Cal. Rptr. at 147, 793 P.2d at 480.

Legal Ramifications

35. See note 25 above.
36. *Id.*
37. *Id.*
38. *Id.*
39. *Id.*
40. *Id.*, 271, Cal. Rptr. at 148, 793 P.2d at 481.
41. *Id.* at 125-126, 271 Cal. Rptr. 147, 793 P.2d at 480.
42. *Id.*
43. See note 25 above.
44. *Id.*
45. *Id.*
46. *Id.*
47. *Id.*
48. *Id.*, at 127, 271 Cal. Rptr. 149, 793 P.2d at 481-82.
49. *Id.*, at 127-128, 271 Cal. Rptr. at 149, 793 P.2d at 482.
50. See note 40 above.
51. *Id.*, at 131-132, 271 Cal. Rptr. at 152, 793 P.2d at 485.
52. *Brown v. Wood*, 202 So. 2d 125 (Fla. App. 1967); *Nishi v. Hartwell,* 52 Hawaii 188, 473 P.2d 116 (1970).
53. *Moore* at 129-12, 271 Cal. Rptr. at 146-152, 793 P.2d at 483-485.
54. *Id.*, at 132-133, 271 Cal. Rptr. at 152, 793 P.2d at 485.
55. *Id.*, at 133-134, 271 Cal. Rptr. at 154, 793 P.2d at 487.
56. *Conversion* refers to the wrongful possession of another's property. Black's Law Dictionary (7th Edition 1999).
57. *Id.*, at 136-137, 271 Cal. Rptr. at 154, 793 P.2d at 487.
58. *Id.*, at 147, 271 Cal. rptr. at 164, 793 P.2d at 497.
59. *Id.*, at 136-142, 271 Cal.Rptr. at 154-160, 793 P.2d at 487-495.
60. *Id.*, at 142, 271 Cal. Rptr. at 146, 793 P.2d at 493.
61. See note 55 above.
62. L Daniels discusses the effect of both of these statutory provisions as catalysts in changing incentives in research, thereby ultimately changing the nature of the relationship between physicians and patients. L Daniels. *Commercialization of Human Tissues: Has Biotechnology Created the Need for an Expanded Scope of Informed Consent?* 27 Calif. W. L. Rev. 209, 210 (quoting) L. Rosenberg. *Using Patient Materials for Product Development: A Dean's Prospective.* Clinical Research 1985; 33:452-53.

63. 35 U.S.C. §201 (1988).
64. 447 U.S. 303, 309. [*Diamond v. Chakrabarty*]
65. Daniels at 212, see note 62 above.
66. Quoting M Rodwin. The organized American medical profession's response to financial conflicts of interest: 1890-1992, 70 Milbank Q 703, 705 (1992).
67. The Drug Amendments of 1952 require researchers to disclose the investigative purpose of experimental medications. *Id.* at 220, and regulations enacted regarding research funded by the National Institutes of Health require prospective review of research methods by an institutional review board that is to assure that appropriate means to obtain informed consent from research subjects are included in research protocols. *Id.* (citing) 21 CFR §50.1(a) (1990); 45 CFR §46.116 (a)(6) (1990); 21 CFR §50.25(a)(6); 45 CFR §46.102(g); 21 CFR §50.3(1); 45 CFR §46.116(a)(1-8); 21 CFR §50.25(a)(1-8).
68. Daniels at 214.
69. *See generally* 61 Am Jur 2d § 188.
70. *Stacey v. Pantano*, 177 Neb. 694, 131 N.W.2d 163 (1964).
71. EH Morreim. Conflicts of Interest. JAMA (1989); 262: 390.
72. Morreim at 391.
73. *Moore*, 271 Cal. Rptr. at 148, 793 P.2d at 481.
74. A Relman. Economic Incentives in Clinical Investigation. New Engl J Med 1989; 320:933.
75. A. Relman. Dealing with Conflicts of Interest NEJM 1985; 313: 749-50.
76. J Brainard. Physician May Lead New Human-Research Office. Chron Higher Educ. May 26, 200 at A41.
77. Hippocrates. The Oath. Written 400 BCE. Translated by Francis Adams. Available at *http://classics.mit.edu.*
78. H.R. 4697 107th Congress 2d Session. May 9, 2002.
79. The "Common Rule," Subpart A, 45 CFR § 46 (56 FR 803) *http://www.hhs.gov/ohrp/humansubjects/guidance/45cfr46.htm;* see appendix D of this volume.

6

A Recent Clinical Trial Involving Financial Conflicts of Interest: Applying Traditional Legal Theories

> This is all about money, prestige. . . . We forgot the basic point of it all: people.
> — *Paul Gelsinger*

Recently, several lawsuits have been filed involving clinical trials in which investigators and/or study institutions have a financial conflict of interest. This and the following chapter provide several examples of such cases. The cases are presented not to provide a litany of horror stories, but instead to provide insight into how legal theories are being applied to cases involving financial conflicts of interest.

Many of these cases are being brought on the traditional malpractice theories of failure to obtain informed consent, including the failure to disclose financial conflicts of interest and/or assault and battery. Attorneys for injured plaintiffs are also proceeding on the basis of fraud/intentional misrepresentation, claiming that, by intentionally failing to adequately disclose financial conflicts of interest, investigators and study institutions have led research subjects to participate in research studies in which they otherwise would not have enrolled.

These cases have been noteworthy for several reasons. One is that some of the legal theories advanced have been novel, as will be discussed in the next chapter. Another is that defendants have been named in these suits who heretofore have not been considered targets, including a bioethicist and members of IRBs. The following provides a discussion of the first and perhaps most publicly visible case of recent vintage that was brought on the basis of traditional legal theories.

THE JESSE GELSINGER CASE

Just as the Tuskegee experiments,[1] in which Black men were deceptively denied treatment for syphilis, led to major reforms, the Jesse Gelsinger case has been a turning point for the protection of human subjects of clinical research. The case shook the foundations of the research world and was a catalyst for revisiting how human research subjects are protected. By bringing national attention and public scrutiny to the numerous shortcomings in the federal system to protect research subjects, the case prompted several congressional hearings and served as an impetus for efforts by the FDA, NIH, and DHHS to better protect human research subjects.

An NIH inquiry regarding dangerous adverse reaction, conducted after the Gelsinger case, prompted researchers around the country to reveal more than 650 dangerous adverse reactions that had previously been kept secret — including many deaths.[2]

The Gelsinger case involved gene therapy, one of medicine's most promising treatments. It also, unfortunately, exposed some tragic deficiencies in the way we protect those who volunteer to participate in research. As one CBS News reporter commented, "A mountaintop grave near Tucson, Arizona calls into question the wisdom and hope of gene therapy experiments in the hunt for medical breakthroughs."[3] This case illustrates that ethical breaches related to financial conflicts of interest can have deadly consequences. As one commentator wrote, this case demonstrates how "Law gives ethics power; that is, it may make ethics enforceable."[4] It also indicates that the promise and progress of gene therapy research has been quashed, to some degree, because financial conflicts of interest have not been appropriately managed.

6

A Recent Clinical Trial Involving Financial Conflicts of Interest: Applying Traditional Legal Theories

> This is all about money, prestige. . . . We forgot the basic point of it all: people.
> — *Paul Gelsinger*

Recently, several lawsuits have been filed involving clinical trials in which investigators and/or study institutions have a financial conflict of interest. This and the following chapter provide several examples of such cases. The cases are presented not to provide a litany of horror stories, but instead to provide insight into how legal theories are being applied to cases involving financial conflicts of interest.

Many of these cases are being brought on the traditional malpractice theories of failure to obtain informed consent, including the failure to disclose financial conflicts of interest and/or assault and battery. Attorneys for injured plaintiffs are also proceeding on the basis of fraud/intentional misrepresentation, claiming that, by intentionally failing to adequately disclose financial conflicts of interest, investigators and study institutions have led research subjects to participate in research studies in which they otherwise would not have enrolled.

These cases have been noteworthy for several reasons. One is that some of the legal theories advanced have been novel, as will be discussed in the next chapter. Another is that defendants have been named in these suits who heretofore have not been considered targets, including a bioethicist and members of IRBs. The following provides a discussion of the first and perhaps most publicly visible case of recent vintage that was brought on the basis of traditional legal theories.

THE JESSE GELSINGER CASE

Just as the Tuskegee experiments,[1] in which Black men were deceptively denied treatment for syphilis, led to major reforms, the Jesse Gelsinger case has been a turning point for the protection of human subjects of clinical research. The case shook the foundations of the research world and was a catalyst for revisiting how human research subjects are protected. By bringing national attention and public scrutiny to the numerous shortcomings in the federal system to protect research subjects, the case prompted several congressional hearings and served as an impetus for efforts by the FDA, NIH, and DHHS to better protect human research subjects.

An NIH inquiry regarding dangerous adverse reaction, conducted after the Gelsinger case, prompted researchers around the country to reveal more than 650 dangerous adverse reactions that had previously been kept secret — including many deaths.[2]

The Gelsinger case involved gene therapy, one of medicine's most promising treatments. It also, unfortunately, exposed some tragic deficiencies in the way we protect those who volunteer to participate in research. As one CBS News reporter commented, "A mountaintop grave near Tucson, Arizona calls into question the wisdom and hope of gene therapy experiments in the hunt for medical breakthroughs."[3] This case illustrates that ethical breaches related to financial conflicts of interest can have deadly consequences. As one commentator wrote, this case demonstrates how "Law gives ethics power; that is, it may make ethics enforceable."[4] It also indicates that the promise and progress of gene therapy research has been quashed, to some degree, because financial conflicts of interest have not been appropriately managed.

Except when otherwise cited, the following report was taken from pleadings filed in a lawsuit by the estate of Jesse Gelsinger.[5] Jesse Gelsinger was 18 years old when he died while participating in a gene transfer experiment at the University of Pennsylvania. He suffered from a rare metabolic disorder, partial ornithine transcarbamylase (OTC), which prevented him from properly metabolizing ammonia, so he was in danger of accumulating toxic levels of it in his blood. His condition was controlled with a low-protein diet and medication, and he was relatively healthy when he began participation in the experiment. He knew that the trial he agreed to be a part of would not benefit him, but he was led to believe that participation in the experiment posed little risk, while it held the potential to yield important benefits in the future for infants born with OTC. According to his father, "he wanted to be a hero."[6]

The experiment involved injecting Gelsinger with adenovirus, a pathogen that causes the common cold, as a vehicle known as a vector to deliver corrective genes for OTC by invading cells. In this case, the adenovirus vector was developed at the University of Pennsylvania. The goal of the experiment was to replace defective genes with healthy ones.

In September 1999, Gelsinger enrolled in the study. Following injection with the OTC gene attached to the adenovirus, he developed a fever and began to experience flu-like symptoms, which were expected. However, within hours, Paul Gelsinger, his father, received a call telling him that his son's immune system was raging out of control. His eyes and ears swelled shut. Ultimately, he suffered irreversible multiple organ system failure and brain death, and was removed from life support. His death was the first reported that was directly attributable to a gene therapy experiment.

According to the pleadings, this research involved numerous financial conflicts of interest involving both James M. Wilson, MD, the physician and researcher involved in this case, and the University of Pennsylvania that were unknown to Gelsinger and his family.

Wilson was the director of the Institute for Human Gene Therapy Research (IHGT) at the University of Pennsylvania.

At the same time, he was the founder and employee of Genovo, a corporation that provided about 25 percent of the budget for IHGT, with more than $4 million annually for five years to conduct genetic research. Wilson controlled up to 30 percent of Genovo's stock. Reportedly, he made $13.5 million when the company was sold.[7]

In return for Genovo's research sponsorship, the University of Pennsylvania granted Genovo licenses for the lung and liver applications for existing technologies developed by Wilson. In addition, Genovo retained an option to negotiate for licenses for future developments by IHGT or Wilson, which included full patent reimbursement, milestone payments, and royalties on product sales. Genovo shareholders included numerous past and present university and IHGT employees.

The ensuing lawsuit, seeking both dollars to compensate the family for the loss of Gelsinger's life as well as punitive damages, revealed a tangled maze of financial conflicts of interest. The eight-count lawsuit alleged wrongful death, strict product liability, intentional assault and battery, intentional and negligent infliction of emotional distress, and fraud. The complaint was noteworthy in that it named not only the institution and investigators as defendants, but also an ethicist at the University of Pennsylvania.

One of the central theories upon which the suit was premised was lack of informed consent as set out in the plaintiffs' pleadings, which were based on the following.

> 110. The lack of informed consent includes, but is not limited to:
>   a. understating the risks of the toxic effects of the injection of the adenovirus particles;
>   b. failing to inform plaintiff's decedent regarding the fact that monkeys injected with the virus had become ill and/or died;
>   c. failing to inform plaintiff's decedent that patients who had previously participated in the trial suffered serious adverse effects;
>   d. misrepresenting the fact that prior participants in the study had achieved certain efficacy with respect to the treatment of OTC;

Applying Traditional Legal Theories

    e. failing to adequately disclose the extent to which Dr. Wilson and the University had a conflict of interest;
    f. failing to adequately disclose the financial interest that Dr. Wilson and the University had in relation to the study;
    g. allowing the vectors to sit and/or be stored on lab shelves for 25 months before being tested in animals, making them less potent then [sic] they could have been. The vectors administered to the plaintiff's decedent were only stored for two months. The 25 month storage in turn, may have resulted in an underestimation of the vectors [sic] potency in humans. Additionally, the animals who received the vector stored for 25 months would have been given a dose of vector from 52.2% to 65.3% below the vector dose specified in the FDA protocol.[8]

Following Jesse's death, the FDA found numerous violations of its guidelines; the following were cited in the lawsuit.

    a. failing to tell the National Institute [sic] of Health Recombinant DNA Advisory Committee ("the RAC") of a change in the way the virus was to be delivered to patients;
    b. changing the informed consent form from what had been approved by the FDA by removing information concerning the death or illness of several monkeys during a similar study;
    c. failing to report to the FDA that patients prior to Jesse suffered significant liver toxicity which required that the study be put on hold;
    d. failing to follow the study protocol which mandated that in each cohort at least two women be subject to injection before any male;
    e. admitting Jesse in the trial when his blood ammonia level on the day before he received the gene transfer exceeded the limit set out in the FDA protocol; and
    f. allowing the vectors to sit and/or be stored on lab

shelves for 25 months before being tested in animals, making them less potent then [sic] they could have been. The 25 month storage in turn, may have resulted in an underestimation of the vectors [sic] potency in humans. Additionally, the animals who received the vector stored for 25 months would have been given a dose of vector from 52.2% to 65.3% below the vector dose specified in the FDA protocol.[9]

Following this case, all gene therapy trials, not only at the University of Pennsylvania but around the country, were put on hold. President Bill Clinton demanded improvements in informed consent procedures and access to information on gene therapy research.

Not surprisingly, the case was settled out of court, and details of the settlement remained confidential. Parties to the settlement included the University of Pennsylvania, Wilson and his co-investigators, Batshaw and Raper, and their institutions. The bioethicist who was named as a defendant because he had provided advice that led to the experiment's focus on healthy adults instead of critically ill newborns was released from the suit, as was the former medical dean of the University of Pennsylvania.

When and if cases such as Gelsinger's proceed to trial on the basis of lack of informed consent or medical malpractice, it will no doubt be difficult to prove that a financial conflict of interest caused the injury, a requisite requirement to prove a tort claim, as discussed in chapter 5. However, from a legal perspective, such conflicts have significant evidentiary value in demonstrating that there was a motive to withhold such information, which, in turn, caused a patient to enroll in a trial or continue in a trial that the patient would not have otherwise consented to, and which led to the commission of other acts that caused the patient's injury.[10]

The presence of financial conflicts of interest will no doubt significantly enhance the settlement value of such cases, if for no other reason than such conflicts present a public relations nightmare for defendants that will encourage swift resolution.

Following Gelsinger's case, several other lawsuits involving clinical trials that were plagued by conflicts of interest have been filed. As discussed in the following chapters, it is within the context of these cases that the attorneys for the plaintiffs have made novel application of legal theories to their claims.

NOTES

The epigraph at the beginning of this chapter is from S Lehrman. The Gelsinger Story. GeneLetter. May 1, 2000.

  1. CH Coleman. Rationalizing risk assessment in human subject research. Ariz L Rev 2004; 46: 1.
  2. A Relman. Economic Incentives in Clinical Investigation. New Engl J Med 1989; 320:933.
  3. E Shiff (reporter), P Webster. In the Service of Science. CBS News — The Magazine. March 6, 2000. Available at *http://www.cbc.ca/national/magazine.*
  4. R Collins. Regulating Dr. Frankenstein: Money, Lax Ethics, & Clinical Trials. Integrity in Science, Center for Science in the Public Interest, available at *http://www.cspinet.org/integrity/regulate_frank.html.*
  5. Available at *http://www.sskrplaw.com.*
  6. S. Lehrman. The Gelsinger Story, GeneLetter. May 1, 2000.
  7. D Wilson and D Heath. The Prospects for Change: System's Serious Flaws Have Led Many to Call for Regulatory Reform. March 15, 2001. The Seattle Times at A1.
  8. See note 5 above.
  9. *Id.*
  10. P Harrington. Faculty conflicts of interest in an age of academic entrepreneurialism: An analysis of the problem, the law, and selected university policies. J College and Univ L 2001; 27:775.

7

Is There a Constitutional Right to Be Treated with Dignity within the Context of Medical Experimentation?

> It was a perfect lesson on how not to run a clinical trial.
> — *Cherlynn Mathias*

Preservation of bodily integrity is not a new concept under tort law. Likewise, as described below, experimentation on an unknowing human subject has long been recognized as unconstitutional. It has been characterized as "an intentional constitutional tort" by Supreme Court Justice Brennan.[1] However, it is novel to make constitutional claims in the context of financial conflicts of interest that were unknown to research subjects when they consented to participate in an experiment, and cases are just now being brought that test such theories.

In 2001, 14 patients and their family members filed a federal lawsuit alleging a variety of injuries resulting from a clinical trial of a melanoma vaccine.[2] The suit was noteworthy in that the named defendants included not only the study's lead clinical investigator and corporate cosponsor, but also the IRB of the Oklahoma Health Sciences Center in Tulsa. The suit followed a whistleblower's complaint to the Office for Human Research Protections (OHRP) and made national news. *Time Magazine* characterized the circumstances as follows.

By the time Cherlynn Mathias was ready to blow the whistle on Dr. Michael McGee two years ago, it had been clear for quite a while that something fishy was going on. For one thing, there were the hokey infomercials touting his experimental vaccine for malignant melanoma, a particularly nasty form of cancer, as if it were a Veg-O-Matic. Thanks to the vaccine, a patient declared onscreen, my cancer is in total remission. Then there was the sales pitch McGee delivered in person. When she and the doctor met with a prospective patient, says Mathias, who worked as his research nurse, he would come on like a used-car salesman: "We have the best vaccine out there," she remembers his saying. "Two-thirds of my patients have responded to the treatment." He was even giving the drug to his father-in-law, he would tell people; that's how good it was.[3]

Mathias asserted that most of the patients enrolled in the trial believed it was their best hope for recovery from an otherwise usually fatal disease. She claims this is why patients were surprised when McGee sent them a letter that read in part, "Patients have enrolled in this study more rapidly than originally expected. . . . Due to this interest, the sponsor has exceeded its capacity to supply the experimental Melanoma Vaccine and is unable to provide material for further injections at this time." Mathias knew this was a lie, and that the trial was suspended because of concern by McGee's superiors that the vaccine might have been doing more harm than good. Mathias then wrote a letter to OHRP reporting that McGee had, "among other things, stored the vaccine improperly, exposing it to potential contamination; failed to maintain adequate records and track its consistency from batch to batch; mislabeled vials of the stuff; and worst of all, kept most of the data on adverse side effects secret."[4]

A subsequent investigation by the FDA noted more than 20 deficiencies. A lawsuit following this series of events made 122 claims for recovery.[5]

This case and other similar cases that followed received public attention because of the novel claims or legal theories the plaintiffs' attorneys sought to apply. Traditionally, cases involving experiments involving human subjects that have

A Constitutional Right to Dignity?

gone awry have been brought as malpractice cases, and thus have received limited public scrutiny. Among the theories advanced in this case were ones that had been around for a long time, but their application to the clinical trials setting is unique.

Several applications of embryonic theories were set forth; one theory was that the plaintiff had a constitutional right to human dignity not to be the subject of an unethical human experiment.[6] Invoking the Fourteenth Amendment to the Constitution, the plaintiffs (McGee acknowledged he was a state actor) argued that the state shall not deprive any person of life, liberty, or property without due process of law, and that this guarantees more than absence from physical restraint.[7]

Citing constitutional law cases decided by the U.S. Supreme Court such as *Moore v. City of East Cleveland Ohio*[8] and *Griswold v. Connecticut*,[9] among others, the plaintiffs argued that rights are protected under the Constitution's Due Process Clause if they are "so rooted in the tradition and conscience of our people as to be ranked as fundamental," or if such rights reflect "basic values implicit in the concept of ordered liberty" such that "neither liberty nor justice would exist if they were sacrificed." The plaintiffs went on to argue that the right to bodily integrity has long been recognized as a fundamental right guaranteed by the Constitution.[10]

The U.S. District Court for the Northern District of Oklahoma considered the plaintiffs' constitutional claims and dismissed the case on the grounds that the plaintiffs failed to establish federal subject matter jurisdiction. That is, the plaintiffs were not able to provide a statutory basis for federal jurisdiction by showing that the dispute arose under the Constitution, laws, or treaties of the United States.[11] In this case, the plaintiffs contended that the court had jurisdiction pursuant to a federal law (hereinafter referred to as Section 1983).[12] Section 1983 provides that liability will be imposed on anyone, who under "color of state law, deprives a person of any rights, privileges or immunities secured by the Constitution and Laws."

In this case, the claim was made that the constitutional right to be treated with dignity in the context of medical experimentation, as guaranteed by the Fourteenth Amendment to the U.S. Constitution, had been violated, and also that there was an implied private cause of action under federal regulations.[13]

In dismissing the case under Section 1983, the court held:

> The due process clause cannot be interpreted to impose federal rights that are more appropriately state tort claims. The cases cited by plaintiffs primarily involve non-consensual administration of medication or lack of consent to medical experiments. In this instance, the plaintiffs volunteered to be participants in the melanoma vaccine study. *At the onset, the plaintiff's participation in the study was consensual*, even though the study was ultimately closed for failure to comply with federal standards. To have a Section 1983 claim, it is not sufficient to show that a physician exposed a person to an unreasonable risk of harm, ordinary negligence, or medical malpractice. Such allegations do not rise to the level of a constitutional claim or fundamental right guaranteed by the Fourteenth Amendment. *See, Daniels v. Gilbreadth*, 668 F.2d 477, 486 (19th Super. Cir. 1982).[14] [Emphasis added.]

The court's analysis contained a serious flaw, which, unfortunately, formed the basis for its opinion, and that is its finding, as quoted above: that at the outset, participation in this research study was consensual. Amazingly, the court overlooked the "informed" part of "informed consent." It is interesting that it did not use the phrase "informed consent" in its opinion. This interpretation erodes the essence of "informed consent" as it has evolved through common law and federal regulatory regulations.[15] Apparently, the court believed that because the plaintiffs signed consent forms, even though the consent forms were misleading and deceptive, this meant that their participation in the study was consensual.[16]

But how can "uninformed consent" be seen as consensual? Uninformed consent is a misnomer, a legal nullity. If consent is not "informed," then it amounts to *non-consensual experimentation*.

The court appears to make a distinction between cases in which research subjects are not told that they are being ex-

A Constitutional Right to Dignity?

perimented upon and those in which subjects are given erroneous and misleading information to induce them to consent to experimentation.

In reality, such a distinction is a fiction. The fundamental right to preservation of bodily integrity is equally violated when a research subject is not told about the experimentation as when researchers knowingly and willingly dupe subjects to agree to participate in a study. And, as the plaintiffs in this case pointed out, the right to be free from unethical human experimentation or the right to human dignity should be considered a distinct, fundamental right of all humans.

The plaintiffs' brief went to great pains to explain the nature of this right, examining the historical context in which human subject protection evolved, particularly emphasizing *The Nuremberg Code*.[17] *The Nuremberg Code* was drafted by a doctor who worked with the prosecution during the trial of *USA v. Karl Brandt,* following the Holocaust, and was submitted as a memorandum to the United States Counsel for War Crimes. It outlined six points defining legitimate research. The verdict in the case reiterated almost all of the points in a section called "Permissible Medical Experiments," and expanded the original six points to 10.

The plaintiffs' counsel argued that an understanding of *The Nuremberg Code* was essential because an examination of "our Nation's history, legal traditions and practices is critical to determination of the scope of the liberty interest under the Due Process Clause."[18] In this regard, the plaintiffs argued that there were a number of cases in which the courts expressly held that *The Nuremberg Code* may be applied by U.S. Courts, and in which it was clear that the protections offered by *The Nuremberg Code* are "a fundamental right rooted in the conscience and history of the people of the world, in general, and of the United States, in particular."

For example, *In re Cincinnati Radiation Litigation* involved a suit that was brought by subjects who had unknowingly been involved in radiation experiments.[19] The court held that this claim was cognizable under the Constitution's Due Process Clause, and, in doing so, found, "The Nuremberg Code is part of the law of humanity. It may be applied in both civil and criminal cases by the federal courts in the United States."[20]

The court went on to hold that if the Constitution did not establish a right under which these clients could establish their case, then a gaping hole in the Constitution had been exposed.

A closer evaluation by the *Robertson* court of this well-reasoned holding would have been instructive for several reasons. First, while it is true that in the beginning that *Cincinnati* was a case in which the research subjects were unwitting participants, and no consent to the involved experimentation was given in the first five years of the radiation experiments, beginning in 1965, consent forms were used, but failed to state the real risk — a circumstance remarkably similar to the *Robertson* case. Therefore, at the outset, the distinction the *Robertson* court made between cases such as this and the circumstances in *Robertson* was at least in part an artificial one. However, for reasons set out above, such distinction, even to the extent it did exist, was superfluous as to whether or not a constitutionally protected liberty interest had been violated.

Secondly, the defendants in *Cincinnati* attempted to confine the case to the medical malpractice/ordinary tort case arena — a position that the *Roberston* court upheld. But, as the court in *Cincinnati*[21] points out, this argument is without merit and

> ... reveals an interpretation of the Constitution that would vitiate the fundamental constitutional principles just described. The distinction between this case and an ordinary tort case is not one of degree, but rather, of kind. Government actors in cases such as this violate a different kind of duty from that owed by a private tort defendant. Individuals in our society are largely left free to pursue their own ends without regard for others, save a general duty not to harm others by negligent conduct. This is the "ordinary" tort case. The relationship between government and the individual is fundamentally different. In a free society, government is neither an autonomous actor nor a master to whom the people must acquiesce. The function of government is to serve the people and to enhance the quality of life. The broad purpose of all constitutional limits on government power is to ensure that government does not stray from that role or abuse its power.[22]

Likewise, in *Stadt v. University of Rochester*, the plaintiff brought a lawsuit under the Federal Tort Claims Act, alleging that she had been injected with plutonium without her informed consent.[23] In rejecting a motion to dismiss the case, the court stated, "This case does not involve the right to refuse medical treatment, but instead the right to be free from nonconsensual experimentation on one's body . . . the right to bodily integrity . . . a right which has been recognized throughout this nation's history."[24] The court held, "The Constitution and, more specifically, the Due Process Clause of the Fifth Amendment clearly established the right to be free from nonconsensual government experimentation on one's body."[25]

In 1999, a federal district court in Massachusetts[26] stated, in a case involving experimental treatment with terminally ill patients without their consent, that a breach of the principles of *The Nuremberg Code* by the government constituted a violation of the Due Process Clause of the Constitution. The court stated, "Similar conduct that 'shocks the conscience' includes the use of false promises of therapeutic hope to terminally ill patients in order to lure them into becoming human subjects for the benefit of curious scientists rather than the health of the test subjects."[27] This court noted that, while such a claim may be analyzed under the legal standards governing ordinary medical treatment, "This does not, however, obviate the possibility that medical experimentation conducted under false pretenses by government actors can rise to the level of a constitutional violation."[28]

It seems clear that the authority in this area allows for both a state claim under ordinary malpractice or tort law, as well as a constitutional claim under certain circumstances when a liberty interest has been implicated. While the definition of the exact type of liberty interest that must be violated to trigger a valid constitutional claim has not been explicitly set forth by the courts, one guidepost is a state action that "shocks the conscience."[29]

What is it in cases that shocks the conscience? A careful reading of cases involving experimentation with human subjects, and their predecessors in other areas involving constitutional claims for non-consensual medical intervention, leads to a common thread that allows an ordinary tort claim to also encompass a constitutional one. This thread is state action, by which subjects are deceived or misled to induce them to consent to experimentation or to participate in treatment that they might otherwise have refused.

The *Robertson* court also appears to have been misguided in finding that "plaintiffs are contending that by defendants conducting the melanoma study in violation of federal regulations for the protection of human subjects, such conduct gives rise to an independent private cause of action by incorporating the Declaration of Helsinki and the Nuremberg Code. . . . the standards in the United States for conducting research on human subjects is contained in the Code of Federal Regulations and, thus, there is no need for the courts to resort to international law to impute a standard."[30]

Here the court misses the point altogether. The plaintiff's claim in *Robertson* was asserted under the Constitution, not under *The Nuremberg Code* or *The Declaration of Helsinki*. (*Helsinki* is a "statement of ethical principles to provide guidance to physicians and other participants in medical research" created by the World Medical Association).[31] The plaintiffs never claimed that these international laws created a private cause of action. These documents were relied upon by the plaintiff solely to demonstrate the historical context from which the rights of all citizens to bodily integrity have been recognized as a fundamental right. However, even if plaintiffs contended that a private action was created by these international codes, at least one court would likely disagree with the *Robertson* holding.

The *Krieger* case discussed in chapter 5 held, admittedly within a different context (negligence rather than constitutional claim), that the breach of obligations imposed on researchers by *The Nuremberg Code* "might well support actions sounding in negligence. . . ."[32] The court held:

> The Nuremberg Code is the "most complete and authoritative statement of the law of informed consent to human experimentation." It is also "part of international common law and may be applied, in both civil and criminal cases by state, federal and municipal courts in the United States." However, even though the courts in the United States may

A Constitutional Right to Dignity? 117

use the Nuremberg Code to set criminal and civil standards of conduct, none have used it in a criminal case and only a handful have even cited it in the civil context. [N]o United States court has ever awarded damages to an injured experimental subject, or punished an experimenter, on the basis of a violation of the Nuremberg Code. There have, however, been very few court decisions involving human experimentation. It is therefore very difficult for a "common law" of human experimentation to develop. This absence of judicial precedent makes codes, especially judicially-crafted codes like the Nuremberg Code, all the more important. [Footnotes omitted and emphasis added by the court].[33]

The *Krieger* court noted that one reason *The Nuremberg Code* was not immediately adopted by U.S. Courts as setting the minimum standard of care for human experimentation is that there has been little opportunity to do so until now, noting that almost no experiments resulted in lawsuits in the 1940s, 1950s, and 1960s. Additionally, the court stated that a second reason may be that the Nazi experiments were considered so extreme as to be considered irrelevant to the U.S. Consequently, physician groups, finding *The Nuremberg Code* too legalistic, developed alternatives to guide medical researchers such as *The Declaration of Helsinki*.[34]

While the *Robertson* case did not involve a claim involving financial conflict of interest, the constitutional claims described above are now being employed in subsequent cases, such as the "Hutch" cases, described below, which involve financial conflicts of interest.

THE "HUTCH" LITIGATION

The "Hutch" cases involve the Fred Hutchinson Cancer Research Center in Seattle (hereafter, the Center). According to an investigative report in the *Seattle Times* on the circumstances surrounding these cases, the Center was founded as a tax-supported nonprofit organization that spawned private companies worth more than $18 billion and an estimated $100 million in personal wealth for its doctors; further, at least 20 of its researchers left the Center to start private ventures based on the government-funded work they undertook at the Center.[35] Others, particularly senior management, stayed at the Center but supplemented their salaries with private consulting, stock deals, and drug development rights. Noting in this article how conflict of interest policies have "been weakened and walls between taxpayer-funded science and for-profit science have crumbled" at the Center, the article questioned the wisdom of awarding the financial benefits of science to the scientists who conduct the research.[36]

The *Wright* Case

The *Wright* complaint is a class action, a lawsuit in which one person or a small number of individuals represent the interests of a much larger group, brought on behalf of individuals who participated in a study known as "Protocol 126" between 1981 and 1993 at the Center. Becky Wright, the lead plaintiff in the case, had leukemia. At the time of study enrollment, she was a 36-year-old mother of three. She was told that with a standard bone marrow transplant, chances were good that she would live to see her then five-year-old daughter grow up.[37] Her husband, who owned a local drugstore in Alabama, searched for the best place for her treatment and chose the Center. The researchers and three of the defendants in the case were E. Donnall Thomas, MD, a co-founder of the Center and a 1990 Nobel Prize winner, John Hansen, MD, who was head of a tissue-typing lab and later clinical director of the Center, and a young oncologist, Paul Martin, MD.[38] When Wright arrived at the Center in 1985 for treatment, she was not given the standard transplant. Instead, as described in an investigative report published in the *Seattle Times,* her experience was as follows.

> [Becky Wright was] thrust unwittingly into a world where the quest for cure gets tangled in the pursuit of fame and fortune....
>
> At the urging of her Hutchinson Center doctors, Becky Wright joins an experiment in which eight man-made proteins are added to her sister's bone marrow before it is transplanted.

Some of those proteins belong to a Seattle biotech company — a company named Genetic Systems. Some of Wright's doctors at the Hutch were among David Blech's recruits. [Blech is the founder of Genetic Systems.] The doctors — and the Hutch itself — had financial ties to the company Blech and his family had invented in their Flatbush flat.

By the time Wright was enrolled in the clinical trial, the doctors knew it wasn't working. Transplants were being rejected at alarming rates. New cancers were appearing and old ones reappearing far more than they normally would.

All were problems directly attributable to the experimental treatment.

The doctors didn't tell the Wrights any of that. Not about the 11 patients who had already died.

Not about other, less-dangerous ways of treating her disease.

Not about their own financial interests. . . .

Odds are high that some of them [referring to the deceased participants] would otherwise have survived a standard transplant and lived full lives. Many of the others likely would have lived at least a year or two longer than they did — a year or two they would have shared with their spouses, their children, their families and friends.

The story of Protocol 126 . . . has never been told. Federal and state investigators looked into Protocol 126 for a while, then closed their investigations half completed — leaving one investigator "saddened and alarmed" at the lack of follow-through.

During the 12-year span of the trial, several doctors at the Hutch tried to curb it. They said it was hurting rather than helping patients, and that mice or dogs rather than humans should be the test subjects. They complained that patients weren't being told about the risks, the alternatives, the researchers' financial conflicts.[39]

Wright lost her life, along with 79 of the other 82 patients in the study from what the plaintiffs claim was graft failure and/or leukemic relapse attributable to the treatment.

The ensuing lawsuit alleged, among other things, that the defendants misrepresented the risks of participating in the trial. The pleadings contend that the consent forms that were signed by the study participants minimized the risk of graft failure and suggested that a second bone marrow transplant could be undertaken with little difficulty, even though the investigators knew that the salvage rate from second transplants was only 5 to 10 percent. Of the 82 patients who enrolled in the study, 80 died from graft failures and/or leukemic relapse attributable to the treatment.

The following facts, unless otherwise noted, are taken from the pleadings filed on behalf of the plaintiffs.[40] The lawsuit claims the following.

- At no time prior to Becky Wright's participation in the study was she informed of the true nature of the risks that she would encounter.
- The defendants had a financial interest in the study.
- The salvage rate of second transplants was only 5 to 10 percent.
- Becky Wright was not informed that the first nine patients who used one of the antibodies in Protocol 126 suffered new cancers and died or that the experimental procedure increased the chance of relapse because graft versus host disease has an anti-leukemic effect, and that the relapses were usually fatal.

According to the *Seattle Times*, Genetic Systems Corporation recruited physicians to treat cancer patients in exchange for a position on their board; the corporation was formed by David Blech, whose "fall from grace is no more fascinating than his ascension as a brash 24-year-old who turned a family dream into reality. . . . Blech helped create a situation at the Center in which the care of cancer patients might be compromised by business relationships." Blech, who later was sentenced to five years of probation and community services for securities fraud for executing sham and unauthorized stock sales, suffers from manic depression and has spent time in a mental institution.[41]

Defendant researchers Hansen, Thomas, and Martin submitted Protocol 126 to the IRB of the Center for review in De-

A Constitutional Right to Dignity?

cember 1980. The goal of Protocol 126 was to prevent graft-versus-host disease (GVHD), an immune system reaction that affects about half of bone marrow transplants from siblings.

One month after Protocol 126 was submitted to the Center's IRB, Genetic Systems gave Hansen 250,000 shares of its stock and an $18,000 consulting fee. It gave 100,000 shares of stock and a $3,000 per year board position to Thomas and 10,000 shares of stock to Martin. Pleadings filed by the plaintiffs' attorneys stated that at the time suit was filed, Thomas' stock holdings in Genetic Systems were valued at about $5 million; the foundation's holdings were worth $2.5 million; Martin's were worth $525,000; and Hansen's were worth $9 million.

In January 1981, the IRB rejected the protocol due to concerns that it might cause graft rejections and cancer relapses. In March 1981, Genetic Systems executed a 20-year deal with the Center for commercial rights to 37 substances, three of which were to be tested in Protocol 126. In return, the Center received money, a royalty agreement, and an affiliated foundation received Genetic Systems stock.

In April 1981, Hansen resubmitted Protocol 126, which was then approved by the IRB. At no time was the IRB told that Hansen, Thomas, Martin, or the Center had financial interests in Genetic Systems.

In March 1983, the Center adopted a conflict of interest policy prohibiting scientists from participating in research involving the Center in which the members had a financial interest. Yet Hansen, Thomas, and Martin continued to participate in Protocol 126. In April 1983, the IRB tried to institute criteria to stop the trial if subjects in the trial died; the IRB also tried to change the consent form to include a warning of unexpected new cancers. Despite these efforts, and the deaths of numerous subjects, the defendants did not report the deaths to the IRB. In 1983, the IRB again approved the trial and the consent form did not disclose the risks of new cancers, relapse, or graft failure. At about the same time, Hansen was named vice president for research at Genetic Systems.

In September 1983, the IRB asked for clarification of animal studies, human risks, and financial interests involved in Protocol 126. In response, Thomas denied any conflict of interest, refused the request for separate tests on antibodies, and warned the IRB not to impede the research. In April 1985, the IRB approved Protocol 126.2, and the consent form did not mention the known risks associated with Protocol 126. In April 1985, Martin, Hansen, and Thomas applied for Protocol 126.3, which combined T-cell depletion with other chemicals. The IRB asked for outside review, which was denied, as its previous requests had been.

In September 1985, Martin told colleagues that Protocol 126 had prevented GVHD, but was associated with between 25 to 40 percent graft failures, compared to the expected 1 percent failure rate. In October 1985, Genetic Systems was bought by Bristol-Myers for $294 million. In April 1988, Martin presented a paper claiming that T-cell depletion in certain leukemia patients led to a 100 percent relapse rate, instead of the expected 25 percent rate.

During the 12 years in which the trial was conducted, several physicians at the Center attempted to stop the study. In 1998, John Pesando, MD, a member of the Center's IRB, wrote to federal officials, "Many patients died at the Fred Hutchinson Cancer Research Center when the Institutional Review Board charged with protecting them was shamelessly used and abused by senior staff."[42] He added that the Center's management "denied the existence of financial conflicts of interest, refused to halt the protocols, and refused to have protocols reviewed by independent outside examiners."[43]

The Berman (Kathryn Hamilton) Case

In a case similar to Wright's involving egregious financial conflicts of interest, Allan Berman, husband of the late Kathryn Hamilton, brought suit against the Center. However, this case involved a different experimental study — Protocol 681, which researchers at the Center theorized would protect a patient's organs from the damaging effects of high-dose chemotherapy.

Hamilton was diagnosed with breast cancer when she was 34 and underwent a lumpectomy, radiation, and chemotherapy. She was cancer-free for 10 years, but in year 11 her cancer returned, this time in the form of bone cancer.[44] After additional treatment and surgery, the cancer was eradicated but returned two years later, which indicated Hamilton was dying.[45] Desperate to spend more time with her family, par-

A Constitutional Right to Dignity? 123

ticularly her 14-year-old daughter, she thought her best hope for survival was a stem cell transplant at the Center, in which patients were infused with immature cells taken from their own blood that were turned into bone marrow cells.[46]

The following facts were taken from pleadings filed on behalf of the plaintiff in this case, unless otherwise cited.[47] James Bianco, MD, who at that time, working with the Center, conducted preliminary research with 30 patients on pentoxifylline (PTX), a drug used for treating leg cramps. His preliminary results indicated the drug would shield the liver, kidney, and digestive system from toxicity associated with chemotherapy. Bianco claimed that only 3 percent of patients taking PTX suffered kidney damage. The study was considered a breakthrough, and PTX was seen as the new miracle drug. However, Bianco was unable to replicate the first set of study results, and, in a second study, more research subjects (39 percent) suffered kidney damage than those in a control group who received chemotherapy and a placebo.

A year before Hamilton was admitted to the study, Bianco knew that not only was PTX not a miracle drug, but there was evidence that it may have made patients sicker.

Bianco went on to pull charts of patients who received PTX in combination with other drugs that altered the way drugs metabolize, and found that patients had also been given the antibiotic Cipro® and the steroid prednisone. He concluded that none of the 10 subjects had suffered damage to their kidneys, liver, or lungs. Based on a woefully inadequate sample of only 10, this data was used in part as justification to enroll patients into Protocol 681, the study in which Hamilton took part in 1993.

Bianco, along with Jack Singer, MD, worked with Blech to found Cell Therapeutics, Incorporated (CTI). Bianco and Singer left the Center to work full time in their new start-up company to develop treatment for breast cancer patients with PTX, Cipro, and prednisone. They sought to collaborate with the Center in researching the treatment. Robert Day, president of the Center, cut the following deal with Bianco and Singer: the Center would receive about $20,000 in stock shares and $50,000 a year in licensing fees in return for their collaboration, to increase to at least $100,000 plus a percentage of sales if the company successfully sold the treatment. Consequently, the Center stood to make millions if the drug combination worked. Two Center co-founders, Donnall Thomas, MD, and C. Dean Buckner, MD, who would later become Hamilton's physicians, were included on the company's scientific advisory board and received stock options.

In the meantime, another researcher, William Bensinger, MD, was experimenting at the Center with stem cell transplants in patients with advanced breast cancer. Soon into his experiment, high-dose anti-cancer drugs killed two of four patients. Bensinger knew about Bianco's research and sought investigation of Bianco's drug combination in Center patients. Buckner, who also joined Cell Therapeutics' board, was working with Bensinger on Protocol 681. Knowing that PTX alone did not work, they hoped its combination with other drugs would work. Consequently, Bensinger submitted Protocol 681 with its combined drug regimen to the IRB, but made no mention of the generally known negative results concerning PTX.

According to a report in the *Seattle Times,* Bianco had given up on the use of PTX in combination with other drugs.[48] It is believed that he reached this conclusion because:
- The FDA resists the idea of combining two drugs into one, since the way drugs interact may differ among patients.
- Cipro increased the risk that patients might develop resistance to antibiotics.
- Business difficulties have been associated with combining drugs from competing manufacturers. Therefore, Bianco and CTI patented a compound of the drugs PTX and Cipro, known as lysofylline.

In 1992, a study was published that attempted to replicate Bianco's first PTX study and concluded that the drug did not work. In spite of this and Bianco's negative results from his own follow-up study, he defended the efficacy of PTX on the basis that the results of the European study were different because it relied on intravenous administration of PTX, which Bianco and Singer claimed was not as effective. It is interesting that this public support of the drug came when CTI was concluding its first major stock sale, raising $38.5 million.[49]

A Constitutional Right to Dignity?

In June 1993, CTI reported that research results suggested PTX and Cipro were wonder drugs, and claimed that 74 percent of the sickest patients lived one year after treatment, versus 7 percent of those who did not take the drugs, although no peer-reviewed article supporting these results appeared in the literature. Stock analysts have been quoted as saying that the commercial value of such a drug would be difficult to overstate and that anyone with convincing proof would have a market cap of $1 billion.[50]

At the very same time that CTI was publicly announcing these results, it was shutting down the research, which caused the Center to lose its supply of the intravenous (IV) form of PTX. Bianco had received permission from the FDA to use the IV form in clinical research, and all the Center had to do was ask for permission to use it. Instead, Bensinger decided to stop using the IV form in Protocol 681, and accordingly sent a revised protocol to the IRB. The IRB ordered that this be mentioned in the consent forms.

The following day, Kathryn Hamilton met with a Center physician, Frederick Appelbaum, MD, to decide if she should enter the study. Appelbaum was one of the investigators for Protocol 681 and a co-author of two articles about PTX: one showing promise and another that had not been submitted for publication that showed the drug did not work. But Appelbaum never mentioned the new findings to Hamilton, and the informed consent form therefore incorrectly stated that recent findings suggested that PTX prevented kidney, lung, and liver damage. In addition, the informed consent form mentioned the availability of the IV version of PTX, even though the Center no longer had this version available.

Hamilton was admitted to the study in early January 1993, and orally took PTX and Cipro, and shortly thereafter she became nauseated and vomited. She was supposed to receive PTX for 31 days, but could not tolerate the medication and threw up each time she took it. The Center did not seek FDA permission to use the IV form of the drug because it would have involved increased paperwork.

In mid-January, Hamilton underwent a stem cell transplant and within days developed a fever, suggesting an infection. She became jaundiced as a result of the liver damage she suffered. She had difficulty breathing and began bleeding from vessels in her eyes, ears, and nose. This was followed by kidney failure and finally death on 19 February, as she pleaded with her husband not to let her die.

Six days following her death, 17 Center researchers, including Bensinger, Appelbaum, Bianco, and Singer, submitted an article they had been preparing for months to a medical journal, reporting that PTX was not efficacious in protecting against the toxic effects of chemotherapy — while the defendants had continued their participation in Protocol 681.

The clinical trial continued, involving decisions that shock the conscience. For example, even after the deaths of Hamilton and another subject, the researchers not only continued the trial but *increased* the doses given to the other women enrolled, leading David Lepay, MD, PhD, director of the FDA Division of Scientific Investigation, to state; "I can't imagine such a scenario occurring."[51] Following Hamilton's death, at least two more women died from the treatment. Center researchers attributed the four deaths in 68 subjects to the treatment, rather than to the cancer. The rate of regimen-related deaths was almost 12 times higher than that experienced in these types of cancer trials.[52] Bensinger shut down the study in 1998, one week after CTI reported disappointing results for the drug it derived from the drugs used in Protocol 681.[53] The complete findings of the study were never published.[54] Bianco and CTI have moved on to developing other drugs, and in 2001 were reported to be worth more than $764 million.[55]

These lawsuits are premised on several legal theories including violation of the right to be treated with dignity, violation of federal regulations, breach of *The Belmont Report*[56] as incorporated in the assurance agreement, fraud/intentional misrepresentation, assault and battery, and strict products liability, which is commonly known as *liability without fault,* and "refers to when a seller is liable for any and all defective or hazardous products which unduly threaten a consumers personal safety."[57] In addition, there are claims of violation of the Washington State Consumer Protection Act and HealthCare Provider Act. The lawsuits claim that the failure to obtain informed consent constituted battery and negligent and wrongful conduct in violation of this act. As in some of the other cases discussed earlier, the cases are also noteworthy in that the *suits named individual IRB members*. This has only happened very rarely in the past. As to some of the outcomes, in *Wright*, the trial court dismissed the constitutional and international claims. This is in contrast to what a New York District Court did in a similar case in which such claims were allowed,[58] and a trial court ruled in favor of Berman.[59]

FINANCIAL CONFLICTS OF INTEREST AND FEDERAL REGULATORY REQUIREMENTS

The *Robertson* case discussed in the preceding chapter, as well as several of the other cases discussed, proceed on the legal theory that the conduct of the defendants violated federal regulations concerning the protection of human research subjects.[60] Among other things, *45 Code of Federal Regulations (CFR)* Part 46 and forward of the federal regulations that govern the safety of human research subjects requires that risks to research participants be minimized and that subjects not be unnecessarily exposed to risks (see appendix D). It also requires that risks must be reasonable in relation to anticipated benefits, and that informed consent must be obtained from each subject. The research protocol must contain adequate provisions for monitoring study data to insure the safety of subjects and to insure the privacy of subjects through assuring confidentiality for study data. In addition, the regulations contain special provisions to assure protection of those subjects who are particularly vulnerable to coercion or undue influence.

The major point of contention in asserting this legal claim is whether or not an individual may bring a private right of action under these regulations. The defendants in cases proceeding on this theory argue that only OHRP and FDA may enforce the rights that are assured under these regulations. The regulations themselves are silent on the issue.

The U.S. Supreme Court has set out a four-part test to determine whether or not an individual can bring a lawsuit claiming a violation of this federal regulation.[61] First, the plaintiff must be one in the class for whose benefit the statute or regulation was enacted. Second, it must be determined whether any legislative intent to create or deny a private right exists. Third, it must be determined if a private right of action or lawsuit would frustrate or be consistent with the purpose of the legislative scheme. Fourth, it must be determined whether a private cause of action is usually relegated to state law, as opposed to federal law, so that it would be inappropriate to infer a cause of action based only on federal law.

The court in the *Robertson* case, discussed earlier, ruled that there is no private right of action under this federal regulatory scheme because there is a comprehensive enforcement scheme provided to the FDA.[62] The court's decision is misguided. Defendants contend, and the *Robertson* court apparently bought the argument, that a private cause of action cannot be brought by the plaintiffs under the Food, Drug and Cosmetic Act (FCA) for unlawful human experimentation. In support, defendants cited cases including *Merrell Dow Pharmaceuticals, Inc. v. Thompson*[63] and *Kemp v. Medtronic*.[64] These cases do hold that a private cause of action cannot be brought under the FCA, but are not factually applicable here. As the plaintiffs' claim in this matter is predicated on federal claims, that is, the *Code of Federal Regulations*, the defendant's reliance on *Merrell Dow Pharmaceuticals, Inc., v. Thompson* is misplaced, in addition to being irrelevant. For example, the plaintiffs' brief states, "Plaintiffs do not dispute that the FCA does not provide a private cause of action. . . . Plaintiffs do not seek a private cause of action under the FCA and have never sought such relief. . . . Thus, defendant's reliance on precedent that there is no private cause of action under the FCA while correct is irrelevant."[65]

As the plaintiffs argue in their brief, "the rights at issue here are Constitutional rights rooted in this nation's history and conscience. That there are state causes of action applicable to defendants' conduct does not negate the viability of a federal cause of action." As the court stated *in re Cincinnati Radiation Litigation,* a case also involving unethical human experimentation, "The distinction between this case and an ordinary tort case is not one of degree, but rather of kind."[66] Thus, a private right of action arguably should exist for the failure to abide by 45 *CFR* Part 46 when such failure causes harm to human subjects.

NOTES

The epigraph at the beginning of this chapter is from MD Lemonick and A Goldstein. At Your Own Risk. Time. April 14, 2002.

1. *U.S. v. Stanley*, 483 U.S. 669 (1987). J. Brennan dissenting.
2. *Robertson et al. v. McGee et al.* (N.D. Okla., No. 01CV 00GH(M)).
3. MD Lemonick and A Goldstein. At Your Own Risk. Time. April 14, 2002.
4. P Harrington. Faculty conflicts of interest in an age of academic entrepreneurialism: An analysis of the problem, the law, and selected university policies. J College and Univ L 2001; 27:775.
5. *Robertson et al. v. McGee et al.* No. 01CV60 (D.C. Okla.) Jan. 28 2002. Slip Copy. 2002 WL 535045.
6. The Financier. No Wonder They Call the Place 'Mother Hutch,' March 14, 2001. Seattle Times at A9.
7. *Id.*
8. *Moore v. City of East Cleveland, Ohio*, 431 U.S. 494, 503 (1977).
9. *Griswold v. Connecticut*, 381 U.S. 479, 500 (1965).
10. In support of this position the plaintiffs provide the following:

> The right to bodily integrity has long been recognized as a fundamental right protected by the constitution. See *Albright v. Oliver*, 510 U.S. 266 (1994) (due process accorded to matters involving marriage, family, procreation and the right to bodily integrity); *Planned Parenthood of Southeastern Pennsylvania v. Casey*, 505 U.S. 388 (1992), (constitutional liberty interest includes right to bodily integrity, a right to control one's person); *Schmerber v. California*, 384 U.S. 757 (1966) integrity of an individual's person is cherished value of our society); *Union Pacific R. Co. V. Botsford*, 141 U.S. 250 (1891) (no right held more sacred or more carefully guarded than right of every individual

to be in possession and control of his own person, free from restraint or interference of others). Courts have particularly recognized such constitutional autonomy rights in the medical context. See, e.g., *Cruzan v. Director, Missouri Department of Health*, 497 U.S. 261 (1990) (Constitution grants competent person right to refuse life-saving hydration and nutrition); *Roe v. Wade*, 410 U.S. 113 (1973) women have constitutional right to control decision on whether to obtain an abortion); *Griswold v. Connecticut*, 381 U.S. 479 (1965) (restriction on citizens from receiving contraceptives from their physician an unconstitutional intrusion); *Rochin v. California*, 342 U.S. 165 (1952) (forcible stomach pumping of accused violates due process and is conduct which "shocks the conscience"); *Skinner v. State of Oklahoma*, 316 U.S. 535 (1942) (sterilization performed without consent deprives individual of basic liberty). As Justice Cordoza stated in *Schloendorff v. The Society of New York Hospital*, 211 N.Y. 125, 105 N.E. 92, 93 (1914), a case against a surgeon for performing an operation without consent: "Every human being of adult years and sound mind has a right to determine what should be done with his own body." *Id.*, 211 N.Y. at 129-130.

11. 28 USC Section 1331.
12. 42 USC Section 1983.
13. 45 *CFR* Part 46, see appendix D of this volume.
14. D Wilson and D Heath. The Prospects for Change: System's Serious Flaws Have Led Many to Call for Regulatory Reform. March 15, 2001. The Seattle Times at A1.
15. 45 *CFR* Section 46.116.
16. Plaintiff's complaint sets forth the following ways in which the consent forms were misleading:

1. The consent form falsely implied that the FDA approved the Trial of the Vaccine and GM-CSF and their experimental use when the Trial that was actually implemented was different than the proposed Trial submitted for approval to the FDA. 2. The consent form falsely stated that "[t]he medical and scientific basis for the use of such a vaccine

A Constitutional Right to Dignity?

comes from studies in both animals and humans showing that, from these cells, factors are obtained that appear to assist the body to reject cancer." In actuality, no proper studies were conducted on either animals or humans. 3. The consent form falsely stated that risks subjects could expect included only local skin reddening; itching, swelling, and pain; and occasional temporary fever. In addition, the consent form provided that "fever, weakness, headache, bone and muscle pain, and chills have occurred with GM-CSF and can be prevented or reduced with Tylenol or Advil. Additional side effects may include swelling in the feet and hands due to water retention, difficulty breathing and rash." In fact, Plaintiff Participants suffered through much more dangerous and painful side effects. 4. The consent form stated that "records of the Trial would be kept confidential and that the subject would not be identifiable by name or description in any reports or publications." In actuality, the records of the Trial were not kept confidential and the subjects were identified by name in reports. 5. Dr. McGee, the principal investigator, failed to adequately discuss the consent form with the plaintiffs, failed to advise them of the true nature of the Trial, and instead advised that he had the cure for their cancer. 6. Certain versions of the consent form indicated that pregnant women were prohibited from participating in the Trial and that participants in the Trial should not become pregnant or impregnate women while in the Trial, while other drafts of the consent form did not contain this provision. As a result of these and other misrepresentations, Plaintiff Participants were led to believe the risks of the Trial were minimal and the potential benefits of their participation for themselves and the future treatment of melanoma were enormous. The effects of such misrepresentations and nondisclosures were that Plaintiff Participants agreed to participate and continue in the Trial.

17. The Nuremberg Code. Excerpted from Permissible Medical Experiments. Trials of War Criminals before the Nuernberg Military Tribunals under Control Council Law No.

10: Nuernberg, October 1946-1949, vol. 2 (Washington, D.C.: U.S. Government Printing Office, n.d.), 181-2; see appendix A of this volume.

18. *Washington v. Glucksberg*, 521 U.S. y02 (1997); *Collins v. Harker Heights*, 503 U.S. 115, 125 (1992).

19. 874 F. Supp. 796 (S.D. Ohio 1995).

20. See note 16 above.

21. *Id.*

22. 874 F. Supp. at 817.

23. 921 F. Supp. 1023 (W.D.N.Y. 1996).

24. See note 18 above.

25. *Id.*

26. *Grimes v. Kennedy Krieger Institute, Inc.* (366 Md. 29, 782 A.2d 807 2001).

27. See note 23 above.

28. *Id.*

29. See note 10 above; see note 26 above.

30. See note 3 above.

31. The section of the *Code of Federal Regulations* concerning experimentation with human subjects is 45 *CFR* Part 46; see appendix D of this volume.

The *World Medical Association Declaration of Helsinki* can be found at *http://www.wma.net/e/policy/63.htm*; see appendix B of this volume.

32. *West Virginia Central RR Co. v. Fuller*, 96 Md. 652, 666, 54 A. 669 671 (1903).

33. *Canterbury*, 464 F.2d at 786 (footnote 20).

34. *World Medical Association Declaration of Helsinki*, see note 31 above.

35. See note 6 above.

36. *Id.*

37. D Huff and D Heath. Patients never knew the full danger of trials they staked their lives on. March 11, 2001. Seattle Times at A1.

38. See note 6 above.

39. See note 37 above.

40. Available at *http://www.sskrplaw.com.*

41. D Wilson and D Heath. He Helped Create the Biotech Boom and When It Went Bust, So Did He. March 14, 2001.

A Constitutional Right to Dignity? 133

Seattle Times at A1.

42. *World Medical Association Declaration of Helsinki*, see note 30 above; The Financier, see note 6 above.

43. *Id.*

44. D Wilson and D Heath. With a Year or Two to Live, Woman Joined Test in Which She Was Misled — and Died. March 13, 2001. Seattle Times at A1.

45. Wilson and Heath, see note 41 above.

46. *Id.*

47. See note 40 above.

48. Wilson and Heath, see note 41 above.

49. *Id.*

50. *Id.*

51. *Id.*

52. *Id.*

53. *Id.*

54. *Id.*

55. *Id.*

56. On 12 July 1974, the National Research Act created the National Commission for the Protection of Human Subjects, which was charged with identifying the basic ethical principles that underlie the conduct of biomedical and behavioral research involving human subjects and with developing guidelines to assure research is conducted in accordance with these principles. *The Belmont Report* summarizes these basic ethical principles. It is reprinted as appendix C in this volume, and is also available at *http://ohrp.osophs.dhhs.gov/humansubjects/guidance/belmont.htm.*

57. PM Tereskerz. Changes in products liability law: The impact on patient safety and physician liability. J Healthcare Safety Quarterly. 1:1-6 Winter 2003.

58. MM Mello, DM Studdert, and TA Brennan. The Rise of Litigation in Human Subjects Research. Ann Intern Med 2003; 139:40-45.

59. D Heath. Judge: Hutch didn't reveal study's risk to patient. Seattle Times. 9 August 2002:A1.

60. Lemonick, see note 3 above.

61. *Cort v. Ash*, 422 U.S. 66 (1975).

62. Lemonick, see note 3 above.

63. *Merrell Dow Pharmaceuticals, Inc. v. Thompson,* 478 U.S. 804, 106 S.Ct 3229 (1986).
64. *Kemp v. Medtronic, Inc.,* 231 F.3d 216, 2000 Fed. App 0381P (6th Cir. 2000).
65. See note 40 above.
66. *Washington v. Glucksberg,* see note 18 above.

8

Financial Conflicts of Interest and Potential Statutory or Regulatory Violations

> One cannot work simultaneously as an inventor-entrepreneur and a physician or other health care provider and maintain the trust of patients and the public. . . . I believe that institutions such as academic medical centers must remain true to their primary mission to promote human health. Without this commitment, I fear that we will not continue to enjoy strong public support for our research efforts, and in the end, will achieve far less than our potential.
>
> — *R.P. Kelch*

In addition to PHS, FDA, and NSF regulations, there are a number of other statutory requirements that apply when a financial conflict of interest occurs in a research setting. The preceding chapters describe the potential liability that financial conflicts of interest in research create under common law. This chapter likewise will describe how these conflicts may violate regulatory and statutory provisions that, on their surface, may not seem to apply to financial conflicts of interest in industry-sponsored research.

STATUTORY PROVISIONS

False Claims Act

If an institutional administrator and/or a principal investigator signs a federal grant application that certifies that proposed research complies with all federal regulations, and later it is determined that financial conflicts of interest were not fully disclosed in violation of federal regulations, the university and investigator could be liable for violating the False Claims Act.[1] The act requires actual knowledge, deliberate ignorance of the truth or falsity, or reckless disregard of the truth for liability to be imposed.[2] If liability is found under the act, with limited exceptions, the actor will be liable to the U.S. government for a civil penalty of not less than $5,000 and not more than $10,000, plus three times the amount of damages that the government sustains because of the failure to disclose.

The case of *Cantekin v. University of Pittsburgh* is illustrative.[3] This case was discussed in chapter 3, and involved a medical researcher evaluating the treatment of otitis media, who failed to disclose industry funding of his research on a number of NIH grant applications, including several million dollars from pharmaceutical companies making the drugs that NIH paid the researcher to evaluate. The court denied the defendant's motion for summary judgment,[4] ruling there was plenty of evidence that NIH disclosure instructions were clear concerning outside funding, so that an issue of fact existed as to whether the defendant knowingly submitted false claims. The court found that an affidavit stating that the researcher's colleague had specifically told him he should disclose private funding, and that he refused to do so, created a genuine dispute as to whether the applicant knowingly omitted industry funding, and that he had the specific intent to defraud, proof of which is not even required to prove a violation of the False Claims Act. The court also found that failure to disclose industry funding qualified as material.

Insider Trading

Another area of potential liability for financial conflicts of interest associated with clinical research is violation of insider trading laws. Consider the recent example of the former chief executive officer of ImClone, Samuel Waksal, who was arrested and subsequently indicted for insider trading, and who since has pled guilty to several charges including securities fraud.[5]

The *Wall Street Journal* graphically described the sequence of events leading to Waksal's arrest as follows.[6] Waksal gave up his career as an immunology researcher to become a biotechnology entrepreneur, and ultimately became CEO of ImClone. Only a short while before his arrest, ImClone was a hot commodity with a promising cancer drug, Erbitux. However, on 26 December 2002, Waksal found out that the FDA would refuse to review his company's application for Erbitux. On 27 December, Waksal's family members sold more than $9 million in ImClone stock, and his friend, Martha Stewart, the home-decorating diva, sold 3,928 shares. Waksal himself tried to sell almost $5 million of shares on this date, but two brokerage firms refused to execute the sell order.

On 28 December, the FDA announced it had refused to review Erbitux's application. This announcement was followed by a 16 percent drop in ImClone stock, with a trading volume increase of 177 percent on 31 December, the first day of trading after the FDA announcement.

Waksal pled guilty to insider trading/securities fraud and received a seven-year prison term;[7] Martha Stewart was convicted by a jury of obstructing justice and lying to investigators during the investigation of this case.[8]

Following the public revelation of the insider trading allegations, it was also revealed that the M.D. Anderson Cancer Center in Houston enrolled 195 people in an experimental treatment involving Erbitux without informing the participants that the institution's president, John Mendelsohn, MD, held a financial interest in ImClone that could earn him millions of dollars. Mendelsohn invented Erbitux and served on ImClone's board; he earned $6.3 million on the sale of a stake in his stock ownership to Bristol-Myers on an offer open to all ImClone shareholders.[9] Unfortunately, Mendelsohn also was caught up in two major corporate disasters, both of which occurred around the same time. He served as a director and a member of the audit committee for Enron, now in bankruptcy and the subject of a major investigation of accounting practices.

Although it appears that Mendelsohn took steps to distance himself from ongoing research involving Erbitux, a former coinvestigator who worked on Erbitux at M.D. Anderson, who now is chief of medical oncology at Albert Einstein College of Medicine in New York, Roman Perez-Soler, MD, was quoted in the *Washington Post* as stating, "the results of any medical test conducted under such conditions must be viewed cautiously, since the financial interests involved would likely translate into pressure on faculty members to produce favorable results. . . . You need a promotion. You need a salary increase. You need another lab. It distorts the normal conduct of things, because you go all the way to try to please the boss."[10]

Insider Trading Laws

Insider trading laws were enacted by Congress as part of the Securities Exchange Act of 1934, following the 1929 stock market crash.[11] This act has been supplemented by other laws containing specific sanction and enforcement provisions.[12]

There are serious criminal and civil penalties for insider trading. Prentice provided the following example of potential penalties for trading on insider information by a physician who personally profited $100,000, and who also passed the information on to friends and family who profited another $200,000. Under this scenario, the physician could face the following penalties:

> (a) a civil order to disgorge profits earned by the physician and tippees ($300,000); (b) a civil fine in the amount of three times those profits ($900,000); (c) a felony criminal conviction carrying (i) a criminal fine (up to $1,000,000) and (ii) a jail term (as much as 10 years) and (these are cumulative); (d) civil damages action by a class of investors who traded at the same time that the physician traded if the class members believe that the physician profited by a greater sum than the SEC recovered in its disgorgement action. [Citation omitted.] This is not to mention felony charges of mail fraud and wire fraud, and if applicable, perjury that are often tacked on by prosecutors in egregious criminal cases. [Citation omitted.][13]

The first case brought against a biomedical researcher for insider trading violations by the Securities and Exchange Com-

Potential Statutory or Regulatory Violations 139

mission (SEC) was in 1997.[14] The suit was filed against Milton Mutchnick, MD, a gastroenterologist at Wayne State University in Michigan who was the lead investigator for a clinical trial of an experimental antihepatitis drug, and his assistant. The suit alleged that the researchers tipped off friends and relatives that the clinical trial failed to show the drug was effective. It was claimed that these tips allowed friends and relatives to sell their stock in the pharmaceutical company before the results were made public, allowing them to avoid more than $160,000 in losses. After the results were made public, the stock value plummeted by about 66 percent. Mutchnick and those who received his advice consented to a judgment and civil penalties without admitting or denying the allegation.

The issue of insider trading has been discussed in the medical literature, where it has been noted that stock of publicly owned companies has increased by more than 50 percent in value following publication that a product may be effective, or has plunged significantly following disclosure of negative results from clinical trials of the companies' products.[15]

The prospect of being caught up in an insider trading scandal poses a greater risk to researchers today than in the past. Among new businesses that have emerged are "matchmakers" between investment firms and experts such as physician researchers. A *New York Times* article identified Gerson Lehrman Group of New York and a subsidiary of Leerink Swann & Company of Boston as two companies that arrange for physicians to speak with investors. The authors quote an article in the *Seattle Times* that reported 26 instances in which doctors revealed confidential to investment analysts.[16] Other articles have discussed researchers, and particularly physicians, in their role of advising investment firms.[17]

In particular, an article by Eric J. Topol, MD, in the *Journal of the American Medical Association* highlighted the potential for the problems that these relationships bring through his own experience with an investment fund that had a medical advisory board.[18] The fund sold Merck stock short, and profited from this sale because of the withdrawal of rofecoxib

(Vioxx®) from the market. The fund's newsletter celebrated its decision and provided Topol's name as a physician advisor who had been outspoken about safety issues concerning rofecoxib. Topol's article stated there had been no discussion between Topol and the fund about rofecoxib and Merck, but the firm's publication created the appearance that the fund had proprietary information and that Topol had a conflict of interest. He added that while he was not an investor with the fund, had no interest in the fund, or any idea that Merck was an investment fund, the appearance of potential conflict was "troublesome," and the experience illustrated how an investment company can entangle physician advisors unwittingly.

Some biotech analysts will go to extreme measures to obtain confidential information on preliminary results of clinical drug trials. The *Wall Street Journal* has reported that some stock analysts have gone so far as to impersonate patients and doctors to gain a peek into how well a drug is faring in a clinical trial.[19] For example, an article in the *Wall Street Journal* recounted the following scenario.

> On Feb. 15, David Risk drove his black BMW into the Palm Beach Research Center and signed up as a patient in a clinical trial of a new sleep disorder, he gave blood and urine samples and signed a form agreeing not to disclose anything he had learned about patients.
>
> Five days later, Mr. Risk published a research report recommending that investors sell shares of Neurocrine Bioscience Inc., the company whose drug trial he entered. The Sterling Financial Investment Group report said one patient in the trial had a bad reaction — a middle-aged man couldn't be roused from sleep by his wife for several hours. Neurocrine stock, about $35 at the time, didn't get hit right away but slid through spring and early summer to about $23. . . .
>
> Mr. Risk says . . . he heard of the reaction from a doctor he spoke to while posing as a patient. . . . Such activity could be considered insider trading if the research analysts misappropriated clinical-trial information or obtained it under false pretenses, then traded on it or passed it along to someone who did.[20]

Potential Statutory or Regulatory Violations

During the first 10 months of 1998, the SEC conducted at least five investigations involving alleged violations of insider trading laws by clinical investigators.[21]

What Constitutes Insider Trading?

Obviously, individuals who conduct clinical research or who evaluate drugs or products in association with industries that involve publicly traded stock are at potential risk for insider trading liability because they often have access to research results before they are made public. But what does it take to prove that insider trading has occurred? The following elements are necessary: "(a) trading securities, (b) on the basis of material, nonpublic information, (c) with intent to deceive (scienter), while (d) owing a duty to 'disclose or abstain'."[22]

Insider trading includes both buying and selling on secret good and bad news to profit or to avoid a loss, respectively. It also includes those who do not trade, but who are considered to be "tipsters" by providing material, nonpublic information to others who make trades based on their tips.[23]

Information is considered *material* if it has the potential to move a company's stock in the market. In other words, a "reasonable investor" would consider the information to be important to making an investment decision.[24] As Ferguson pointed out, a determination of whether information is material is difficult within the context of biomedical research because the prospects for success of any product being tested are speculative.[25] Courts have held that materiality is dependent upon: (1) the likelihood that the event will occur, that is, that the product being tested will be approved by the FDA and successfully marketed, and (2) the magnitude of the benefit expected, if the event does occur.[26]

While on its surface the definition of "nonpublic" may appear obvious, determinations of when information is considered public for purposes of establishing insider trading has proven tricky. Originally, the rule was that news was public after a company issued a press release that was carried over the newswires. However, with the advent of the internet and financial screens, it is unclear whether the original rule has become obsolete or still applies.[27] Within this context, however, it appears clear that the results of such trials are not considered public information. In fact, in many instances, investigators are required to sign confidentiality agreements not to disclose study data.

In this context, consider the case of Changnian Liu, MD, a researcher for ImmunoGen. The Securities Exchange Commission (SEC) brought suit again Liu for insider trading of ImmunoGen stock before his report that an Immunogen drug reduced colon cancer in mice was published in a scientific journal. Liu argued that he had reported this research at two scientific meetings before buying the stock, and therefore considered the information to be public. The SEC responded that the CEO of ImmunoGen had advised employees not to trade in the company stock because the research was soon to be published. Although Liu contended that he had not been warned, he settled the case by paying twice his $41,700 profits plus interest.[28]

But what of the required fiduciary duty that is necessary to meet the definition of insider trading within the context of biomedical research? In this regard, there are four potential types of defendants:

1. Company insiders (employees),
2. Temporary insiders,
3. Misappropriators (breach of fiduciary duty to the source of information, not to the company),
4. Those given tips by members of the preceding three groups.[29]

Often researchers are deemed to have a fiduciary duty because they fall into the "temporary insider" category.

A temporary insider is one who has a special relationship with the company that involves access to material, nonpublic information for a business purpose.[30]

For example, in the case of *SEC v. Lange*, one of the defendants was a neurologist who was hired by Cephalon, not only as a clinical researcher to conduct drug trials, which made him a company insider, but also as an independent consultant to review trials, which alone would have been sufficient to make him a temporary insider.[31]

Likewise, in November 1997, the SEC obtained a final judgment requiring Roger Wyatt, a former consultant to Chantal

Potential Statutory or Regulatory Violations

Pharmaceuticals. Wyatt was ordered to pay more than $260,000 in civil penalties and fines for using insider information about the unfavorable results of a clinical trial of Chantal's acne medication to sell his stock and tip off a friend, who also sold his stock. In 1998, the U.S. District Court for the Central District of California sentenced Wyatt to 15 months in prison and ordered him to pay a $20,000 fine for perjury that he committed during the insider trading investigation and civil suit.[32]

It is important to note that the requirement concerning intent does not mean that the SEC (for a civil case) or the U.S. Department of Justice (for a criminal case) must show that a defendant intended to violate a specific law, since ignorance of the law is not a valid legal excuse. However, in the criminal context, it must be shown that the defendants acted "willfully."[33]

ANTI-KICKBACK STATUTES

Federal anti-kickback law prohibits compensation from research sponsors that provide or supply healthcare services or products to researcher-physicians or hospitals for their participation in clinical research if such payments are intended to encourage the purchase of drugs or services paid for by Medicare or Medicaid.[34] Barnes and Krauss have identified the following potential culprits for violating anti-kickback statutes that regularly occur within the research setting.[35]

Concerns about violating the anti-kickback laws arise regarding excessively large honoraria offered to researchers by corporate sponsors for speaking engagements concerning the speaker's research or a free trip for a researcher's family to attend a seminar that is of *de minimus* educational benefit to them. Other areas of trepidation are "enrollment bonuses" or "signing payments" that researchers receive from sponsors for clinical trials. The issue is whether these payments are related to the value of the research performed or are an attempt to channel extra funds to researchers to induce the purchase of the sponsor's drugs or services. Another potential pitfall is the use of "gag clauses" concerning publication of research results or pre-publication review by a sponsor, which, when accompanied by excessively large payments to researchers, may represent an attempt to buy the researcher's professional silence. In December 2004, the American Medical Association (AMA) required organizations working with industry to eliminate gag clauses and to protect the rights of physician-researchers to publish data from clinical trials.[36]

One study that looked at institutional standards regarding contractual provisions that restrict investigators' control of studies found considerable variation. In 2001, the International Committee of Medical Journal Editors (ICMJE) began to require authors to accept full responsibility for the conduct of the trial, access to data, and the decision to publish, but academic institutions continue to make agreements to sponsor research that do not adhere to these requirements.[37] In 2005, Steinbrook concluded that even after the institution of these remedial measures, nothing changed in actual practice.[38]

Institutional conflict of interest policies prohibiting the use of arrangements such as the ones described above may not only avoid violation of anti-kickback laws, but may also help institutions to insure compliance with the provisions of the U.S. Internal Revenue Service that are related to nonprofit corporations, which recommend that all nonprofit organizations enact conflict of interest policies to assure that the actions taken by their officers, directors, and others (such as faculty) are in keeping with the educational or charitable purpose of the organization.

CONSUMER PROTECTION LAWS AND HEALTHCARE PROVIDER ACTS

Failure to inform research subjects of financial conflicts of interest can result in claims of violation of state consumer protection laws and healthcare provider acts. Such claims are grounded in state law. Although a state may or may not have such laws, and statutory requirements vary among jurisdictions, it is important to be aware of the existence of such statutory schemes.

In the recently filed cases of *Wright et al. v. The Fred Hutchinson Cancer Research Center et al.* and *Berman et al. v. the Fred Hutchinson Cancer Research Center et al.*, discussed in chapter 7, claims for violation of the Washington State Consumer Protection and Health Care Provider Acts have been made. The plaintiffs claim that the defendants' wrongful conduct in marketing or promoting Protocol 126 and in failing to disclose their financial and business interests constituted false and/or unfair business conduct in violation of the act.[39] The act declares unlawful "unfair methods of competition and unfair or deceptive acts or practices in the conduct of any trade or commerce." The act provides both for civil and criminal penalties.[40]

This chapter has outlined various statutory and regulatory provisions that may apply when financial conflicts of interest exist. Investigators and institutions should also keep in mind that many states have conflict of interest statutes that set out requirements that go beyond federal law. The requirements vary among different jurisdictions. In particular, disclosure requirements for financial interests held in a sponsor are often more stringent under such state laws. Therefore, institutions should make sure that investigators are aware of the requirements, because violation of the state laws can be accompanied by both civil and criminal sanctions.

NOTES

The epigraph at the beginning of this chapter is from RP Kelch. Maintaining the Public Trust in Clinical Research. New Engl J Med 2002; 346:285-287.

1. 31 USC Section 3729-3733.
2. *U.S. ex rel Milam v. Regents of University of California*, 912 F. Supp. 868 (D. Md. 1995).
3. *Cantekin v. University of Pittsburgh*, 192 F.3d 402 (3rd Cir 1999).
4. *Summary judgment* refers to a judgment granted when there is no genuine issue of material fact, as a matter of law upon which one can prevail. *Black's Law Dictionary* (7th ed. 1999).
5. L. Beltran. ImClone ex-CEO Pleads Guilty. CBS. Market Watch.com Oct. 15, 2002. Available at *http://cbs.marketwatch.com*.
6. G. Anand, J Markon, C Adams. ImClone's ex-CEO ar-

rested, charged with insider trading. Wall St J, June 13, 2002 at A1.

7. Not a good thing for Martha. A Lie turned her into a convicted felon. The woman known for perfection made mistakes at almost every turn. *Time Magazine*, pg. 60. March 15, 2004.

8. Stewart convicted on all charges. Jury finds style maven, ex-broker guilty of obstructing justice and lying to investigators. *CNNmoney*. March 5, 2004. Available at *http://money.cnn.com*.

9. J Gillis. A hospital's conflict of interest: Patients weren't told of stake in cancer drug. *Washington Post*. June 30, 2002 at A3.

10. J Gillis. A hospital's conflict of interest: Patients weren't told of stake in cancer drug. Washington Post. June 30, 2002 at A01.

11. 15 USC Section 77a et seq. (1988 & Supp. 1993).

12. Pub. L. No. 98-376, 98 Stat. 1264 (codified as amended in various sections of 15 U.S.C.; 17 CFR. Section 240.10b-5 (1997); Pub. L. No. 100-704, 102 Stat. 4677 (codified as amended in various sections of 15 U.S.C.); 17 CFR Section 240.14e-3 (1997).

13. R Prentice. Clinical trial results, physicians, and insider trading. J Leg Med 1999; 20:195-222 (summarizing basic elements of insider trading liability).

14. SEC cites drug researchers in insider trading lawsuits. New York Times. April 11, 1997: D4; *Securities and Exchange Commission v. Milton Mutchnick et al.* Case No. 97 CV00709 (D.C.D.C.) (April 10, 1997).

15. JR Ferguson. Biomedical research and insider trading. New Engl J Med. 1997; 337:631-34; Medical News & Perspectives. SEC going after insider trading based on medical research results. JAMA. 1998; 28:10-11.

16. S Saul, J Anderson. Doctors' links with investors raise concerns. the New York Times. August 16, 2005.

17. R Steinbrook. Wall street and clinical trials. New Engl J Med 2005; 353:1091-93.

18. EJ Topol. Physicians and the investment industry. JAMA 2005; 293:2654-57. See also related correspondence. Hampson and Emanuel. Physicians advising investment firms. JAMA

2004; 294:1897-97; Patmas. Physicians advising investment firms. JAMA 2004; 294:1897-97.

19. G Anand, R Smith. Biotech Analysts Strive to Peek Inside Clinical Tests of Drugs. Wall St J at A1, Aug. 8, 2002.

20. See note 14 above.

21. Cox, SEC Focus: Doctor-Lab Insider Trading, Nat'l L.J., Oct. 26, 1998 at B1.

22. 17 CFR Section 240.14e-3 (1997), see note 12 above.

23. *Id.*

24. *TSC Industries, Inc. v. Northway*, 426 U.S. 438, 449 (1976).

25. *Chiarella v. United States*, 445 U.S. 222 (1980).

26. *Id.*

27. See note 22 above.

28. *Id.*

29. *Id.*

30. *Id.*

31. SEC Litig Rel. No. 15509, 1997 SEC LEXIS 1997 (E.D. Pa. Sept. 25, 1997).

32. See note 22 above.

33. *Id.*

34. 42 USCA Section 1320a-7b(b) (2002).

35. M Barnes, S Krauss. Conflicts of Interest in Human Research: Risks and Pitfalls of "Easy Money" in Research Funding. BHLR 2000; 9:1378.

36. MM Mello, BR Clarridge, DM Studdert. Academic medical centers' standards for clinical-trial agreements with industry. New Engl J Med 2005; 352:2202-10.

37. See note 25 above.

38. R Steinbrook. Gag clauses in clinical-trial agreements. New Engl J Med 2005; 352:2160-2162.

39. RCW 19.86 et seq.

40. RCW 19.85.020.

9

The Other Side of the Coin: Potential Liability for Overly Restrictive Employment Policies

An additional concern associated with financial conflicts of interest is to assure that institutional conflict of interest policies do not infringe upon the constitutional rights of employees, or, in the academic settings, of faculty members. There are very few cases assessing the constitutionality of institutional conflict of interest policies. But, for the few that do exist, it is clear that overly broad policies can violate an employee's constitutional rights to equal treatment and free speech. This chapter explains the basis for such constitutional claims and makes a recommendation for avoiding employment policies that may violate constitutional rights.

Policies that violate constitutional rights are likely to arise in the context of industry-funded research in an academic environment when there is also federal research funding or when the institution is a state university.

Ironically, conflict of interest policies in such settings may be adopted to protect an investigator's or institution's financial arrangements with private industry that are plagued by conflicts of interest.

For example, a senior faculty member or institution that is supported by industry may exert undue influence or pressure on subordinate faculty members to preclude them from participating in litigation or not to engage in projects, write reports, or take a public position that is contrary to the interests of an industry sponsor, and thereby contrary to the employing institution and/or the investigator. Many times such pressure is exerted under the guise of adopting an internal conflict of interest policy, because it is in a senior investigator's or the institution's best interest to prevent scrutiny of the institution's or senior investigator's financial conflicts of interest.

Such actions or policies have been found to violate the Equal Protection Clause of the Constitution under the Fourteenth Amendment, and the First Amendment guarantee of free speech. *Tristor v. University of Miss.* is illustrative.[1] In this case, a federal circuit court found that the University of Mississippi violated the equal protection rights of two part-time law professors when it tried to prevent them from continuing a part-time employment relationship with a legal services organization, representing clients who had sued the state. The court found that the faculty members' instruction efforts were not compromised as a result of their outside work, and that the plaintiff faculty members were being treated differently than other part-time faculty. The court held that the basis for different treatment of these faculty members was representation of unpopular clients, and this was impermissible under the Fourteenth Amendment of the Constitution.

More recently, a federal case holds particular significance for public universities that have state loyalty provisions encompassed within their faculty conflict of interest policies.[2] This case involves policies enacted by Texas A&M University that bar professors and other university employees from serving as expert witnesses in legal disputes and engaging in outside employment when these activities bring them into conflict with state interests. Three of the plaintiffs bringing the case were retained as expert witnesses for the tobacco industry in a case brought against the industry by the State of Texas. The fourth plaintiff is a law professor who volunteered his services to an environmental group that opposed the state's approval of a waste facility. The plaintiffs won a preliminary injunction barring the university from enforcing its conflict of interest policies, and the university appealed. The Fifth Circuit Court of Appeals upheld the lower court's decision, ruling that the university's conflict of interest policies were "impermissibly overbroad" and that the state's "amorphous interest" in "preventing state employees from speaking in a manner contrary to the state's interests, "was not a sufficiently compelling interest to outweigh the professors' First Amendment rights to free speech."

Legal counsel for research institutions should be aware of cases such as these, and take steps to remedy any overly broad conflict of interest policies. Notwithstanding the appropriate drafting of global institutional conflict of interest policies or state statutory schemes to comport with constitutional requirements, the greatest risk that large research institutions will likely face today is that individual centers or departments that are encompassed within an institution will independently draft their own overly broad conflict of interest policies to keep potential whistleblowers in check.

Clearly, when it can be proven that conflict of interest policies are related to the state's legitimate interest in promoting and assuring the safety of research subjects, they do not violate any constitutionally protected right.

The decisive factor is whether the purpose of the conflict of interest policy in question is to protect a legitimate state interest. Lucrative financial arrangements with private industry that pose a conflict of interest for a researcher and/or research institution clearly do not protect a legitimate state interest. On the contrary, such arrangements exist only to line the coffers and enhance the financial viability and wealth of investigators and institutions, to the possible detriment of the safety of research subjects and the validity and integrity of clinical research.

It is therefore recommended that universities not allow individual departments and centers to draft their own conflict of interest policies, but instead to adopt a uniform policy that applies to the entire institution. In situations when a separate policy is warranted, departments or centers should submit the draft policy to the institution's legal counsel for review and approval before it is instituted.

NOTES

1. *Tristor v. University of Miss.*, 420 F.2d 499 (5th Cir. 1969).
2. *Hoover v. Morales*, 164 F.3d 221, 1998.

10

Developing a New Model: Preserving Scientific Objectivity, Trust, and the Informed Choices of Human Subjects

> The cat's out of the bag. . . . It's not just a problem with five doctors or 25, or a single institution; it's the system.
> — *Vera Hassner Sharav*
> *Alliance for Human Research Protection*

The passage of legislation discussed in chapter 2 promoted partnerships between industry and academia, resulting in a technology boom. The conflicts of interest that accompanied these unions are of a magnitude that likely was not anticipated.

The general consensus appears to be that conflicts of interest should be better managed, because the safety of human subjects has been and will continue to be jeopardized by the current "laissez-faire" environment.[1] Financial conflicts of interest within the realm of clinical research may lead to actions that seriously harm society. They likely will never be completely eliminated, but potential conflicts must be prevented to the extent possible.

This book centers on the argument that the current regulatory and legal frameworks regarding managing conflicts of interest in clinical research are inadequate, and that a new approach is needed. The Bayh-Dole Act served as the impetus for collaboration between industry and academia, and, in the process, created a legislative structure that unintentionally fostered new financial conflicts of interest in clinical research.[2] Financial conflicts of interest in clinical research exist primarily because the methods currently embraced by statutory, regulatory, and policy frameworks to manage conflicts are reactive or palliative, rather than preventive or curative.

Both empirical and anecdotal evidence have been used to illustrate how financial conflicts that exist under the current regimen adversely affect research and undermine public trust in the research enterprise and to demonstrate the need for a new model to address financial conflicts of interests. This chapter will propose a new model to address conflicts of interest — a model that is conceptually different, in that it emphasizes prevention of conflicts of interest, rather than reaction to them.

A price has been paid for removing the wall between research institutions and industry. Unfortunately, in some instances, there has been a compromise in the integrity of clinical research. Universities are essential to the functioning of a democracy and free society, as Francis H. Miller noted, in the "provision and dissemination of knowledge essential to culture, science, medicine, commerce and government — widely viewed as being critical to society."[3] Consequently, it is important to consider attendant concerns raised about the credibility of the researchers and research institutions that are involved in the race to commercialize technology, and to assure that this does not become a race to disgrace.

IS "THE DEAL" A GOOD ONE?

It is easy to understand why many researchers, particularly those in universities, have turned to private industry for funding, and why industry has enthusiastically obliged. Chapter 2 outlined the reasons for this union. First, there was a need to facilitate the transfer of the technology of new drugs and devices from the laboratory to the marketplace. Second, academic medical centers need the money; as Marcia Angell

A New Model

noted, many are "bleeding red ink as a result of reduction in Medicare and the hard bargaining of other third-party payers to keep hospital costs down."[4] Third, in the past, academic institutions had a monopoly on performing clinical trials for industry for several reasons:
- A lack of in-house expertise in industry;
- Available populations of patient research subjects at academic hospitals;
- The credibility and prestige of academic publications necessary to market industry's products.[5]

However, the model has changed, and academia's position has been substantially weakened by competition from for-profit contract-research organizations and site-management organizations.

It is true that the share of clinical research supported by public funds has decreased, while the portion supported by private funds has increased. It is also the case that the pharmaceutical industry has allocated an increasing portion of revenues to research. However, this should not automatically lead to the conclusion that increased spending by pharmaceutical enterprises has been associated with great innovative breakthroughs. Of the new drugs approved by the FDA in the last decade, only about 15 percent represent novel or innovative chemicals that are a significant improvement over older drugs. The majority are modified versions of existing medicines.[6] Universities continue to be the birthplace of the biotechnology that fuels industry. Pharmaceuticals are the industry that is most dependent on university research: 44 percent of the pharmaceutical industry's new products and 37 percent of its processes are created by academia.[7]

While there are individual anecdotal reports of highly successful licensing agreements between universities and industry, even those universities with successful licensing programs receive only 0.5 percent to 2 percent of their total research budget from licensing revenues, and plan to receive only 5 percent from such agreements in the long term.[8] Even in universities with highly successful economic track records from licensing, the return is usually a result of a single "blockbuster" patent.⁹ Yet these funds are more valuable to universities than the absolute dollar amount would suggest, because they represent discretionary resources that can be spent as the university sees fit without the constraints that attend most other funding sources.

The bottom line is that revenues from licensing fees or corporate funding provide only a small amount of the financial support required by research universities, when compared to total operational budgets. As Kenneth Sutherland Dueker stated in 1997, "Licensing revenue, however, has not made nor is likely to ever make a substantial contribution to the overall research budgets of U.S. universities."¹⁰ Dueker quotes Joyce Brinton, director of Harvard University's technology transfer program: "Most people who are even reasonably optimistic think it's highly unlikely that very many institutions will ever realize more than five percent for their research budget from this source."¹¹

Bhaven Sampat notes that two questions concerning the success of the Bayh-Dole Act remain unresolved. The first is whether the Bayh-Dole Act has achieved its intended purpose of enhancing commercialization of academic research funded by the federal government. Second, and argued to be the more important, is whether the act has had unintended or potentially negative effects on university research.¹² Sampat concludes that there is only limited evidence that the act has improved technology transfer in the United States.¹³ Most licensed inventions are currently not commercially useful and require significantly more development before they will be. Sampat argues that, prior to enactment of Bayh-Dole, universities patented and licensed federally funded inventions via institutional patent agreements (IPAs) and case by case petitions. The act served to reduce the cost of these activities. Accordingly, Sampat makes the point that the main impact of the act is most likely upon "marginal" inventions for which anticipated profitability is low.¹⁴

Notwithstanding these limitations, there is no doubt that funding for industry is important to continuing technological growth and development. The issue, when distilled, is whether there is a way that academia and industry can enjoy the benefits of collaboration without financial conflicts of interest.

A New Model

HOW TO APPROACH THE PROBLEM: LAYING THE CONCEPTUAL FRAMEWORK

First-year law students are given sage advice: Never argue your case within the box drawn by the opposing party. Get outside of the box and argue within the parameters you create. This advice has application in the context of managing conflicts of interest in clinical research.

In the past, the management of conflicts of interest has been discussed within the limitation of the tools that have been traditionally used to manage such conflicts. Looking to other professions, Marc Rodwin, for example, identified three regulatory approaches to conflicts of interest:

- Prohibition of certain activities,
- Regulation and monitoring of conduct, and
- Provision of penalties for improper conduct.[15]

Recommendations thus far concerning the management of financial conflicts of interest in clinical research have primarily revolved around these methods. We should not be limited to these options. The time has come to consider alternatives outside of the traditional box. With this in mind, a new model is proposed with a different mindset that addresses the cause of the problem, rather than the symptoms.

Most current management strategies are palliative. A successful model will go as far as possible to cure or remove the conflict. The first step is to identify those conflicts that can be removed without seriously compromising the viability of continued research and technological advancements between industry and academia. Can conflict be eliminated without putting continued research in serious jeopardy? If so, then it should be eliminated. Palliative measures should only be considered when removing the conflict will seriously jeopardize continued viability of clinical research.

Disclosure is an example of a palliative measure that may be applied, when appropriate. As noted scholars have commented, disclosure will not cure that which is morally wrong;[16] in such cases, disclosure would be like treating fever with aspirin. Aspirin ameliorates the symptom but does not eradicate the underlying disease. Informing research participants of a conflict and allowing them to include this in the calculus of risk in choosing to take part in a study only ameliorates the potential harm by allowing subjects to choose whether to assume the risk of harm the conflict poses.

As discussed earlier, given the limited medical knowledge that patients have and the dependence and trust that they place in researchers, disclosure does not insure that patients will truly appreciate the ramifications of conflicts of interest.[17] Given the imbalance of knowledge and the perceived power of researchers and physicians, it is morally unjust to place this burden on research participants. Of all the involved parties, research participants are the least likely to be knowledgeable about the ramifications of financial conflicts of interest — and, at the same time, the most vulnerable to harm.

As discussed in detail, it is obvious that professionals in the research enterprise and policy makers struggle over how best to handle financial conflicts in clinical research. When the experts are floundering because the problem is so complex, it is morally indefensible to shift the burden to research subjects, except under extraordinary circumstances. It is conceivable that there may be some circumstances in which an investigator who has a financial conflict of interest is the only qualified surgeon available, for example, in a rural area, to perform a lifesaving operation; in such circumstances, disclosure may be appropriate.

UNDERLYING ETHICAL PRINCIPLES

Any model must, first and foremost, preserve the public's trust in clinical research. It must assure that the judgment of researchers is not impaired by financial incentives that compromise or have the appearance of compromising their judgment. Even though conflicts of interest do not necessarily impair researchers' judgment, if it appears that they *may* impair researchers' judgment, this is sufficient to compromise the public's trust, and ultimately the public's support of and participation in clinical research. Hence, the definition of financial conflicts of interest includes not only any activity that actually does impair researchers' judgment so as to actually

A New Model

cause injury to a research participant, but also any activity that has only *the appearance* of impropriety.

There is concern that such conflicts cannot be eliminated because this might destroy partnerships between academia and industry that are necessary to sustain synergistic technologic advances. The model proposed attempts to ameliorate this concern.

THE PROPOSED MODEL

With these underlying principles in mind, the proposed model calls for the creation of a separate entity — a U.S. government research brokerage firm or clearing house. Here is how it would work.

All private pharmaceutical and products companies seeking to have a product or drug tested by an independent research entity would develop a request for proposal (RFP) and submit it to the research brokerage firm (hereinafter, the National Research Brokerage Institute or NRBI). The RFP would be modeled after those currently used by NIH. The RFP would be published and distributed to all interested parties. Products undergoing clinical trials generally already have patent applications pending or are already patented; therefore, the proposed arrangement would not compromise industry's ability to market an efficacious product.

Following the NIH model for evaluation of applications, a study section whose membership is selected based on their reputation within the scientific community would evaluate and rank all the proposals it receives, based on scientific merit. Study section members who may have a conflict in reviewing a proposal would be bound to follow rules governing such conflicts. In developing such rules, guidance may be sought by looking at regulations and rules used by government and professional organizations such as NIH, for example. The NIH model is suggested because it is a proven model that has an established track record. However, it is only a suggested mechanism, and others should be considered.

The requesting sponsor would ask for a clinical trial of Drug X or Product X. The sponsor would be asked to specify the purpose of the study in broad terms. For example, *the pur-*

pose of the study is to test the efficacy of X in preventing or treating a given disease or condition. Otherwise, the design of the study would be left completely to the discretion of the competing investigators, including the composition of the study population, how the new product should be compared (to placebo or other similar product), dose, and route of administration. Analysis of data and presentation of data for publication of results would also be within the investigator's complete control. However, there would be a requirement that the results of completed studies would be available for public review. Investigators participating in multi-institutional trials would be obligated to share their data with other participating investigators. No financial incentives for investigators or referring physicians for enrollment of patients, for example, signing bonuses or referring fees, would be allowed.

Investigators would be required to disclose any and all financial arrangements, including, but not limited to, those discussed in this book. Disclosures of financial agreements would be considered by the reviewers in assessment of grant proposals. Financial relationships, including financial agreements with sponsors for a defined period of time prior to submitting the application, would be factors that determine which applicants and proposals would be selected for funding.

A scoring system could be developed in which points are given for various types of financial agreements, placing applicants with direct financial agreements at a competitive disadvantage. So, for example, if an investigator held a chair endowed by an industrial sponsor, or an investigator had a significant equity interest in the sponsor, the investigator's application would not be competitive with those similarly situated in terms of scientific merit that include no financial agreements. Guidelines would need to be developed to guide NRBI in declining any application for a RFP in which there are an insufficient number of applicants without serious financial arrangements.

How would a research brokerage institute address institutional conflicts of interest? As with investigators, institutions would be required to disclose financial arrangements with sponsors, and these arrangements would be taken into consideration by the reviewers in the competitive ranking of

A New Model

proposals. Institutional investments that involve equity interests in sponsors should be managed through blind trusts, and the institution would have to certify this. In addition, if any members of an institution's control group sat on the board or were employees of or consultants for the sponsor, this would be taken into account when scoring applications. This would provide an incentive for institutions to avoid direct financial relationships with industry to remain competitive in attracting top faculty.

Investigators and institutions that submitted proposals would not be allowed to acquire any financial interest in a sponsor for a defined period during and following the study.

All proposals would be required to comply with federal IRB regulations. Budgets would be required to break down all costs, and be based on actual costs to conduct a study, including an appropriate indirect cost rate for the research institution. After the NRBI ranked the proposals on scientific merit, the proposals would be evaluated for economic efficiency. Proposals of comparable scientific merit would be ranked on cost-effectiveness.

HOW TO GET INDUSTRY "ON BOARD"

There appear to be few incentives for industry, investigators, and research institutions to support this model. Each has been a fiscal beneficiary of financial conflicts of interest. The financial arrangements that industry makes with researchers and research institutions are likely some of its best investments. What will it take for industry to sign on?

One strategy would be to link use of NRBI to the approval of new drugs and devices. FDA approval for products requiring a clinical trial could include the use of NRBI. Or the clearing house could be mandated by legislation.

Professional standards could mandate use of NRBI. For example, if journals required the use of the model for any publication of clinical trial results, or if professional organizations and institutions required investigators to employ the model as a condition of membership, then the model would become the new standard against which all other research would be measured. Research conducted outside of the model that involves financial agreements between researchers and institutions would lack the equivalent of a "Good Housekeeping Seal of Approval," and would be considered less credible, leaving those who did not employ the model with exposure for legal liability in the face of bad outcomes.

If such a system were in place, the NRBI would in essence become a requirement, establishing a higher standard by which to judge clinical research. Research involving direct financial agreements between industry and the researcher or institution would come up short on the scale of credibility. It could be inferred that only those products that could not withstand the rigorous demands of objective testing would be evaluated outside of the NRBI.

It could mean that it would become difficult, if not impossible, to obtain FDA approval for a product evaluated or studied outside of this system, or to have the findings that result from such research published in a peer-reviewed scientific or medical journal.

ADVANTAGES OF THE MODEL

The primary advantage of this model, and what distinguishes it from other proposals, is its potential to *eliminate* many conflicts of interest. Since proposals channeled through NRBI would compete and be judged solely on the basis of scientific merit, investigators would no longer have an incentive to consider the ramifications of their research on the involved company's profits.

Industry would bear the risk of testing a product that would not be able to withstand rigorous clinical evaluation. Currently, when industry funds clinical research outside the company, product performance becomes linked to the financial incentives that are provided to researchers and/or research institutions. In essence, conflicts of interest allow the financial risks that are associated with poor product performance in a clinical trial *to be spread among all three parties.* Under the proposed model, industry alone will assume this risk, and is thereby encouraged to produce the best product possible before clinical trials are begun.

A New Model

LIMITATIONS OF THE MODEL

It is acknowledged that there are many disincentives for industry to sign on to the proposed model, and it will, no doubt, protest loudly. Industry is one of the primary economic beneficiaries of financial conflicts of interest and so has reasons to strenuously object to the employment of such an intervention. The road to profitability will become more arduous when the standard to prove efficacy of a given drug or device is made more stringent. The model requires the evaluation of drugs and devices by vigorous scientific methods that are not contaminated or diluted by financial conflicts of interest.

There could be a concern that industry might turn to foreign institutions that use less stringent requirements to test their products. This would not be likely, because clinical trials that did not comply with the higher U.S. standards would not obtain FDA approval, and the U.S. market is too large and lucrative to risk this outcome. Despite criticism from some consumers, there is already ample precedent for the FDA to impose more stringent requirements for drug approval than exist in other parts of the world, and it is unlikely that this will change, because the risks to the safety of patients are too great.

While the proposed model has the potential to eliminate many conflicts of interest, it is still conceptual, and is intended to stimulate discussion on how to best address the ethical concerns associated with financial conflicts of interest. It is not offered as a definitive solution. There are countless pragmatic issues to be decided before such a model could be put into actual practice, and it is far beyond the scope of this book to address these. For example, to name but one, a mechanism to monitor ongoing studies funded through NRBI would have to be created. If such a model were implemented, it would be imperative to avoid the kinds of draconian bureaucracy that accompanied technology transfer prior to passage of the Bayh-Dole Act. Congress should establish a multi-disciplinary national committee or task force to undertake these tasks.

This is not to suggest that research supported by other entities such as foundations or the government does not embrace its own conflicts. These must also be discussed, but that is not the purpose of this book.

However, there are also advantages for the drug and medical device industry. First, for those who develop excellent products that receive favorable outcomes after clinical testing using the model, there is enhanced credibility in marketing their products, as they will have withstood rigorous testing from some of the best and brightest in a given area. Second, those who develop truly good and innovative products may receive economic benefit from using the model, although this would need to be empirically studied. When the cost of "perks" for investigators and institutions is removed from the equation — referral fees, bonuses, expensive trips, inflated drug study budgets — conducting clinical trials will become less costly.

This should encourage, rather than discourage, additional clinical trials of worthwhile products. It may discourage trials of products that are known from the outset to be unlikely to pass muster — but this would be highly desirable, because resources and effort would not be channeled into testing and marketing products developed only to profit stockholders, not patients. Finally, adherence to a standard model will provide manufacturers some shelter from product liability claims.

WHO WOULD PAY FOR THE CLEARING HOUSE?

The clearing house could be supported through a required indirect cost rate added to all study budgets. In addition to supporting NRBI, a portion of the indirect cost fees collected could be used to fund selected competitive proposals that are initiated by new investigators, so that they may develop the expertise needed to become competitive with established investigators. A portion of the funds could also be dedicated to supporting institution- or researcher-initiated proposals for research that is deemed to be valuable, but for which there is no other source of funding available.

These funds could also be used to support related educational grants and to subsidize the cost of RFPs that are initiated by nonprofit institutions, such as universities, that need to have drugs or devices that have been developed internally to be tested through NRBI. The mechanism for funding each

A New Model

of these would be as described above, and would be competitive.

CONCLUSION

Clinical research must be grounded in championing human dignity and freedom of choice. Universities and other academic research institutions that perform this research must muster the moral strength to remain objective and dedicated to the pursuit of knowledge, untainted by financial conflicts of interest. As a government and as a society, we must create policies that will make this happen. Regardless of the corrective approach ultimately implemented – the model proposed here is only one – the strengths and weaknesses of each alternative should be carefully evaluated.

Conflicts of interest must not be allowed to trammel the high ethical standards to which most researchers are dedicated. The greed of a few cannot be allowed to damage the integrity of research for years to come.

The proposed model is intended to eliminate many conflicts of interest in the current clinical research environment. It is limited to clinical research because research involving human subjects presents unique circumstances. As such, clinical research involving human subjects should be and is appropriately distinguished from basic research,[18] and a model that is designed to address the unique characteristics of clinical research is necessary and warranted.

Is it possible that such a model may reduce the amount of dollars industry currently channels to academia to evaluate its products? Maybe, but this is unlikely, because private industry will always need the credibility of trials conducted by independent researchers. A brokerage firm of this sort would act as a Chinese Wall or barrier between the researcher/study institution and private funding entities and, at the same time, will allow the flow of research dollars from private industry. It is a mechanism to preserve private funding and allow industry continued access to the intellectual resources of academia and other professional research organizations. The model will channel research dollars in a manner that minimizes the serious conflicts of interest that emerge when there is direct interaction among research institutions, researchers, and private industry.

The use of such a brokerage institute would minimize any incentives that investigators might now encounter to design a study, analyze data, or withhold results to serve the best interests of a sponsor, but not the best interests of science or of society. The yardstick for success will have changed. Success will be gauged by scientific progress, not profits.

This system offers the added benefit of pushing industry to develop "a better mousetrap." The expectation that a drug or device will undergo rigorous clinical evaluation will encourage industry to develop better products and not sacrifice quality for turning a quick profit — to the benefit of society.

Industry will no doubt protest about such an intervention. Profitability will become more difficult when the standard used to prove the efficacy of a given drug or device is raised. Such a model requires the evaluation of drugs and products by vigorous scientific methods that are not diluted by the perks that financial conflicts of interest may provide. It is fair, however, as all competitors will face the same challenge.

Investigators and research organizations or universities that have become accustomed to being in the back pocket of private industry will protest such an arrangement. The likely winners will be those who have exercised restraint in the current laissez-faire environment, avoided financial agreements involving conflicts of interest, and continued to be successful in competing for funds from the federal government or from non-industry affiliated foundations.

The conflicts of interest dilemma faced by researchers brings to mind a statement made by Justice Holmes almost 100 years ago, in his recitation on the "Path of the Law": "When you get the dragon out of his cave onto the plain and in the daylight, you can count his teeth and claws, and see just what is his strength. But to get him out is only the first step. The next is either to kill him, or to tame him and make him a useful animal."[19] This dragon has seen the light of day, and it is unlikely to be put back in its cave. We now must tame the dragon, so that financial support from the private sector can be channeled into research settings in a way that promotes the public good. Otherwise, the jaws of the dragon may swallow clinical research, to the detriment of all.

NOTES

The epigraph at the beginning of this chapter is a quote from Vera Hassner Sharav, founder and president of the Alliance for Human Research Protection, *http://www.ahrp.org*.

1. FH Miller. Trusting Doctors: Tricky business when it comes to clinical research. BU L Rev. 2001; 81:423-43.
2. 35 U.S.C. § 200-212, 1980.
3. Miller, see note 1 above.
4. M Angell. Is academic medicine for sale? New Engl J Med 2000; 342: 1516-18.
5. *Id.*
6. Associated Press. FDA Approved Fewer New Drugs Over Decade. Augusta Chron. A07. May 29, 2002.
7. J Drazen, G Curfman. Financial associations of authors. N Engl J Med 2002; 346 (24):1901-02.
8. Association of University Technology Managers (AUTM). "The AUTM Licensing Survey: FY 2000."
9. L Nelson. The lifeblood of biotechnology: University-industry technology transfer, in the business of giotechnology: From the bench to the street 39 (R. Dana Ono ed. 1991).
10. KS Dueker. Biobusiness on Campus: Commercialization of University-Developed Biomedical Technologies. Food & Drug Law J. 1997; 52: 453-510.
11. *Id.*
12. BN Sampat. Patenting and US academic research in the 20th century: The world before and after Bayh-Dole. Research Policy July 2006; 35: 772-89.
13. *Id.*
14. *Id.*
15. General Accounting Office (GAO) Report to the Ranking Minority Member, Subcommittee on Public Health, Committee on Health, Education, Labor, and Pensions, U.S. Senate. GAO-02-89. November 2001.
16. *Id.*

17. EH Morreim. Conflicts of interest. JAMA 1989; 262:390.

18. JB Martin. DL Kasper. In whose best interest? Breaching the academic-industrial wall. New Engl J Med 2000; 343:1646-49.

19. J Holmes. The Path of the Law, Harv L Rev 1897; 10:457, 469.

Appendix A
The Nuremberg Code

Excerpted from "Permissable Medical Experiments," *Trials of War Criminals before the Nuernberg Military Tribunals under Control Council Law No. 10: Nuernberg, October 1946 -1949,* vol. 2 (Washington, D.C.: U.S. Government Printing Office, n.d.), 181-2.

1. The voluntary consent of the human subject is absolutely essential. This means that the person involved should have legal capacity to give consent; should be so situated as to be able to exercise free power of choice without the intervention of any element of force, fraud, deceit, duress, overreaching, or other ulterior form of constraint or coercion; and should have sufficient knowledge and comprehension of the elements of the subject matter involved as to enable him to make an understanding and enlightened decision. This latter element requires that before the acceptance of an affirmative decision by the experimental subject there should be made known to him the nature, duration, and purpose of the experiment; the method and means by which it is to be conducted; all inconveniences and hazards reasonably to be expected; and their effects upon his health or person which may possibly come from his participation in the experiment.
The duty and responsibility for ascertaining the quality of the consent rests upon each individual who initiates, directs, or engages in the experiment. It is a personal duty and responsibility which may not be delegated to another with impunity.

2. The experiment should be such as to yield fruitful results for the good of society, unprocurable by other methods or means of study, and not random and unnecessary in nature.
3. The experiment should be so designed and based on the results of animal experimentation and a knowledge of the natural history of the disease or other problem under study that the anticipated results will justify the performance of the experiment.
4. The experiment should be so conducted as to avoid all unnecessary physical and mental suffering and injury.
5. No experiment should be conducted where there is an *a priori* reason to believe that death or disabling injury will occur, except perhaps, in those experiments where the experimental physicians also serve as subjects.
6. The degree of risk to be taken should never exceed that determined by the humanitarian importance of the problem to be solved by the experiment.
7. Proper preparations should be made and adequate facilities provided to protect the experimental subject against even remote possibilities of injury, disability or death.
8. The experiment should be conducted only by scientifically qualified persons. The highest degree of skill and care should be required through all stages of the experiment of those who conduct or engage in the experiment.
9. During the course of the experiment the human subject should be at liberty to bring the experiment to an end if he has reached the physical or mental state where continuation of the experiment seems to him to be impossible.
10. During the course of the experiment the scientist in charge must be prepared to terminate the experiment at any stage, if he has probable cause to believe, in the exercise of the good faith, superior skill, and careful judgment required of him, that a continuation of the experiment is likely to result in injury, disability, or death to the experimental subject.

Appendix B
World Medical Association Declaration of Helsinki

Ethical Principals for Medical Research Involving Human Subjects

World Medical Association Declaration of Helsinki: Ethical Principals for Medical Research Involving Human Subjects is © 2006 by the World Medical Association.
Used with permission. All rights reserved.

Adopted by the 18th WMA General Assembly, Helsinki, Finland, June 1964, and amended by the
29th WMA General Assembly, Tokyo, Japan, October 1975
35th WMA General Assembly, Venice, Italy, October 1983
41st WMA General Assembly, Hong Kong, September 1989
48th WMA General Assembly, Somerset West,
Republic of South Africa, October 1996 and the
52nd WMA General Assembly, Edinburgh, Scotland, October 2000
Note of Clarification on Paragraph 29 added by the
WMA General Assembly, Washington 2002
Note of Clarification on Paragraph 30 added by the
WMA General Assembly, Tokyo, 2004

A. INTRODUCTION

    1. The World Medical Association has developed the Declaration of Helsinki as a statement of ethical principles to provide guidance to

physicians and other participants in medical research involving human subjects. Medical research involving human subjects includes research on identifiable human material or identifiable data.

2. It is the duty of the physician to promote and safeguard the health of the people. The physician's knowledge and conscience are dedicated to the fulfillment of this duty.

3. The Declaration of Geneva of the World Medical Association binds the physician with the words, "The health of my patient will be my first consideration," and the International Code of Medical Ethics declares that, "A physician shall act only in the patient's interest when providing medical care which might have the effect of weakening the physical and mental condition of the patient."

4. Medical progress is based on research which ultimately must rest in part on experimentation involving human subjects.

5. In medical research on human subjects, considerations related to the well-being of the human subject should take precedence over the interests of science and society.

6. The primary purpose of medical research involving human subjects is to improve prophylactic, diagnostic and therapeutic procedures and the understanding of the aetiology and pathogenesis of disease. Even the best proven prophylactic, diagnostic, and therapeutic methods must continuously be challenged through research for their effectiveness, efficiency, accessibility and quality.

7. In current medical practice and in medical research, most prophylactic, diagnostic and therapeutic procedures involve risks and burdens.

8. Medical research is subject to ethical standards that promote respect for all human beings and protect their health and rights. Some research populations are vulnerable and need special protection. The particular needs of the economically and medically disadvantaged must be recognized. Special attention is also required for those who cannot give or refuse consent for themselves, for those who may be subject to giving consent under duress, for those who will not benefit personally from the research and for those for whom the research is combined with care.

9. Research Investigators should be aware of the ethical, legal and regulatory requirements for research on human subjects in their own countries as well as applicable international requirements. No national ethical, legal or regulatory requirement should be allowed to reduce or eliminate any of the protections for human subjects set forth in this Declaration.

WMA Declaration of Helsinki

B. BASIC PRINCIPLES FOR ALL MEDICAL RESEARCH

10. It is the duty of the physician in medical research to protect the life, health, privacy, and dignity of the human subject.
11. Medical research involving human subjects must conform to generally accepted scientific principles, be based on a thorough knowledge of the scientific literature, other relevant sources of information, and on adequate laboratory and, where appropriate, animal experimentation.
12. Appropriate caution must be exercised in the conduct of research which may affect the environment, and the welfare of animals used for research must be respected.
13. The design and performance of each experimental procedure involving human subjects should be clearly formulated in an experimental protocol. This protocol should be submitted for consideration, comment, guidance, and where appropriate, approval to a specially appointed ethical review committee, which must be independent of the investigator, the sponsor or any other kind of undue influence. This independent committee should be in conformity with the laws and regulations of the country in which the research experiment is performed. The committee has the right to monitor ongoing trials. The researcher has the obligation to provide monitoring information to the committee, especially any serious adverse events. The researcher should also submit to the committee, for review, information regarding funding, sponsors, institutional affiliations, other potential conflicts of interest and incentives for subjects.
14. The research protocol should always contain a statement of the ethical considerations involved and should indicate that there is compliance with the principles enunciated in this Declaration.
15. Medical research involving human subjects should be conducted only by scientifically qualified persons and under the supervision of a clinically competent medical person. The responsibility for the human subject must always rest with a medically qualified person and never rest on the subject of the research, even though the subject has given consent.
16. Every medical research project involving human subjects should be preceded by careful assessment of predictable risks and burdens in comparison with foreseeable benefits to the subject or to others. This does not preclude the participation of healthy volunteers in medical research. The design of all studies should be publicly available.
17. Physicians should abstain from engaging in research projects involv-

ing human subjects unless they are confident that the risks involved have been adequately assessed and can be satisfactorily managed. Physicians should cease any investigation if the risks are found to outweigh the potential benefits or if there is conclusive proof of positive and beneficial results.
18. Medical research involving human subjects should only be conducted if the importance of the objective outweighs the inherent risks and burdens to the subject. This is especially important when the human subjects are healthy volunteers.
19. Medical research is only justified if there is a reasonable likelihood that the populations in which the research is carried out stand to benefit from the results of the research.
20. The subjects must be volunteers and informed participants in the research project.
21. The right of research subjects to safeguard their integrity must always be respected. Every precaution should be taken to respect the privacy of the subject, the confidentiality of the patient's information and to minimize the impact of the study on the subject's physical and mental integrity and on the personality of the subject.
22. In any research on human beings, each potential subject must be adequately informed of the aims, methods, sources of funding, any possible conflicts of interest, institutional affiliations of the researcher, the anticipated benefits and potential risks of the study and the discomfort it may entail. The subject should be informed of the right to abstain from participation in the study or to withdraw consent to participate at any time without reprisal. After ensuring that the subject has understood the information, the physician should then obtain the subject's freely-given informed consent, preferably in writing. If the consent cannot be obtained in writing, the non-written consent must be formally documented and witnessed.
23. When obtaining informed consent for the research project the physician should be particularly cautious if the subject is in a dependent relationship with the physician or may consent under duress. In that case the informed consent should be obtained by a well-informed physician who is not engaged in the investigation and who is completely independent of this relationship.
24. For a research subject who is legally incompetent, physically or mentally incapable of giving consent or is a legally incompetent minor, the investigator must obtain informed consent from the legally authorized representative in accordance with applicable law. These groups

should not be included in research unless the research is necessary to promote the health of the population represented and this research cannot instead be performed on legally competent persons.
25. When a subject deemed legally incompetent, such as a minor child, is able to give assent to decisions about participation in research, the investigator must obtain that assent in addition to the consent of the legally authorized representative.
26. Research on individuals from whom it is not possible to obtain consent, including proxy or advance consent, should be done only if the physical/mental condition that prevents obtaining informed consent is a necessary characteristic of the research population. The specific reasons for involving research subjects with a condition that renders them unable to give informed consent should be stated in the experimental protocol for consideration and approval of the review committee. The protocol should state that consent to remain in the research should be obtained as soon as possible from the individual or a legally authorized surrogate.
27. Both authors and publishers have ethical obligations. In publication of the results of research, the investigators are obliged to preserve the accuracy of the results. Negative as well as positive results should be published or otherwise publicly available. Sources of funding, institutional affiliations and any possible conflicts of interest should be declared in the publication. Reports of experimentation not in accordance with the principles laid down in this Declaration should not be accepted for publication.

C. ADDITIONAL PRINCIPLES FOR MEDICAL RESEARCH COMBINED WITH MEDICAL CARE

28. The physician may combine medical research with medical care, only to the extent that the research is justified by its potential prophylactic, diagnostic or therapeutic value. When medical research is combined with medical care, additional standards apply to protect the patients who are research subjects.
29. The benefits, risks, burdens and effectiveness of a new method should be tested against those of the best current prophylactic, diagnostic, and therapeutic methods. This does not exclude the use of placebo, or no treatment, in studies where no proven prophylactic, diagnostic or therapeutic method exists. See footnote
30. At the conclusion of the study, every patient entered into the study

should be assured of access to the best proven prophylactic, diagnostic and therapeutic methods identified by the study. See footnote

31. The physician should fully inform the patient which aspects of the care are related to the research. The refusal of a patient to participate in a study must never interfere with the patient-physician relationship.
32. In the treatment of a patient, where proven prophylactic, diagnostic and therapeutic methods do not exist or have been ineffective, the physician, with informed consent from the patient, must be free to use unproven or new prophylactic, diagnostic and therapeutic measures, if in the physician's judgement it offers hope of saving life, re-establishing health or alleviating suffering. Where possible, these measures should be made the object of research, designed to evaluate their safety and efficacy. In all cases, new information should be recorded and, where appropriate, published. The other relevant guidelines of this Declaration should be followed.

Note: Note of clarification on paragraph 29 of the WMA Declaration of Helsinki
The WMA hereby reaffirms its position that extreme care must be taken in making use of a placebo-controlled trial and that in general this methodology should only be used in the absence of existing proven therapy. However, a placebo-controlled trial may be ethically acceptable, even if proven therapy is available, under the following circumstances:
- Where for compelling and scientifically sound methodological reasons its use is necessary to determine the efficacy or safety of a prophylactic, diagnostic or therapeutic method; or
- Where a prophylactic, diagnostic or therapeutic method is being investigated for a minor condition and the patients who receive placebo will not be subject to any additional risk of serious or irreversible harm.

All other provisions of the Declaration of Helsinki must be adhered to, especially the need for appropriate ethical and scientific review.

Note: Note of clarification on paragraph 30 of the WMA Declaration of Helsinki
The WMA hereby reaffirms its position that it is necessary during the study planning process to identify post-trial access by study participants to prophylactic, diagnostic and therapeutic procedures identified as beneficial in the study or access to other appropriate care. Post-trial access arrangements or other care must be described in the study protocol so the ethical review committee may consider such arrangements during its review.

WMA Declaration of Helsinki

The Declaration of Helsinki (Document 17.C) is an official policy document of the World Medical Association, the global representative body for physicians. It was first adopted in 1964 (Helsinki, Finland) and revised in 1975 (Tokyo, Japan), 1983 (Venice, Italy), 1989 (Hong Kong), 1996 (Somerset-West, South Africa) and 2000 (Edinburgh, Scotland). Note of clarification on Paragraph 29 added by the WMA General Assembly, Washington 2002.

Appendix C
The Belmont Report

Ethical Principles and Guidelines for the Protection of Human Subjects of Research

Report of the National Commission for the Protection of Human Subjects of Biomedical and Behavioral Research, Department of Health, Education, and Welfare.
18 April 1979

Scientific research has produced substantial social benefits. It has also posed some troubling ethical questions. Public attention was drawn to these questions by reported abuses of human subjects in biomedical experiments, especially during the Second World War. During the Nuremberg War Crime Trials, the Nuremberg code was drafted as a set of standards for judging physicians and scientists who had conducted biomedical experiments on concentration camp prisoners. This code became the prototype of many later codes[1] intended to assure that research involving human subjects would be carried out in an ethical manner.

The codes consist of rules, some general, others specific, that guide the investigators or the reviewers of research in their work. Such rules often are inadequate to cover complex situations; at times they come into conflict, and they are frequently difficult to interpret or apply. Broader ethical principles will provide a basis on which specific rules may be formulated, criticized and interpreted.

Three principles, or general prescriptive judgments, that are relevant to research involving human subjects are identified in this statement. Other principles may also be relevant. These three are comprehensive, however, and are stated at a level of generalization that should assist scientists, subjects, reviewers and interested citizens to understand the ethical issues inherent in research involving human subjects. These principles cannot always be applied so as to resolve beyond dispute particular ethical problems. The objective is to provide an analytical framework that will guide the resolution of ethical problems arising from research involving human subjects.

This statement consists of a distinction between research and practice, a discussion of the three basic ethical principles, and remarks about the application of these principles.

A. Boundaries Between Practice and Research

It is important to distinguish between biomedical and behavioral research, on the one hand, and the practice of accepted therapy on the other, in order to know what activities ought to undergo review for the protection of human subjects of research. The distinction between research and practice is blurred partly because both often occur together (as in research designed to evaluate a therapy) and partly because notable departures from standard practice are often called "experimental" when the terms "experimental" and "research" are not carefully defined.

For the most part, the term "practice" refers to interventions that are designed solely to enhance the well being of an individual patient or client and that have a reasonable expectation of success. The purpose of medical or behavioral practice is to provide diagnosis, preventive treatment or therapy to particular individuals.[2] By contrast, the term "research" designates an activity designed to test an hypothesis, permit conclusions to be drawn, and thereby to develop or contribute to generalizable knowledge (expressed, for example, in theories, principles, and statements of relationships). Research is usually described in a formal protocol that sets forth an objective and a set of procedures designed to reach that objective.

When a clinician departs in a significant way from standard or accepted practice, the innovation does not, in and of itself, constitute research. The fact that a procedure is "experimental," in the sense of new, untested or different, does not automatically place it in the category of research. Radically new procedures of this description should, however, be made the object of formal research at an early stage in order to determine whether they are safe and effective. Thus, it is the responsibility of medical practice committees, for example, to insist that a major innovation be incorporated into a formal research project.[3]

Research and practice may be carried on together when research is designed to evaluate the safety and efficacy of a therapy. This need not cause any confusion regarding whether or not the activity requires review; the general rule is that if there is any element of research in an activity, that activity should undergo review for the protection of human subjects.

B. Basic Ethical Principles

The expression "basic ethical principles" refers to those general judgments that serve as a basic justification for the many particular ethical prescriptions and evaluations of human actions. Three basic principles, among those generally accepted in our cultural tradition, are particularly relevant to the ethics of research involving human subjects: The principles of respect for persons, beneficence and justice.

1. Respect for Persons.—Respect for persons incorporates at least two ethical convictions: first, that individuals should be treated as autonomous agents, and second, that persons with diminished autonomy are entitled to protection. The principle of respect for persons thus divides into two separate moral requirements: The requirement to acknowledge autonomy and the requirement to protect those with diminished autonomy.

An autonomous person is an individual capable of deliberation about personal goals and of acting under the direction of such deliberation. To respect autonomy is to give weight to autonomous persons' considered opinions and choices while refraining from obstructing their actions unless they are clearly detrimental to others. To show lack of respect for an autonomous agent is to repudiate that person's considered judgments, to deny an individual the freedom to act on those considered judgments, or to withhold information necessary to make a considered judgment, when there are no compelling reasons to do so.

However, not every human being is capable of self-determination. The capacity for self-determination matures during an individual's life, and some individuals lose this capacity wholly or in part because of illness, mental disability, or circumstances that severely restrict liberty. Respect for the immature and the incapacitated may require protecting them as they mature or while they are incapacitated.

Some persons are in need of extensive protection, even to the point of excluding them from activities which may harm them; other persons require little protection beyond making sure they undertake activities freely and with awareness of possible adverse consequences. The extent of protection afforded should depend upon the risk of harm and the likelihood of benefit. The judgment that any individual lacks autonomy should be periodically reevaluated and will vary in different situations.

In most cases of research involving human subjects, respect for persons demands that subjects enter into the research voluntarily and with adequate information. In some situations, however, application of the principle is not obvious. The involvement of prisoners as subjects of research provides an instructive example. On the one hand, it would seem that the principle of respect for persons requires that prisoners not be deprived of the opportunity to volunteer for research. On the other hand, under prison conditions they may be subtly coerced or unduly influenced to engage in research activities for which they would not otherwise volunteer. Respect for persons would then dictate that prisoners be protected. Whether to allow prisoners to "volunteer" or to "protect" them presents a dilemma. Respecting persons, in most hard cases, is often a matter of balancing competing claims urged by the principle of respect itself.

2. *Beneficence.*—Persons are treated in an ethical manner not only by respecting their decisions and protecting them from harm, but also by making efforts to secure their well being. Such treatment falls under the principle of beneficence. The term "beneficence" is often understood to cover acts of kindness or charity that go beyond strict obligation. In this document, beneficence is understood in a stronger sense, as an obligation. Two general rules have been formulated as complementary expressions of beneficent actions in this sense: (1) do not harm and (2) maximize possible benefits and minimize possible harms.

The Hippocratic maxim "do no harm" has long been a fundamental principle of medical ethics. Claude Bernard extended it to the realm of research, saying that one should not injure one person regardless of the benefits that might come to others. However, even avoiding harm requires learning what is harmful; and, in the process of obtaining this information, persons may be exposed to risk of harm. Further, the Hippocratic Oath requires physicians to benefit their patients "according to their best judgment." Learning what will in fact benefit may require exposing persons to risk. The problem posed by these imperatives is to decide when it is justifiable to seek certain benefits despite the risks involved, and when the benefits should be foregone because of the risks.

The obligations of beneficence affect both individual investigators and society at large, because they extend both to particular research projects and to the entire enterprise of research. In the case of particular projects, investigators and members of their institutions are obliged to give forethought to the maximization of benefits and the reduction of risk that might occur from the research investigation. In the case of scientific research in general, members of the larger society are obliged to recognize the longer term benefits and risks that may result from the improvement of knowledge and from the development of novel medical, psychotherapeutic, and social procedures.

The principle of beneficence often occupies a well-defined justifying role in many areas of research involving human subjects. An example is found in research involving children. Effective ways of treating childhood diseases and fostering healthy development are benefits that serve to justify research involving children—even when individual research subjects are not direct beneficiaries. Research also makes is possible to avoid the harm that may result from the application of previously accepted routine practices that on closer investigation turn out to be dangerous. But the role of the principle of beneficence is not always so unambiguous. A difficult ethical problem remains, for example, about research

The Belmont Report

that presents more than minimal risk without immediate prospect of direct benefit to the children involved. Some have argued that such research is inadmissible, while others have pointed out that this limit would rule out much research promising great benefit to children in the future. Here again, as with all hard cases, the different claims covered by the principle of beneficence may come into conflict and force difficult choices.

3. Justice.—Who ought to receive the benefits of research and bear its burdens? This is a question of justice, in the sense of "fairness in distribution" or "what is deserved." An injustice occurs when some benefit to which a person is entitled is denied without good reason or when some burden is imposed unduly. Another way of conceiving the principle of justice is that equals ought to be treated equally. However, this statement requires explication. Who is equal and who is unequal? What considerations justify departure from equal distribution? Almost all commentators allow that distinctions based on experience, age, deprivation, competence, merit and position do sometimes constitute criteria justifying differential treatment for certain purposes. It is necessary, then, to explain in what respects people should be treated equally. There are several widely accepted formulations of just ways to distribute burdens and benefits. Each formulation mentions some relevant property on the basis of which burdens and benefits should be distributed. These formulations are (1) to each person an equal share, (2) to each person according to individual need, (3) to each person according to individual effort, (4) to each person according to societal contribution, and (5) to each person according to merit.

Questions of justice have long been associated with social practices such as punishment, taxation and political representation. Until recently these questions have not generally been associated with scientific research. However, they are foreshadowed even in the earliest reflections on the ethics of research involving human subjects. For example, during the 19th and early 20th centuries the burdens of serving as research subjects fell largely upon poor ward patients, while the benefits of improved medical care flowed primarily to private patients. Subsequently, the exploitation of unwilling prisoners as research subjects in Nazi concentration camps was condemned as a particularly flagrant injustice. In this country, in the 1940's, the Tuskegee syphilis study used disadvantaged, rural black men to study the untreated course of a disease that is by no means confined to that population. These subjects were deprived of demonstrably effective treatment in order not to interrupt the project, long after such treatment became generally available.

Against this historical background, it can be seen how conceptions of justice are relevant to research involving human subjects. For example, the selection of research subjects needs to be scrutinized in order to determine whether some classes (e.g., welfare patients, particular racial and ethnic minorities, or persons confined to institutions) are being systematically selected simply because of their easy availability, their compromised position, or their manipulability, rather than for reasons directly related to the problem being studied. Finally, whenever research supported by public funds leads to the development of therapeutic devices and procedures, justice demands both that these not provide advantages only to those who can afford them and that such research should not unduly involve persons from groups unlikely to be among the beneficiaries of subsequent applications of the research.

C. Applications

Applications of the general principles to the conduct of research leads to consideration of the following requirements: Informed consent, risk/benefit assessment, and the selection of subjects of research.

1. Informed Consent.—Respect for persons requires that subjects, to the degree that they are capable, be given the opportunity to choose what shall or shall not happen to them. This opportunity is provided when adequate standards for informed consent are satisfied.

While the importance of informed consent is unquestioned, controversy prevails over the nature and possibility of an informed consent. Nonetheless, there is widespread agreement that the consent process can be analyzed as containing three elements: information, comprehension and voluntariness.

Information. Most codes of research establish specific items for disclosure intended to assure that subjects are given sufficient information. These items generally include: the research procedure, their purposes, risks and anticipated benefits, alternative procedures (where therapy is involved), and a statement offering the subject the opportunity to ask questions and to withdraw at any time from the research. Additional items have been proposed, including how subjects are selected, the person responsible for the research, etc.

However, a simple listing of items does not answer the question of what the standard should be for judging how much and what sort of information should be provided. One standard frequently invoked in medical practice, namely the information commonly provided by practitioners in the field or in the locale, is inadequate since research takes place precisely when a common understanding does not exist. Another standard, currently popular in malpractice law, requires the practitioner to reveal the information that reasonable persons would wish to know in order to make a decision regarding their care. This, too, seems insufficient since the research subject, being in essence a volunteer, may wish to know considerably more about risks gratuitously undertaken than do patients who deliver themselves into the hand of a clinician for needed care. It may be that a standard of "the reasonable volunteer" should be proposed: The extent and nature of information should be such that persons, knowing that the procedure is neither necessary for their care nor perhaps fully understood, can decide whether they wish to participate in the furthering of knowledge. Even when some direct benefit to them is anticipated, the subjects should understand clearly the range of risk and the voluntary nature of participation.

A special problem of consent arises where informing subjects of some pertinent aspect of the research is likely to impair the validity of the research. In many cases, it is sufficient to indicate to subjects that they are being invited to participate in research of which some features will not be revealed until the research is concluded. In all cases of research involving incomplete disclosure, such research is justified only if it is clear that (1) incomplete disclosure is truly necessary to accomplish the goals of the research, (2) there are no undisclosed risks to subjects that are more than minimal, and (3) there is an adequate plan for debriefing subjects, when appropriate, and for dissemination of research results to them. Information about risks should never be withheld for the purpose of eliciting the cooperation of subjects, and truthful answers should always be given to direct questions about the research. Care should be taken to distinguish cases in which disclosure would destroy or invalidate the research from cases in which disclosure would simply inconvenience the investigator.

Comprehension. The manner and context in which information is conveyed is as important as the information itself. For example, presenting information in a disorganized and rapid fashion, allowing too little time for consideration or curtailing opportunities for questioning, all may adversely affect a subject's ability to make an informed choice.

Because the subject's ability to understand is a function of intelligence, rationality, maturity and language, it is necessary to adapt the presentation of the information to the subject's capacities. Investigators are responsible for ascertaining that the subject has comprehended the information. While there is always an obligation to ascertain that the information about risk to subjects is complete and adequately comprehended, when the risks are more serious, that obligation increases. On occasion, it may be suitable to give some oral or written tests of comprehension.

Special provision may need to be made when comprehension is severely limited—for example, by conditions of immaturity or mental disability. Each class of subjects that one might consider as incompetent (e.g., infants and young children, mentally disabled patients, the terminally ill and the comatose) should be considered on its own terms. Even for these persons, however, respect requires giving them the opportunity to choose to the extent they are able, whether or not to participate in research. The objections of these subjects to involvement should be honored, unless the research entails providing them a therapy unavailable elsewhere. Respect for persons also requires seeking the permission of other parties in order to protect the subjects from harm. Such persons are thus respected both by acknowledging their own wishes and by the use of third parties to protect them from harm.

The third parties chosen should be those who are most likely to understand the incompetent subject's situation and to act in that person's best interest. The person authorized to act on behalf of the subject should be given an opportunity to observe the research as it proceeds in order to be able to withdraw the subject from the research, if such action appears in the subject's best interest.

Voluntariness. An agreement to participate in research constitutes a valid consent only if voluntarily given. This element of informed consent requires conditions free of coercion and undue influence. Coercion occurs when an overt threat of harm is intentionally presented by one person to another in order to obtain compliance. Undue influence, by contrast, occurs through an offer of an excessive, unwarranted, inappropriate or improper reward or other overture in order to obtain compliance. Also, inducements that would ordinarily be acceptable may become undue influences if the subject is especially vulnerable.

Unjustifiable pressures usually occur when persons in positions of authority or commanding influence—especially where possible sanctions are involved—urge a course of action for a subject. A continuum of such influencing factors exists, however, and it is impossible to state precisely where justifiable persuasion ends and undue influence begins. But undue influence would include actions such as manipulating a person's choice through the controlling influence of a close relative and threatening to withdraw health services to which an individual would otherwise be entitled.

2. Assessment of Risks and Benefits.—The assessment of risks and benefits requires a careful arrayal of relevant data, including, in some cases, alternative ways of obtaining the benefits sought in the research. Thus, the assessment presents both an opportunity and a responsibility to gather systematic and comprehensive information about proposed research. For the investigator, it is a means to examine whether the proposed research is properly designed. For a review committee, it is a method for determining whether the risks that will be presented to subjects are justified. For prospective subjects, the assessment will assist the determination whether or not to participate.

The Nature and Scope of Risks and Benefits. The requirement that research be justified on the basis of a favorable risk/benefit assessment bears a close relation to the principle of beneficence, just as the moral requirement that informed consent be obtained is derived primarily from the principle of respect for persons. The term "risk" refers to a possibility that harm may occur. However, when expressions such as "small risk" or "high risk" are used, they usually refer (often ambiguously) both to the chance (probability) of experiencing a harm and the severity (magnitude) of the envisioned harm.

The term "benefit" is used in the research context to refer to something of positive value related to health or welfare. Unlike "risk," "benefit" is not a term that expresses probabilities. Risk is properly contrasted to probability of benefits, and benefits are properly contrasted with harms rather than risks of harm. Accordingly, so-called risk benefit assessments are concerned with the probabilities and magnitudes of possible harms and anticipated benefits. Many kinds of possible harms and benefits need to be taken into account. There are, for example, risks of psychological harm, physical harm, legal harm, social harm and economic harm and the corresponding benefits. While the most likely types of harms to research subjects are those of psychological or physical pain or injury, other possible kinds should not be overlooked.

Risks and benefits of research may affect the individual subjects, the families of the individual subjects, and society at large (or special groups of subjects in society). Previous codes and Federal regulations have required that risks to subjects be outweighed by the sum of both the anticipated benefit to the subject, if any, and the anticipated benefit to society in the form of knowledge to be gained from the research. In balancing these different elements, the risks and benefits affecting the immediate research subject will normally carry special weight. On the other hand, interests other than those of the subject may on some occasions be sufficient by themselves to justify the risks involved in the research, so long as the subjects' rights have been protected. Beneficence thus requires that we protect against risk of harm to subjects and also that we be concerned about the loss of the substantial benefits that might be gained from research.

The Systematic Assessment of Risks and Benefits. It is commonly said that benefits and risks must be "balanced" and shown to be "in a favorable ratio." The metaphorical character of these terms draws attention to the difficulty of making precise judgments. Only on rare occasions will quantitative techniques be available for the scrutiny of research protocols. However, the idea of systematic, nonarbitrary analysis of risks and benefits should be emulated insofar as possible. This ideal requires those making decisions about the justifiability of research to be thorough in the accumulation and assessment of information about all aspects of the research, and to consider alternatives systematically. This procedure renders the assessment of research more rigorous and precise, while making communication between review board members and investigators less subject to misinterpretation, misinformation and conflicting judgments. Thus, there should first be a determination of the validity of the presuppositions of the research; then the nature, probability and magnitude of risk should be distinguished with as much clarity as possible. The method of ascertaining risks should be explicit, especially where there is no alternative to the use of such vague categories as small or slight risk. It should also be determined whether an investigator's estimates of the probability of harm or benefits are reasonable, as judged by known facts or other available studies.

Finally, assessment of the justifiability of research should reflect at least the following considerations: (i) Brutal or inhumane treatment of human subjects is never morally justified; (ii) Risks should be reduced to those necessary to achieve the research objective. It should be determined whether it is in fact necessary to use human subjects at all. Risk can perhaps never be entirely eliminated, but it can often be reduced by careful attention to alternative procedures; (iii) When research involves significant risk of serious impairment, review committees should be extraordinarily insistent on the justification of the risk (looking usually to the likelihood of benefit to the subject or, in some rare cases, to the manifest voluntariness of the participation); (iv) When vulnerable populations are involved in research, the appropriateness of involving them should itself be demonstrated. A number of variables go into such judgments, including the nature and degree of risk, the condition of the particular population involved, and the nature and level of the anticipated benefits; and (v) Relevant risks and benefits must be thoroughly arrayed in documents and procedures used in the informed consent process.

3. Selection of Subjects.—Just as the principle of respect for persons finds expression in the requirements for consent, and the principle of beneficence in risk/benefit assessment, the principle of justice gives rise to moral requirements that there be fair procedures and outcomes in the selection of research subjects.

Justice is relevant to the selection of subjects of research at two levels: the social and the individual. Individual justice in the selection of subjects would require that researchers exhibit fairness: Thus, they should not offer potentially beneficial research only to some patients who are in their favor or select only "undesirable" persons for risky research. Social justice requires that distinction be drawn between classes of subjects that ought, and ought not, to participate in any particular kind of research, based on the ability of members of that class to bear burdens and on the appropriateness of placing further burdens on already burdened persons. Thus, it can be considered a matter of social justice that there is an order of preference in the selection of classes of subjects (e.g., adults before children) and that some classes of potential subjects (e.g., the institutionalized mentally infirm or prisoners) may be involved as research subjects, if at all, only on certain conditions.

Injustice may appear in the selection of subjects, even if individual subjects are selected fairly by investigators and treated fairly in the course of research. Thus injustice arises from social, racial, sexual and cultural biases institutionalized in society. Thus, even if individual researchers are treating their research subjects fairly, and even if IRBs are taking care to assure that subjects are selected fairly within a particular institution, unjust social patterns may nevertheless appear in the overall distribution of the burdens and benefits of research. Although individual institutions or investigators may not be able to resolve a problem that is pervasive in their social setting, they can consider distributive justice in selecting research subjects.

Some populations, especially institutionalized ones, are already burdened in many ways by their infirmities and environments. When research is proposed that involves risks and does not include a therapeutic component, other less burdened classes of persons should be called upon first to accept these risks of research, except where the research is directly related to the specific conditions of the class involved. Also, even though public funds for research may often flow in the same directions as public funds for health care, it seems unfair that populations dependent on public health care constitute a pool of preferred research subjects if more advantaged populations are likely to be the recipients of the benefits.

One special instance of injustice results from the involvement of vulnerable subjects. Certain groups, such as racial minorities, the economically disadvantaged, the very sick, and the institutionalized may continually be sought as research subjects, owing to their ready availability in settings where research is conducted. Given their dependent status and their frequently compromised capacity for free consent, they should be protected against the danger of being involved in research solely for administrative convenience, or because they are easy to manipulate as a result of their illness or socioeconomic condition.

NOTES

1. Since 1945, various codes for the proper and responsible conduct of human experimentation in medical research have been adopted by different organizations. The best known of these codes are the Nuremberg Code of 1948, the Helsinki Declaration of 1964 (revised in 1975), and the 1971 Guidelines (codified into Federal Regulations in 1974) issued by the U.S. Department of Health, Education, and Welfare Codes for the conduct of social and behavioral research have also been adopted, the best known being that of the American Psychological Association, published in 1973.

2. Although practice usually involves interventions designed solely to enhance the well being of a particular individual, interventions are sometimes applied to one individual for the enhancement of the well-being of another (e.g., blood donation, skin grafts, organ transplants) or an intervention may have the dual purpose of enhancing the well-being of a particular individual, and, at the same time, providing some benefit to others (e.g., vaccination, which protects both the person who is vaccinated and society generally). The fact that some forms of practice have elements other than immediate benefit to the individual receiving an intervention, however, should not confuse the general distinction between research and practice. Even when a procedure applied in practice may benefit some other person, it remains an intervention designed to enhance the well-being of a particular individual or groups of individuals; thus, it is practice and need not be reviewed as research.

3. Because the problems related to social experimentation may differ substantially from those of biomedical and behavioral research, the Commission specifically declines to make any policy determination regarding such research at this time. Rather, the Commission believes that the problem ought to be addressed by one of its successor bodies.

Appendix D
45 Code of Federal Regulations Part 46

Including
Subpart A, the "Common Rule," and Supporting Subparts B, C, and D

http://www.hhs.gov/ohrp/humansubjects/guidance/45cfr46.htm

Code of Federal Regulations

TITLE 45
Public Welfare

DEPARTMENT OF HEALTH AND HUMAN SERVICES

PART 46
PROTECTION OF HUMAN SUBJECTS

* * *

Revised June 23, 3005
Effective June 23, 2005

* * *

<u>Subpart A</u> — Basic HHS Policy for Protection of Human Research Subjects

Sec.
46.101	To what does this policy apply?
46.102	Definitions.
46.103	Assuring compliance with this policy—research conducted or supported by any Federal Department or Agency.
46.104 - 46.106	[Reserved]
46.107	IRB membership.
46.108	IRB functions and operations.
46.109	IRB review of research.
46.110	Expedited review procedures for certain kinds of research involving no more than minimal risk, and for minor changes in approved research.
46.111	Criteria for IRB approval of research.
46.112	Review by institution.
46.113	Suspension or termination of IRB approval of research.
46.114	Cooperative research.
46.115	IRB records.
46.116	General requirements for informed consent.
46.117	Documentation of informed consent.
46.118	Applications and proposals lacking definite plans for involvement of human subjects.
46.119	Research undertaken without the intention of involving human subjects.
46.120	Evaluation and disposition of applications and proposals for research to be conducted or supported by a Federal Department or Agency.
46.121	[Reserved]
46.122	Use of Federal funds.
46.123	Early termination of research support: Evaluation of applications and proposals.
46.124	Conditions.

Subpart B — Additional Protections for Pregnant Women, Human Fetuses and Neonates Involved in Research

Sec.
46.201	To what do these regulations apply?
46.202	Definitions.
46.203	Duties of IRBs in connection with research involving pregnant women, fetuses, and neonates.
46.204	Research involving pregnant women or fetuses.
46.205	Research involving neonates.

45 CFR Part 46 Subparts A, B, C, and D

46.206	Research involving, after delivery, the placenta, the dead fetus or fetal material.
46.207	Research not otherwise approvable which presents an opportunity to understand, prevent, or alleviate a serious problem affecting the health or welfare of pregnant women, fetuses, or neonates.

Subpart C — Additional Protections Pertaining to Biomedical and Behavioral Research Involving Prisoners as Subjects

Sec.

46.301	Applicability.
46.302	Purpose.
46.303	Definitions.
46.304	Composition of Institutional Review Boards where prisoners are involved.
46.305	Additional duties of the Institutional Review Boards where prisoners are involved.
46.306	Permitted research involving prisoners.

Subpart D — Additional Protections for Children Involved as Subjects in Research

Sec.

46.401	To what do these regulations apply?
46.402	Definitions.
46.403	IRB duties.
46.404	Research not involving greater than minimal risk.
46.405	Research involving greater than minimal risk but presenting the prospect of direct benefit to the individual subjects.
46.406	Research involving greater than minimal risk and no prospect of direct benefit to individual subjects, but likely to yield generalizable knowledge about the subject's disorder or condition.
46.407	Research not otherwise approvable which presents an opportunity to understand, prevent, or alleviate a serious problem affecting the health or welfare of children.
46.408	Requirements for permission by parents or guardians and for assent by children.
46.409	Wards.

Authority: 5 U.S.C. 301; 42 U.S.C. 289(a).

Editorial Note: The Department of Health and Human Services issued a notice of waiver regarding the requirements set forth in part 46, relating to protection of human subjects, as they pertain to demonstration projects, approved under section 1115 of the Social Security Act, which test the use of cost—sharing, such as deductibles, copayment and coinsurance, in the Medicaid program. For further information see 47 FR 9208, Mar. 4, 1982.

Note: As revised, Subpart A of the HHS regulations incorporates the Federal Policy for the Protection of Human Subjects (56 FR 28003). Subpart D of the HHS regulations has been amended at Section 46.401(b) to reference the revised Subpart A.

The Federal Policy for the Protection of Human Subjects is also codified at
7 CFR Part 1c	Department of Agriculture
10 CFR Part 745	Department of Energy
14 CFR Part 1230	National Aeronautics and Space Administration
15 CFR Part 27	Department of Commerce
16 CFR Part 1028	Consumer Product Safety Commission
22 CFR Part 225	International Development Cooperation Agency, Agency for International Development
24 CFR Part 60	Department of Housing and Urban Development
28 CFR Part 46	Department of Justice
32 CFR Part 219	Department of Defense
34 CFR Part 97	Department of Education
38 CFR Part 16	Department of Veterans Affairs
40 CFR Part 26	Environmental Protection Agency
45 CFR Part 690	National Science Foundation
49 CFR Part 11	Department of Transportation

* * *

Subpart A	Basic HHS Policy for Protection of Human Research Subjects
	Authority: 5 U.S.C. 301; 42 U.S.C. 289(a); 42 U.S.C.
	Source: 56 FR 28003, June 18, 1991; 70 FR 36325, June 23, 2005.

§46.101 To what does this policy apply?

(a) Except as provided in paragraph (b) of this section, this policy applies to all research involving human subjects conducted, supported or otherwise subject to regulation by any federal department or agency which takes appropriate administrative action to make the policy applicable to such research. This includes research conducted by federal civilian employees or military personnel, except that each department or agency head may adopt such procedural modifications as may be appropriate from an administrative standpoint. It also includes research conducted, supported, or otherwise subject to regulation by the federal government outside the United States.

(1) Research that is conducted or supported by a federal department or agency, whether or not it is regulated as defined in §46.102(e), must comply with all sections of this policy.

(2) Research that is neither conducted nor supported by a federal department or agency but is subject to regulation as defined in §46.102(e) must be reviewed and approved, in compliance with §46.101, §46.102, and §46.107 through §46.117 of this policy, by an institutional review board (IRB) that operates in accordance with the pertinent requirements of this policy.

(b) Unless otherwise required by department or agency heads, research activities in which the only involvement of human subjects will be in one or more of the following categories are exempt from this policy:

(1) Research conducted in established or commonly accepted educational settings, involving normal educational practices, such as (i) research on regular and special education instructional strategies, or (ii) research on the effectiveness of or the comparison among instructional techniques, curricula, or classroom management methods.

(2) Research involving the use of educational tests (cognitive, diagnostic, aptitude, achievement), survey procedures, interview procedures or observation of public behavior, unless: (i) information obtained is recorded in such a manner that human subjects can be identified, directly or through identifiers linked to the subjects; and (ii) any disclosure of the human subjects' responses outside the research could reasonably place the subjects at risk of criminal or civil liability or be damaging to the subjects' financial standing, employability, or reputation.

(3) Research involving the use of educational tests (cognitive, diagnostic, aptitude, achievement), survey procedures, interview procedures, or observation of public behavior that is not exempt under paragraph (b)(2) of this section, if: (i) the human subjects are elected or appointed public officials or candidates for public office; or (ii) federal statute(s) require(s) without exception that the confidentiality of the personally identifiable

information will be maintained throughout the research and thereafter.

(4) Research involving the collection or study of existing data, documents, records, pathological specimens, or diagnostic specimens, if these sources are publicly available or if the information is recorded by the investigator in such a manner that subjects cannot be identified, directly or through identifiers linked to the subjects.

(5) Research and demonstration projects which are conducted by or subject to the approval of department or agency heads, and which are designed to study, evaluate, or otherwise examine: (i) Public benefit or service programs; (ii) procedures for obtaining benefits or services under those programs; (iii) possible changes in or alternatives to those programs or procedures; or (iv) possible changes in methods or levels of payment for benefits or services under those programs.

(6) Taste and food quality evaluation and consumer acceptance studies, (i) if wholesome foods without additives are consumed or (ii) if a food is consumed that contains a food ingredient at or below the level and for a use found to be safe, or agricultural chemical or environmental contaminant at or below the level found to be safe, by the Food and Drug Administration or approved by the Environmental Protection Agency or the Food Safety and Inspection Service of the U.S. Department of Agriculture.

(c) Department or agency heads retain final judgment as to whether a particular activity is covered by this policy.

(d) Department or agency heads may require that specific research activities or classes of research activities conducted, supported, or otherwise subject to regulation by the department or agency but not otherwise covered by this policy, comply with some or all of the requirements of this policy.

(e) Compliance with this policy requires compliance with pertinent federal laws or regulations which provide additional protections for human subjects.

(f) This policy does not affect any state or local laws or regulations which may otherwise be applicable and which provide additional protections for human subjects.

(g) This policy does not affect any foreign laws or regulations which may otherwise be applicable and which provide additional protections to human subjects of research.

(h) When research covered by this policy takes place in foreign countries, procedures normally followed in the foreign countries to protect human subjects may differ from those set forth in this policy. [An example is a foreign institution which complies with guidelines consistent with the World Medical Assembly Declaration (Declaration of Helsinki amended 1989) issued either by sovereign states or by an organization whose function for the protection of human research subjects is internationally recognized.] In these circumstances, if a department or agency head determines that the procedures prescribed by the institution afford protections that are at least equivalent to those provided in this policy, the department or agency head may approve the substitution of the foreign procedures in lieu of the procedural requirements provided in this policy. Except when otherwise required by statute, Executive Order, or the department or agency head, notices of these actions as they occur will be published in the FEDERAL REGISTER or will be otherwise published as provided in department or agency procedures.

(i) Unless otherwise required by law, department or agency heads may waive the applicability of some or all of the provisions of this policy to specific research activities or classes or research activities otherwise covered by this policy. Except when otherwise required by statute or Executive Order, the department or agency head shall forward advance notices of these actions to the Office for Human Research Protections, Department of Health and Human Services (HHS), or any successor office, and shall also publish them in the FEDERAL REGISTER or in such other manner as provided in Department or Agency procedures.[1]

[56 FR 38012, 28022, June 18, 1991; 56 FR 29756, June 28, 1991; 70 FR 36325, June 23, 2005]

§46.102 Definitions.

(a) *Department or agency head* means the head of any federal department or agency and any other officer or employee of any department or agency to whom authority has been delegated.

---

[1] Institutions with HHS-approved assurances on file will abide by provisions of Title 45 CFR part 46 subparts A-D. Some of the other departments and agencies have incorporated all provisions of Title 45 CFR Part 46 into their policies and procedures as well. However, the exemptions at 45 CFR 46.101(b) do not apply to research involving prisoners, subpart C. The exemption at 45 CFR 46.101(b)(2), for research involving survey or interview procedures or observation of public behavior, does not apply to research with children, subpart D, except for research involving observations of public behavior when the investigator(s) do not participate in the activities being observed.

(b) *Institution* means any public or private entity or agency (including federal, state, and other agencies).

(c) *Legally authorized representative* means an individual or judicial or other body authorized under applicable law to consent on behalf of a prospective subject to the subject's participation in the procedure(s) involved in the research.

(d) *Research* means a systematic investigation, including research development, testing and evaluation, designed to develop or contribute to generalizable knowledge. Activities which meet this definition constitute research for purposes of this policy, whether or not they are conducted or supported under a program which is considered research for other purposes. For example, some demonstration and service programs may include research activities.

(e) *Research subject to regulation,* and similar terms are intended to encompass those research activities for which a federal department or agency has specific responsibility for regulating as a research activity, (for example, Investigational New Drug requirements administered by the Food and Drug Administration). It does not include research activities which are incidentally regulated by a federal department or agency solely as part of the department's or agency's broader responsibility to regulate certain types of activities whether research or non-research in nature (for example, Wage and Hour requirements administered by the Department of Labor).

(f) *Human subject* means a living individual about whom an investigator (whether professional or student) conducting research obtains

   (1) Data through intervention or interaction with the individual, or
   (2) Identifiable private information.

Intervention includes both physical procedures by which data are gathered (for example, venipuncture) and manipulations of the subject or the subject's environment that are performed for research purposes. Interaction includes communication or interpersonal contact between investigator and subject. *Private information* includes information about behavior that occurs in a context in which an individual can reasonably expect that no observation or recording is taking place, and information which has been provided for specific purposes by an individual and which the individual can reasonably expect will not be made public (for example, a medical record). Private information must be individually identifiable (i.e., the identity of the subject is or may readily be ascertained by the investigator or associated with the information) in order for obtaining the

45 CFR Part 46 Subparts A, B, C, and D 199

information to constitute research involving human subjects.

(g) *IRB* means an institutional review board established in accord with and for the purposes expressed in this policy.

(h) *IRB approval* means the determination of the IRB that the research has been reviewed and may be conducted at an institution within the constraints set forth by the IRB and by other institutional and federal requirements.

(i) *Minimal risk* means that the probability and magnitude of harm or discomfort anticipated in the research are not greater in and of themselves than those ordinarily encountered in daily life or during the performance of routine physical or psychological examinations or tests.

(j) *Certification* means the official notification by the institution to the supporting department or agency, in accordance with the requirements of this policy, that a research project or activity involving human subjects has been reviewed and approved by an IRB in accordance with an approved assurance.

§46.103 Assuring compliance with this policy — research conducted or supported by any Federal Department or Agency.

(a) Each institution engaged in research which is covered by this policy and which is conducted or supported by a federal department or agency shall provide written assurance satisfactory to the department or agency head that it will comply with the requirements set forth in this policy. In lieu of requiring submission of an assurance, individual department or agency heads shall accept the existence of a current assurance, appropriate for the research in question, on file with the Office for Human Research Protections, HHS, or any successor office, and approved for federalwide use by that office. When the existence of an HHS-approved assurance is accepted in lieu of requiring submission of an assurance, reports (except certification) required by this policy to be made to department and agency heads shall also be made to the Office for Human Research Protections, HHS, or any successor office.

(b) Departments and agencies will conduct or support research covered by this policy only if the institution has an assurance approved as provided in this section, and only if the institution has certified to the department or agency head that the research has been reviewed and approved by an IRB provided for in the assurance, and will be subject to continuing review by the IRB. Assurances applicable to federally supported or conducted research shall at a minimum include:

(1) A statement of principles governing the institution in the discharge of its responsibilities for protecting the rights and welfare of human subjects of research conducted at or sponsored by the institution, regardless of whether the research is subject to Federal regulation. This may include an appropriate existing code, declaration, or statement of ethical principles, or a statement formulated by the institution itself. This requirement does not preempt provisions of this policy applicable to department- or agency-supported or regulated research and need not be applicable to any research exempted or waived under *§46.101* (b) or (i).

(2) Designation of one or more IRBs established in accordance with the requirements of this policy, and for which provisions are made for meeting space and sufficient staff to support the IRB's review and recordkeeping duties.

(3) A list of IRB members identified by name; earned degrees; representative capacity; indications of experience such as board certifications, licenses, etc., sufficient to describe each member's chief anticipated contributions to IRB deliberations; and any employment or other relationship between each member and the institution; for example: full-time employee, part-time employee, member of governing panel or board, stockholder, paid or unpaid consultant. Changes in IRB membership shall be reported to the department or agency head, unless in accord with §46.103(a) of this policy, the existence of an HHS-approved assurance is accepted. In this case, change in IRB membership shall be reported to the Office for Human Research Protections, HHS, or any successor office.

(4) Written procedures which the IRB will follow (i) for conducting its initial and continuing review of research and for reporting its findings and actions to the investigator and the institution; (ii) for determining which projects require review more often than annually and which projects need verification from sources other than the investigators that no material changes have occurred since previous IRB review; and (iii) for ensuring prompt reporting to the IRB of proposed changes in a research activity, and for ensuring that such changes in approved research, during the period for which IRB approval has already been given, may not be initiated without IRB review and approval except when necessary to eliminate apparent immediate hazards to the subject.

(5) Written procedures for ensuring prompt reporting to the IRB, appropriate institutional officials, and the department or agency head of (i) any unanticipated problems involving risks to subjects or others or any serious

or continuing noncompliance with this policy or the requirements or determinations of the IRB; and (ii) any suspension or termination of IRB approval.

(c) The assurance shall be executed by an individual authorized to act for the institution and to assume on behalf of the institution the obligations imposed by this policy and shall be filed in such form and manner as the department or agency head prescribes.

(d) The Department or Agency head will evaluate all assurances submitted in accordance with this policy through such officers and employees of the department or agency and such experts or consultants engaged for this purpose as the department or agency head determines to be appropriate. The department or agency head's evaluation will take into consideration the adequacy of the proposed IRB in light of the anticipated scope of the institution's research activities and the types of subject populations likely to be involved, the appropriateness of the proposed initial and continuing review procedures in light of the probable risks, and the size and complexity of the institution.

(e) On the basis of this evaluation, the department or agency head may approve or disapprove the assurance, or enter into negotiations to develop an approvable one. The department or agency head may limit the period during which any particular approved assurance or class of approved assurances shall remain effective or otherwise condition or restrict approval.

(f) Certification is required when the research is supported by a federal department or agency and not otherwise exempted or waived under §46.101 (b) or (i). An institution with an approved assurance shall certify that each application or proposal for research covered by the assurance and by §46.103 of this Policy has been reviewed and approved by the IRB. Such certification must be submitted with the application or proposal or by such later date as may be prescribed by the department or agency to which the application or proposal is submitted. Under no condition shall research covered by §46.103 of the Policy be supported prior to receipt of the certification that the research has been reviewed and approved by the IRB. Institutions without an approved assurance covering the research shall certify within 30 days after receipt of a request for such a certification from the department or agency, that the application or proposal has been approved by the IRB. If the certification is not submitted within these time limits, the application or proposal may be returned to the institution.

(Approved by the Office of Management and Budget under control number

0990-0260.)

[56 FR 38012, 28022, June 18, 1991; 56 FR 29756, June 28, 1991; 70 FR 36325, June 23, 2005]

§§46.104 - 46.106 [Reserved]

§46.107 IRB membership.

(a) Each IRB shall have at least five members, with varying backgrounds to promote complete and adequate review of research activities commonly conducted by the institution. The IRB shall be sufficiently qualified through the experience and expertise of its members, and the diversity of the members, including consideration of race, gender, and cultural backgrounds and sensitivity to such issues as community attitudes, to promote respect for its advice and counsel in safeguarding the rights and welfare of human subjects. In addition to possessing the professional competence necessary to review specific research activities, the IRB shall be able to ascertain the acceptability of proposed research in terms of institutional commitments and regulations, applicable law, and standards of professional conduct and practice. The IRB shall therefore include persons knowledgeable in these areas. If an IRB regularly reviews research that involves a vulnerable category of subjects, such as children, prisoners, pregnant women, or handicapped or mentally disabled persons, consideration shall be given to the inclusion of one or more individuals who are knowledgeable about and experienced in working with these subjects.

(b) Every nondiscriminatory effort will be made to ensure that no IRB consists entirely of men or entirely of women, including the institution's consideration of qualified persons of both sexes, so long as no selection is made to the IRB on the basis of gender. No IRB may consist entirely of members of one profession.

(c) Each IRB shall include at least one member whose primary concerns are in scientific areas and at least one member whose primary concerns are in nonscientific areas.

(d) Each IRB shall include at least one member who is not otherwise affiliated with the institution and who is not part of the immediate family of a person who is affiliated with the institution.

(e) No IRB may have a member participate in the IRB's initial or continuing review of any project in which the member has a conflicting interest, except to provide information requested by the IRB.

45 CFR Part 46 Subparts A, B, C, and D

(f) An IRB may, in its discretion, invite individuals with competence in special areas to assist in the review of issues which require expertise beyond or in addition to that available on the IRB. These individuals may not vote with the IRB

§46.108 IRB functions and operations.

In order to fulfill the requirements of this policy each IRB shall:

(a) Follow written procedures in the same detail as described in *§46.103*(b)(4) and to the extent required by §46.103(b)(5).

(b) Except when an expedited review procedure is used (see §46.110), review proposed research at convened meetings at which a majority of the members of the IRB are present, including at least one member whose primary concerns are in nonscientific areas. In order for the research to be approved, it shall receive the approval of a majority of those members present at the meeting

§46.109 IRB review of research.

(a) An IRB shall review and have authority to approve, require modifications in (to secure approval), or disapprove all research activities covered by this policy.

(b) An IRB shall require that information given to subjects as part of informed consent is in accordance with §46.116. The IRB may require that information, in addition to that specifically mentioned in §46.116, be given to the subjects when in the IRB's judgment the information would meaningfully add to the protection of the rights and welfare of subjects.

(c) An IRB shall require documentation of informed consent or may waive documentation in accordance with §46.117.

(d) An IRB shall notify investigators and the institution in writing of its decision to approve or disapprove the proposed research activity, or of modifications required to secure IRB approval of the research activity. If the IRB decides to disapprove a research activity, it shall include in its written notification a statement of the reasons for its decision and give the investigator an opportunity to respond in person or in writing.

(e) An IRB shall conduct continuing review of research covered by this policy at intervals appropriate to the degree of risk, but not less than once per year, and shall have authority to observe or have a third party observe the consent process and the research.

(Approved by the Office of Management and Budget under control number 0990-0260.)

§46.110 Expedited review procedures for certain kinds of research involving no more than minimal risk, and for minor changes in approved research.

(a) The Secretary, HHS, has established, and published as a Notice in the FEDERAL REGISTER, a list of categories of research that may be reviewed by the IRB through an expedited review procedure. The list will be amended, as appropriate, after consultation with other departments and agencies, through periodic republication by the Secretary, HHS, in the FEDERAL REGISTER. A copy of the list is available from the Office for Human Research Protections, HHS, or any successor office.

(b) An IRB may use the expedited review procedure to review either or both of the following:

> (1) some or all of the research appearing on the list and found by the reviewer(s) to involve no more than minimal risk,
>
> (2) minor changes in previously approved research during the period (of one year or less) for which approval is authorized.

Under an expedited review procedure, the review may be carried out by the IRB chairperson or by one or more experienced reviewers designated by the chairperson from among members of the IRB. In reviewing the research, the reviewers may exercise all of the authorities of the IRB except that the reviewers may not disapprove the research. A research activity may be disapproved only after review in accordance with the non-expedited procedure set forth in §46.108(b).

(c) Each IRB which uses an expedited review procedure shall adopt a method for keeping all members advised of research proposals which have been approved under the procedure.

(d) The department or agency head may restrict, suspend, terminate, or choose not to authorize an institution's or IRB's use of the expedited review procedure.

§46.111 Criteria for IRB approval of research.

(a) In order to approve research covered by this policy the IRB shall determine that all of the following requirements are satisfied:

(1) Risks to subjects are minimized: (i) By using procedures which are consistent with sound research design and which do not unnecessarily expose subjects to risk, and (ii) whenever appropriate, by using procedures already being performed on the subjects for diagnostic or treatment purposes.

(2) Risks to subjects are reasonable in relation to anticipated benefits, if any, to subjects, and the importance of the knowledge that may reasonably be expected to result. In evaluating risks and benefits, the IRB should consider only those risks and benefits that may result from the research (as distinguished from risks and benefits of therapies subjects would receive even if not participating in the research). The IRB should not consider possible long-range effects of applying knowledge gained in the research (for example, the possible effects of the research on public policy) as among those research risks that fall within the purview of its responsibility.

(3) Selection of subjects is equitable. In making this assessment the IRB should take into account the purposes of the research and the setting in which the research will be conducted and should be particularly cognizant of the special problems of research involving vulnerable populations, such as children, prisoners, pregnant women, mentally disabled persons, or economically or educationally disadvantaged persons.

(4) Informed consent will be sought from each prospective subject or the subject's legally authorized representative, in accordance with, and to the extent required by §46.116.

(5) Informed consent will be appropriately documented, in accordance with, and to the extent required by §46.117.

(6) When appropriate, the research plan makes adequate provision for monitoring the data collected to ensure the safety of subjects.

(7) When appropriate, there are adequate provisions to protect the privacy of subjects and to maintain the confidentiality of data.

(b) When some or all of the subjects are likely to be vulnerable to coercion or undue influence, such as children, prisoners, pregnant women, mentally disabled persons, or economically or educationally disadvantaged persons, additional safeguards have been included in the study to protect the rights and welfare of these subjects.

§46.112 Review by institution.

Research covered by this policy that has been approved by an IRB may be subject to further appropriate review and approval or disapproval by officials of the institution. However, those officials may not approve the research if it has not been approved by an IRB.

§46.113 Suspension or termination of IRB approval of research.

An IRB shall have authority to suspend or terminate approval of research that is not being conducted in accordance with the IRB's requirements or that has been associated with unexpected serious harm to subjects. Any suspension or termination of approval shall include a statement of the reasons for the IRB's action and shall be reported promptly to the investigator, appropriate institutional officials, and the department or agency head.

(Approved by the Office of Management and Budget under control number 0990-0260.)

§46.114 Cooperative research.

Cooperative research projects are those projects covered by this policy which involve more than one institution. In the conduct of cooperative research projects, each institution is responsible for safeguarding the rights and welfare of human subjects and for complying with this policy. With the approval of the department or agency head, an institution participating in a cooperative project may enter into a joint review arrangement, rely upon the review of another qualified IRB, or make similar arrangements for avoiding duplication of effort.

§46.115 IRB records.

(a) An institution, or when appropriate an IRB, shall prepare and maintain adequate documentation of IRB activities, including the following:

> (1) Copies of all research proposals reviewed, scientific evaluations, if any, that accompany the proposals, approved sample consent documents, progress reports submitted by investigators, and reports of injuries to subjects.

> (2) Minutes of IRB meetings which shall be in sufficient detail to show attendance at the meetings; actions taken by the IRB; the vote on these

actions including the number of members voting for, against, and abstaining; the basis for requiring changes in or disapproving research; and a written summary of the discussion of controverted issues and their resolution.

(3) Records of continuing review activities.

(4) Copies of all correspondence between the IRB and the investigators.

(5) A list of IRB members in the same detail as described in §46.103(b)(3).

(6) Written procedures for the IRB in the same detail as described in §46.103(b)(4) and §46.103(b)(5).

(7) Statements of significant new findings provided to subjects, as required by §46.116(b)(5).

(b) The records required by this policy shall be retained for at least 3 years, and records relating to research which is conducted shall be retained for at least 3 years after completion of the research. All records shall be accessible for inspection and copying by authorized representatives of the department or agency at reasonable times and in a reasonable manner.

(Approved by the Office of Management and Budget under control number 0990-0260.)

§46.116 General requirements for informed consent.

Except as provided elsewhere in this policy, no investigator may involve a human being as a subject in research covered by this policy unless the investigator has obtained the legally effective informed consent of the subject or the subject's legally authorized representative. An investigator shall seek such consent only under circumstances that provide the prospective subject or the representative sufficient opportunity to consider whether or not to participate and that minimize the possibility of coercion or undue influence. The information that is given to the subject or the representative shall be in language understandable to the subject or the representative. No informed consent, whether oral or written, may include any exculpatory language through which the subject or the representative is made to waive or appear to waive any of the subject's legal rights, or releases or appears to release the investigator, the sponsor, the institution or its agents from liability for negligence.

(a) Basic elements of informed consent. Except as provided in paragraph (c) or (d) of this section, in seeking informed consent the following information shall be provided to each subject:

> (1) A statement that the study involves research, an explanation of the purposes of the research and the expected duration of the subject's participation, a description of the procedures to be followed, and identification of any procedures which are experimental;
>
> (2) A description of any reasonably foreseeable risks or discomforts to the subject;
>
> (3) A description of any benefits to the subject or to others which may reasonably be expected from the research;
>
> (4) A disclosure of appropriate alternative procedures or courses of treatment, if any, that might be advantageous to the subject;
>
> (5) A statement describing the extent, if any, to which confidentiality of records identifying the subject will be maintained;
>
> (6) For research involving more than minimal risk, an explanation as to whether any compensation and an explanation as to whether any medical treatments are available if injury occurs and, if so, what they consist of, or where further information may be obtained;
>
> (7) An explanation of whom to contact for answers to pertinent questions about the research and research subjects' rights, and whom to contact in the event of a research-related injury to the subject; and
>
> (8) A statement that participation is voluntary, refusal to participate will involve no penalty or loss of benefits to which the subject is otherwise entitled, and the subject may discontinue participation at any time without penalty or loss of benefits to which the subject is otherwise entitled.

(b) Additional elements of informed consent. When appropriate, one or more of the following elements of information shall also be provided to each subject:

> (1) A statement that the particular treatment or procedure may involve risks to the subject (or to the embryo or fetus, if the subject is or may become pregnant) which are currently unforeseeable;

45 CFR Part 46 Subparts A, B, C, and D

(2) Anticipated circumstances under which the subject's participation may be terminated by the investigator without regard to the subject's consent;

(3) Any additional costs to the subject that may result from participation in the research;

(4) The consequences of a subject's decision to withdraw from the research and procedures for orderly termination of participation by the subject;

(5) A statement that significant new findings developed during the course of the research which may relate to the subject's willingness to continue participation will be provided to the subject; and

(6) The approximate number of subjects involved in the study.

(c) An IRB may approve a consent procedure which does not include, or which alters, some or all of the elements of informed consent set forth above, or waive the requirement to obtain informed consent provided the IRB finds and documents that:

(1) The research or demonstration project is to be conducted by or subject to the approval of state or local government officials and is designed to study, evaluate, or otherwise examine: (i) public benefit or service programs; (ii) procedures for obtaining benefits or services under those programs; (iii) possible changes in or alternatives to those programs or procedures; or (iv) possible changes in methods or levels of payment for benefits or services under those programs; and

(2) The research could not practicably be carried out without the waiver or alteration.

(d) An IRB may approve a consent procedure which does not include, or which alters, some or all of the elements of informed consent set forth in this section, or waive the requirements to obtain informed consent provided the IRB finds and documents that:

(1) The research involves no more than minimal risk to the subjects;

(2) The waiver or alteration will not adversely affect the rights and welfare of the subjects;

(3) The research could not practicably be carried out without the waiver or alteration; and

(4) Whenever appropriate, the subjects will be provided with additional pertinent information after participation.

(e) The informed consent requirements in this policy are not intended to preempt any applicable federal, state, or local laws which require additional information to be disclosed in order for informed consent to be legally effective.

(f) Nothing in this policy is intended to limit the authority of a physician to provide emergency medical care, to the extent the physician is permitted to do so under applicable federal, state, or local law.

(Approved by the Office of Management and Budget under control number 0990-0260.)

§46.117 Documentation of informed consent.

(a) Except as provided in paragraph (c) of this section, informed consent shall be documented by the use of a written consent form approved by the IRB and signed by the subject or the subject's legally authorized representative. A copy shall be given to the person signing the form.

(b) Except as provided in paragraph (c) of this section, the consent form may be either of the following:

(1) A written consent document that embodies the elements of informed consent required by §46.116. This form may be read to the subject or the subject's legally authorized representative, but in any event, the investigator shall give either the subject or the representative adequate opportunity to read it before it is signed; or

(2) A short form written consent document stating that the elements of informed consent required by §46.116 have been presented orally to the subject or the subject's legally authorized representative. When this method is used, there shall be a witness to the oral presentation. Also, the IRB shall approve a written summary of what is to be said to the subject or the representative. Only the short form itself is to be signed by the subject or the representative. However, the witness shall sign both the short form and a copy of the summary, and the person actually obtaining consent shall

45 CFR Part 46 Subparts A, B, C, and D

sign a copy of the summary. A copy of the summary shall be given to the subject or the representative, in addition to a copy of the short form.

(c) An IRB may waive the requirement for the investigator to obtain a signed consent form for some or all subjects if it finds either:

(1) That the only record linking the subject and the research would be the consent document and the principal risk would be potential harm resulting from a breach of confidentiality. Each subject will be asked whether the subject wants documentation linking the subject with the research, and the subject's wishes will govern; or

(2) That the research presents no more than minimal risk of harm to subjects and involves no procedures for which written consent is normally required outside of the research context.
In cases in which the documentation requirement is waived, the IRB may require the investigator to provide subjects with a written statement regarding the research.

(Approved by the Office of Management and Budget under control number 0990-0260.)

§46.118 Applications and proposals lacking definite plans for involvement of human subjects.

Certain types of applications for grants, cooperative agreements, or contracts are submitted to departments or agencies with the knowledge that subjects may be involved within the period of support, but definite plans would not normally be set forth in the application or proposal. These include activities such as institutional type grants when selection of specific projects is the institution's responsibility; research training grants in which the activities involving subjects remain to be selected; and projects in which human subjects' involvement will depend upon completion of instruments, prior animal studies, or purification of compounds. These applications need not be reviewed by an IRB before an award may be made. However, except for research exempted or waived under §46.101 (b) or (i), no human subjects may be involved in any project supported by these awards until the project has been reviewed and approved by the IRB, as provided in this policy, and certification submitted, by the institution, to the department or agency.

§46.119 Research undertaken without the intention of involving human subjects.

In the event research is undertaken without the intention of involving human subjects, but it is later proposed to involve human subjects in the research, the research shall first be reviewed and approved by an IRB, as provided in this policy, a certification submitted, by the institution, to the department or agency, and final approval given to the proposed change by the department or agency.

§46.120 Evaluation and disposition of applications and proposals for research to be conducted or supported by a Federal Department or Agency.

(a) The department or agency head will evaluate all applications and proposals involving human subjects submitted to the department or agency through such officers and employees of the department or agency and such experts and consultants as the department or agency head determines to be appropriate. This evaluation will take into consideration the risks to the subjects, the adequacy of protection against these risks, the potential benefits of the research to the subjects and others, and the importance of the knowledge gained or to be gained.

(b) On the basis of this evaluation, the department or agency head may approve or disapprove the application or proposal, or enter into negotiations to develop an approvable one.

§46.121 [Reserved]

§46.122 Use of Federal funds.

Federal funds administered by a department or agency may not be expended for research involving human subjects unless the requirements of this policy have been satisfied.

§46.123 Early termination of research support: Evaluation of applications and proposals.

(a) The department or agency head may require that department or agency support for any project be terminated or suspended in the manner prescribed in applicable program requirements, when the department or agency head finds an institution has materially failed to comply with the terms of this policy.

(b) In making decisions about supporting or approving applications or proposals covered by this policy the department or agency head may take into account, in addition to all other eligibility requirements and program criteria, factors such as whether the applicant has been subject to a termination or suspension under paragraph (a) of this section and whether the applicant or the person or persons who would direct or has/have directed the scientific and technical aspects of an activity has/have, in the judgment of the department or agency head, materially failed to discharge responsibility for the protection of the rights and welfare of human subjects (whether or not the research was subject to federal regulation).

§46.124 Conditions.

With respect to any research project or any class of research projects the department or agency head may impose additional conditions prior to or at the time of approval when in the judgment of the department or agency head additional conditions are necessary for the protection of human subjects.

Subpart B	Additional Protections for Pregnant Women, Human Fetuses and Neonates Involved in Research
	Source: 66 FR 56778, Nov. 13, 2001, unless otherwise noted.

§46.201 To what do these regulations apply?

(a) Except as provided in paragraph (b) of this section, this subpart applies to all research involving pregnant women, human fetuses, neonates of uncertain viability, or nonviable neonates conducted or supported by the Department of Health and Human Services (DHHS). This includes all research conducted in DHHS facilities by any person and all research conducted in any facility by DHHS employees.

(b) The exemptions at §46.101(b)(1) through (6) are applicable to this subpart.

(c) The provisions of §46.101(c) through (i) are applicable to this subpart. Reference to State or local laws in this subpart and in §46.101(f) is intended to include the laws of federally recognized American Indian and Alaska Native Tribal Governments.

(d) The requirements of this subpart are in addition to those imposed under the other subparts of this part.

§46.202 Definitions.

The definitions in §46.102 shall be applicable to this subpart as well. In addition, as used in this subpart:

(a) Dead fetus means a fetus that exhibits neither heartbeat, spontaneous respiratory activity, spontaneous movement of voluntary muscles, nor pulsation of the umbilical cord.

(b) Delivery means complete separation of the fetus from the woman by expulsion or extraction or any other means.

(c) Fetus means the product of conception from implantation until delivery.

(d) Neonate means a newborn.

(e) Nonviable neonate means a neonate after delivery that, although living, is not viable.

(f) Pregnancy encompasses the period of time from implantation until delivery. A woman shall be assumed to be pregnant if she exhibits any of the pertinent presumptive signs of pregnancy, such as missed menses, until the results of a pregnancy test are negative or until delivery.

(g) Secretary means the Secretary of Health and Human Services and any other officer or employee of the Department of Health and Human Services to whom authority has been delegated.

(h) Viable, as it pertains to the neonate, means being able, after delivery, to survive (given the benefit of available medical therapy) to the point of independently maintaining heartbeat and respiration. The Secretary may from time to time, taking into account medical advances, publish in the FEDERAL REGISTER guidelines to assist in determining whether a neonate is viable for purposes of this subpart. If a neonate is viable then it may be included in research only to the extent permitted and in accordance with the requirements of subparts A and D of this part.

§46.203 Duties of IRBs in connection with research involving pregnant women, fetuses, and neonates.

In addition to other responsibilities assigned to IRBs under this part, each IRB shall review research covered by this subpart and approve only research which satisfies the conditions of all applicable sections of this subpart and the other subparts of this part.

§46.204 Research involving pregnant women or fetuses.

Pregnant women or fetuses may be involved in research if all of the following conditions are met:

(a) Where scientifically appropriate, preclinical studies, including studies on pregnant animals, and clinical studies, including studies on nonpregnant women, have been conducted and provide data for assessing potential risks to pregnant women and fetuses;

(b) The risk to the fetus is caused solely by interventions or procedures that hold out the prospect of direct benefit for the woman or the fetus; or, if there is no such prospect of benefit, the risk to the fetus is not greater than minimal and the purpose of the research is the development of important biomedical knowledge which cannot be obtained by any other means;

(c) Any risk is the least possible for achieving the objectives of the research;

(d) If the research holds out the prospect of direct benefit to the pregnant woman, the prospect of a direct benefit both to the pregnant woman and the fetus, or no prospect of benefit for the woman nor the fetus when risk to the fetus is not greater than minimal and the purpose of the research is the development of important biomedical knowledge that cannot be obtained by any other means, her consent is obtained in accord with the informed consent provisions of subpart A of this part;

(e) If the research holds out the prospect of direct benefit solely to the fetus then the consent of the pregnant woman and the father is obtained in accord with the informed consent provisions of subpart A of this part, except that the father's consent need not be obtained if he is unable to consent because of unavailability, incompetence, or temporary incapacity or the pregnancy resulted from rape or incest.

(f) Each individual providing consent under paragraph (d) or (e) of this section is fully informed regarding the reasonably foreseeable impact of the research on the fetus or neonate;

(g) For children as defined in §46.402(a) who are pregnant, assent and permission are obtained in accord with the provisions of subpart D of this part;

(h) No inducements, monetary or otherwise, will be offered to terminate a pregnancy;

(i) Individuals engaged in the research will have no part in any decisions as to the timing, method, or procedures used to terminate a pregnancy; and

(j) Individuals engaged in the research will have no part in determining the viability of a neonate.

§46.205 Research involving neonates.

(a) Neonates of uncertain viability and nonviable neonates may be involved in research if all of the following conditions are met:

(1) Where scientifically appropriate, preclinical and clinical studies have been conducted and provide data for assessing potential risks to neonates.

(2) Each individual providing consent under paragraph (b)(2) or (c)(5) of this section is fully informed regarding the reasonably foreseeable impact of the research on the neonate.

(3) Individuals engaged in the research will have no part in determining the viability of a neonate.

(4) The requirements of paragraph (b) or (c) of this section have been met as applicable.

(b) Neonates of uncertain viability. Until it has been ascertained whether or not a neonate is viable, a neonate may not be involved in research covered by this subpart unless the following additional conditions have been met:

(1) The IRB determines that:

(i) The research holds out the prospect of enhancing the probability of survival of the neonate to the point of viability, and any risk is the least

45 CFR Part 46 Subparts A, B, C, and D

possible for achieving that objective, or

(ii) The purpose of the research is the development of important biomedical knowledge which cannot be obtained by other means and there will be no added risk to the neonate resulting from the research; and

(2) The legally effective informed consent of either parent of the neonate or, if neither parent is able to consent because of unavailability, incompetence, or temporary incapacity, the legally effective informed consent of either parent's legally authorized representative is obtained in accord with subpart A of this part, except that the consent of the father or his legally authorized representative need not be obtained if the pregnancy resulted from rape or incest.

(c) Nonviable neonates. After delivery nonviable neonate may not be involved in research covered by this subpart unless all of the following additional conditions are met:

(1) Vital functions of the neonate will not be artificially maintained;

(2) The research will not terminate the heartbeat or respiration of the neonate;

(3) There will be no added risk to the neonate resulting from the research;

(4) The purpose of the research is the development of important biomedical knowledge that cannot be obtained by other means; and

(5) The legally effective informed consent of both parents of the neonate is obtained in accord with subpart A of this part, except that the waiver and alteration provisions of §46.116(c) and (d) do not apply. However, if either parent is unable to consent because of unavailability, incompetence, or temporary incapacity, the informed consent of one parent of a nonviable neonate will suffice to meet the requirements of this paragraph (c)(5), except that the consent of the father need not be obtained if the pregnancy resulted from rape or incest. The consent of a legally authorized representative of either or both of the parents of a nonviable neonate will not suffice to meet the requirements of this paragraph (c)(5).

(d) Viable neonates. A neonate, after delivery, that has been determined to be viable may be included in research only to the extent permitted by and in accord with the requirements of subparts A and D of this part.

§46.206 Research involving, after delivery, the placenta, the dead fetus or fetal material.

(a) Research involving, after delivery, the placenta; the dead fetus; macerated fetal material; or cells, tissue, or organs excised from a dead fetus, shall be conducted only in accord with any applicable federal, state, or local laws and regulations regarding such activities.

(b) If information associated with material described in paragraph (a) of this section is recorded for research purposes in a manner that living individuals can be identified, directly or through identifiers linked to those individuals, those individuals are research subjects and all pertinent subparts of this part are applicable.

§46.207 Research not otherwise approvable which presents an opportunity to understand, prevent, or alleviate a serious problem affecting the health or welfare of pregnant women, fetuses, or neonates.

The Secretary will conduct or fund research that the IRB does not believe meets the requirements of §46.204 or §46.205 only if:

(a) The IRB finds that the research presents a reasonable opportunity to further the understanding, prevention, or alleviation of a serious problem affecting the health or welfare of pregnant women, fetuses or neonates; and

(b) The Secretary, after consultation with a panel of experts in pertinent disciplines (for example: science, medicine, ethics, law) and following opportunity for public review and comment, including a public meeting announced in the FEDERAL REGISTER, has determined either:

(1) That the research in fact satisfies the conditions of §46.204, as applicable; or

(2) The following:

(i) The research presents a reasonable opportunity to further the understanding, prevention, or alleviation of a serious problem affecting the health or welfare of pregnant women, fetuses or neonates;

(ii) The research will be conducted in accord with sound ethical principles;

and

(iii) Informed consent will be obtained in accord with the informed consent provisions of subpart A and other applicable subparts of this part.

Subpart C	Additional Protections Pertaining to Biomedical and Behavioral Research Involving Prisoners as Subjects
	Source: 43 FR 53655, Nov. 16, 1978, unless otherwise noted.

§46.301 Applicability.

(a) The regulations in this subpart are applicable to all biomedical and behavioral research conducted or supported by the Department of Health and Human Services involving prisoners as subjects.

(b) Nothing in this subpart shall be construed as indicating that compliance with the procedures set forth herein will authorize research involving prisoners as subjects, to the extent such research is limited or barred by applicable State or local law.

(c) The requirements of this subpart are in addition to those imposed under the other subparts of this part.

§46.302 Purpose.

Inasmuch as prisoners may be under constraints because of their incarceration which could affect their ability to make a truly voluntary and uncoerced decision whether or not to participate as subjects in research, it is the purpose of this subpart to provide additional safeguards for the protection of prisoners involved in activities to which this subpart is applicable.

§46.303 Definitions.

As used in this subpart:

(a) *Secretary* means the Secretary of Health and Human Services and any other officer or employee of the Department of Health and Human Services to whom authority has been delegated.

(b) *DHHS* means the Department of Health and Human Services.

(c) *Prisoner* means any individual involuntarily confined or detained in a penal institution. The term is intended to encompass individuals sentenced to such an institution under a criminal or civil statute, individuals detained in other facilities by virtue of statutes or commitment procedures which provide alternatives to criminal prosecution or incarceration in a penal institution, and individuals detained pending arraignment, trial, or sentencing.

(d) *Minimal risk* is the probability and magnitude of physical or psychological harm that is normally encountered in the daily lives, or in the routine medical, dental, or psychological examination of healthy persons.

§46.304 Composition of Institutional Review Boards where prisoners are involved.

In addition to satisfying the requirements in §46.107 of this part, an Institutional Review Board, carrying out responsibilities under this part with respect to research covered by this subpart, shall also meet the following specific requirements:

(a) A majority of the Board (exclusive of prisoner members) shall have no association with the prison(s) involved, apart from their membership on the Board.

(b) At least one member of the Board shall be a prisoner, or a prisoner representative with appropriate background and experience to serve in that capacity, except that where a particular research project is reviewed by more than one Board only one Board need satisfy this requirement.

[43 FR 53655, Nov. 16, 1978, as amended at 46 FR 8366, Jan. 26, 1981]

§46.305 Additional duties of the Institutional Review Boards where prisoners are involved.

(a) In addition to all other responsibilities prescribed for Institutional Review Boards under this part, the Board shall review research covered by this subpart and approve such research only if it finds that:

> (1) The research under review represents one of the categories of research permissible under §46.306(a)(2);

(2) Any possible advantages accruing to the prisoner through his or her participation in the research, when compared to the general living conditions, medical care, quality of food, amenities and opportunity for earnings in the prison, are not of such a magnitude that his or her ability to weigh the risks of the research against the value of such advantages in the limited choice environment of the prison is impaired;

(3) The risks involved in the research are commensurate with risks that would be accepted by nonprisoner volunteers;

(4) Procedures for the selection of subjects within the prison are fair to all prisoners and immune from arbitrary intervention by prison authorities or prisoners. Unless the principal investigator provides to the Board justification in writing for following some other procedures, control subjects must be selected randomly from the group of available prisoners who meet the characteristics needed for that particular research project;

(5) The information is presented in language which is understandable to the subject population;

(6) Adequate assurance exists that parole boards will not take into account a prisoner's participation in the research in making decisions regarding parole, and each prisoner is clearly informed in advance that participation in the research will have no effect on his or her parole; and

(7) Where the Board finds there may be a need for follow-up examination or care of participants after the end of their participation, adequate provision has been made for such examination or care, taking into account the varying lengths of individual prisoners' sentences, and for informing participants of this fact.

(b) The Board shall carry out such other duties as may be assigned by the Secretary.

(c) The institution shall certify to the Secretary, in such form and manner as the Secretary may require, that the duties of the Board under this section have been fulfilled.

§46.306 Permitted research involving prisoners.

(a) Biomedical or behavioral research conducted or supported by DHHS may involve prisoners as subjects only if:

(1) The institution responsible for the conduct of the research has certified to the Secretary that the Institutional Review Board has approved the research under §46.305 of this subpart; and

(2) In the judgment of the Secretary the proposed research involves solely the following:

(i) Study of the possible causes, effects, and processes of incarceration, and of criminal behavior, provided that the study presents no more than minimal risk and no more than inconvenience to the subjects;

(ii) Study of prisons as institutional structures or of prisoners as incarcerated persons, provided that the study presents no more than minimal risk and no more than inconvenience to the subjects;

(iii) Research on conditions particularly affecting prisoners as a class (for example, vaccine trials and other research on hepatitis which is much more prevalent in prisons than elsewhere; and research on social and psychological problems such as alcoholism, drug addiction, and sexual assaults) provided that the study may proceed only after the Secretary has consulted with appropriate experts including experts in penology, medicine, and ethics, and published notice, in the FEDERAL REGISTER, of his intent to approve such research; or
(iv) Research on practices, both innovative and accepted, which have the intent and reasonable probability of improving the health or well-being of the subject. In cases in which those studies require the assignment of prisoners in a manner consistent with protocols approved by the IRB to control groups which may not benefit from the research, the study may proceed only after the Secretary has consulted with appropriate experts, including experts in penology, medicine, and ethics, and published notice, in the FEDERAL REGISTER, of the intent to approve such research.
(b) Except as provided in paragraph (a) of this section, biomedical or behavioral research conducted or supported by DHHS shall not involve prisoners as subjects.

Subpart D	**Additional Protections for Children Involved as Subjects in Research**
	Source: 48 FR 9818, March 8, 1983, unless otherwise noted.

45 CFR Part 46 Subparts A, B, C, and D

§46.401 To what do these regulations apply?

(a) This subpart applies to all research involving children as subjects, conducted or supported by the Department of Health and Human Services.

(1) This includes research conducted by Department employees, except that each head of an Operating Division of the Department may adopt such nonsubstantive, procedural modifications as may be appropriate from an administrative standpoint.

(2) It also includes research conducted or supported by the Department of Health and Human Services outside the United States, but in appropriate circumstances, the Secretary may, under paragraph (i) of §46.101 of subpart A, waive the applicability of some or all of the requirements of these regulations for research of this type.

(b) Exemptions at §46.101(b)(1) and (b)(3) through (b)(6) are applicable to this subpart. The exemption at §46.101(b)(2) regarding educational tests is also applicable to this subpart. However, the exemption at §46.101(b)(2) for research involving survey or interview procedures or observations of public behavior does not apply to research covered by this subpart, except for research involving observation of public behavior when the investigator(s) do not participate in the activities being observed.

(c) The exceptions, additions, and provisions for waiver as they appear in paragraphs (c) through (i) of §46.101 of subpart A are applicable to this subpart.

[48 FR 9818, Mar. 8, 1983; 56 FR 28032, June 18, 1991; 56 FR 29757, June 28, 1991.]

§46.402 Definitions.

The definitions in §46.102 of subpart A shall be applicable to this subpart as well. In addition, as used in this subpart:

(a) *Children* are persons who have not attained the legal age for consent to treatments or procedures involved in the research, under the applicable law of the jurisdiction in which the research will be conducted.

(b) *Assent* means a child's affirmative agreement to participate in research. Mere failure to object should not, absent affirmative agreement, be construed as assent.

(c) *Permission* means the agreement of parent(s) or guardian to the participation of their child or ward in research.

(d) *Parent* means a child's biological or adoptive parent.

(e) *Guardian* means an individual who is authorized under applicable State or local law to consent on behalf of a child to general medical care.

§46.403 IRB duties.

In addition to other responsibilities assigned to IRBs under this part, each IRB shall review research covered by this subpart and approve only research which satisfies the conditions of all applicable sections of this subpart.

§46.404 Research not involving greater than minimal risk.

HHS will conduct or fund research in which the IRB finds that no greater than minimal risk to children is presented, only if the IRB finds that adequate provisions are made for soliciting the assent of the children and the permission of their parents or guardians, as set forth in §46.408.

§46.405 Research involving greater than minimal risk but presenting the prospect of direct benefit to the individual subjects.

HHS will conduct or fund research in which the IRB finds that more than minimal risk to children is presented by an intervention or procedure that holds out the prospect of direct benefit for the individual subject, or by a monitoring procedure that is likely to contribute to the subject's well-being, only if the IRB finds that:

(a) The risk is justified by the anticipated benefit to the subjects;

(b) The relation of the anticipated benefit to the risk is at least as favorable to the subjects as that presented by available alternative approaches; and

(c) Adequate provisions are made for soliciting the assent of the children and permission of their parents or guardians, as set forth in §46.408.

§46.406 Research involving greater than minimal risk and no prospect of direct benefit to individual subjects, but likely to yield generalizable knowledge about the subject's disorder or condition.

45 CFR Part 46 Subparts A, B, C, and D

HHS will conduct or fund research in which the IRB finds that more than minimal risk to children is presented by an intervention or procedure that does not hold out the prospect of direct benefit for the individual subject, or by a monitoring procedure which is not likely to contribute to the well-being of the subject, only if the IRB finds that:

(a) The risk represents a minor increase over minimal risk;

(b) The intervention or procedure presents experiences to subjects that are reasonably commensurate with those inherent in their actual or expected medical, dental, psychological, social, or educational situations;

(c) The intervention or procedure is likely to yield generalizable knowledge about the subjects' disorder or condition which is of vital importance for the understanding or amelioration of the subjects' disorder or condition; and

(d) Adequate provisions are made for soliciting assent of the children and permission of their parents or guardians, as set forth in §46.408.

§46.407 Research not otherwise approvable which presents an opportunity to understand, prevent, or alleviate a serious problem affecting the health or welfare of children.

HHS will conduct or fund research that the IRB does not believe meets the requirements of §46.404, §46.405, or §46.406 only if:

(a) The IRB finds that the research presents a reasonable opportunity to further the understanding, prevention, or alleviation of a serious problem affecting the health or welfare of children; and

(b) The Secretary, after consultation with a panel of experts in pertinent disciplines (for example: science, medicine, education, ethics, law) and following opportunity for public review and comment, has determined either:

(1) That the research in fact satisfies the conditions of §46.404, §46.405, or §46.406, as applicable, or (2) the following:

(i) The research presents a reasonable opportunity to further the understanding, prevention, or alleviation of a serious problem affecting the health or welfare of children;

(ii) The research will be conducted in accordance with sound ethical principles;

(iii) Adequate provisions are made for soliciting the assent of children and the permission of their parents or guardians, as set forth in §46.408.

§46.408 Requirements for permission by parents or guardians and for assent by children.

(a) In addition to the determinations required under other applicable sections of this subpart, the IRB shall determine that adequate provisions are made for soliciting the assent of the children, when in the judgment of the IRB the children are capable of providing assent. In determining whether children are capable of assenting, the IRB shall take into account the ages, maturity, and psychological state of the children involved. This judgment may be made for all children to be involved in research under a particular protocol, or for each child, as the IRB deems appropriate. If the IRB determines that the capability of some or all of the children is so limited that they cannot reasonably be consulted or that the intervention or procedure involved in the research holds out a prospect of direct benefit that is important to the health or well-being of the children and is available only in the context of the research, the assent of the children is not a necessary condition for proceeding with the research. Even where the IRB determines that the subjects are capable of assenting, the IRB may still waive the assent requirement under circumstances in which consent may be waived in accord with §46.116 of Subpart A.

(b) In addition to the determinations required under other applicable sections of this subpart, the IRB shall determine, in accordance with and to the extent that consent is required by §46.116 of Subpart A, that adequate provisions are made for soliciting the permission of each child's parents or guardian. Where parental permission is to be obtained, the IRB may find that the permission of one parent is sufficient for research to be conducted under §46.404 or §46.405. Where research is covered by §46.406 and §46.407 and permission is to be obtained from parents, both parents must give their permission unless one parent is deceased, unknown, incompetent, or not reasonably available, or when only one parent has legal responsibility for the care and custody of the child.

(c) In addition to the provisions for waiver contained in §46.116 of subpart A, if the IRB determines that a research protocol is designed for conditions or for a subject population for which parental or guardian permission is not a reasonable

45 CFR Part 46 Subparts A, B, C, and D

requirement to protect the subjects (for example, neglected or abused children), it may waive the consent requirements in Subpart A of this part and paragraph (b) of this section, provided an appropriate mechanism for protecting the children who will participate as subjects in the research is substituted, and provided further that the waiver is not inconsistent with federal, state, or local law. The choice of an appropriate mechanism would depend upon the nature and purpose of the activities described in the protocol, the risk and anticipated benefit to the research subjects, and their age, maturity, status, and condition.

(d) Permission by parents or guardians shall be documented in accordance with and to the extent required by §46.117 of subpart A.

(e) When the IRB determines that assent is required, it shall also determine whether and how assent must be documented.

§46.409 Wards.

(a) Children who are wards of the state or any other agency, institution, or entity can be included in research approved under §46.406 or §46.407 only if such research is:

(1) Related to their status as wards; or

(2) Conducted in schools, camps, hospitals, institutions, or similar settings in which the majority of children involved as subjects are not wards.

(b) If the research is approved under paragraph (a) of this section, the IRB shall require appointment of an advocate for each child who is a ward, in addition to any other individual acting on behalf of the child as guardian or in loco parentis. One individual may serve as advocate for more than one child. The advocate shall be an individual who has the background and experience to act in, and agrees to act in, the best interests of the child for the duration of the child's participation in the research and who is not associated in any way (except in the role as advocate or member of the IRB) with the research, the investigator(s), or the guardian organization.

Last revised: November 17, 2005

Note: The formatting of the original text has been retained, including any inconsistencies in formatting, capitalization, and the underlining of text.